"All Guns Fired at One Time"

"All Guns Fired at One Time" Native Voices of Wounded Knee, 1890

Compiled and Edited by **JEROME A. GREENE**

SOUTH DAKOTA

HISTORICAL

SOCIETY

PRESS Pierre

Dedicated to the memory of

MICHAEL HER MANY HORSES (1950–2019),

friend, historian, and activist for the Lakota Sioux

Contents

Acknowledgments

I extend thanks to Charles E. Rankin, Helena, Mont.; R. Eli Paul and Lori Cox-Paul, Kansas City, Mo.; Paul L. Hedren, Omaha, Nebr.; the late Michael Her Many Horses, Wounded Knee, S.Dak.; and the South Dakota State Historical Society, Pierre.

Introduction

The Wounded Knee Massacre of 29 December 1890, involving the loss of more than two hundred Lakota Sioux men, women, and children in South Dakota, marked the tragic climax of the Indian wars in the American West. It followed myriad conflicts throughout that region before, during, and after the Civil War, but by its horrifically disproportionate loss of lives and property, it embodied one of the worst human tragedies involving American Indians throughout four centuries of contact with European Americans. Most directly, what happened at Wounded Knee highlighted the miscarriage of the United States government's Indian policy, which sought to introduce the tenets of white civilization among the Lakota people—and notably here the Miniconjous—and confine them to reservations.

Wounded Knee thus broadly stemmed from federal enterprise in the West. One of its worst antecedents occurred at Sand Creek, Colorado Territory, where a massacre of Southern Cheyennes by federalized troops in 1864 provoked years of intermittent fighting between soldiers and American Indians—including Lakotas—throughout the Great Plains. In 1867 and 1868, tribal representatives signed treaties with the federal government establishing reservations, but in the wake of gold discoveries and whites' quest for land in the Black Hills, more warfare ensued. Following the Battle of the Little Bighorn in 1876, wherein the Sioux and their allies defeated Lieutenant Colonel George A. Custer's Seventh Cavalry command, government troops intently subdued the Lakotas, consigning them to the Great Sioux Reservation in today's western South Dakota. Appointed agents then sought to acculturate the Lakotas through labor, schooling, and other precepts of white society.

Over time, the quest among settlers, cattlemen, and politicians to open American Indian land for settlement by whites manifested itself politically in the dismantling of the Great Sioux Reservation into several smaller reserves. The Pine Ridge Indian Reservation, a parcel of the former Great Sioux Reservation fashioned by obligatory agreement with the Indians in 1889, forms a significant component of the Wounded Knee story. The Pine Ridge tract comprised a spacious acreage in southwestern Dakota Territory adjoining the northern boundary of Nebraska. The Cheyenne River Indian Reservation, a similar expanse carved from the prior Sioux reserve, began roughly ninety miles north of the Pine Ridge boundary and extended to the North Dakota border. The Standing Rock, Rosebud, and Lower Brule reservations were also established at the time.

The reapportionments increased malaise and fostered further suspicion and unrest among the Lakota people. By late 1889, worsening drought, compounded by reductions in government treaty rations, devastated families and bred uncertainty over their basic survival. Chronic misery, intensified by hunger and crippling disease, ultimately bred desperation among the Lakota people and influenced many, including the Miniconjous, to embrace transcendent help. Amid mounting social distress, many of the Sioux welcomed tenets of the Ghost Dance, an inspirational ritual that had influenced other tribes. Through the Ghost Dance, American Indian peoples sought divine deliverance from white oppression, the opportunity to return to old ways, and, notably, spiritual reunion with dead relatives. Ghost Dances variously took place on the Pine Ridge, Rosebud, and Cheyenne River reservations. Anticipating trouble, the United States War Department sent troops onto the Lakota lands. It became an explosive mix.

On the Standing Rock Indian Reservation, pervasive dancing in mid-December drew the attention of the Indian police, who then killed the principal Hunkpapa Lakota leader, Sitting Bull. Word of the deed spread quickly, and when the news reached Cheyenne River, Chief Big Foot welcomed three dozen frightened Hunkpapa refugees fleeing Standing Rock. Fearful of attack by soldiers patrolling the Cheyenne River, Big Foot hurriedly resolved to avoid trouble by leading his Miniconjous and the newly arrived Hunkpapas south to Pine Ridge Agency, where he had been summoned to council with Oglala chief Red Cloud in hopes of stemming conflict with the soldiers. On the night of 23 December, the apprehensive Big Foot, now sick with pneumonia, headed south with some three hundred people, many of them riding in wagons with others walking alongside monitoring cattle and ponies.

At Pine Ridge, army forces under Brigadier General John R. Brooke occupied camps around the agency. On 26 December, Brooke ordered Colonel James W. Forsyth—who had been alerted of Big Foot's movement—to direct four troops of the Seventh Cavalry under Major Samuel M. Whitside into the field. Oglala scouts and the men of Light Battery E, Fourth Artillery, with two Hotchkiss guns, accompanied the troops. The next day, the command marched eighteen miles northeast of the agency and set up camp near Wounded Knee Creek. On 28 December, Whitside's soldiers rode nine miles northeast, hoping to intercept Big Foot and his people. Scouts soon spotted the Miniconjous east of Porcupine Butte and negotiated with the chief, who was prostrated with illness. The people submitted, and the troops escorted them to the cavalry camp adjoining the west side of Wounded Knee Creek.

The Miniconjous set up their meager tipis, wickiups, and wagons with their ponies and dogs immediately north of a wide, deep ravine extending from high ground on the west down to Wounded Knee Creek, seven hundred feet east of the Indian camp. The Seventh Cavalry bivouacked atop a broad ridge on the north. That evening, the troops issued bacon, hardtack, coffee, and sugar to the people as their ponies grazed nearby. The ailing Big Foot was placed in an army tent on level ground below the cavalry camp, where doctors attended him. Unknown to Big Foot's people, the army planned to conduct them to Nebraska where trains would swiftly remove them from the region. Whitside, in a dispatch to Forsyth at Pine Ridge Agency, announced the capture of Big Foot and called for the remaining four Seventh Cavalry troops to bolster his men during the planned disarmament of the Miniconjous in the morning. Whitside also asked for the remaining two Hotchkiss guns and the accompanying soldiers of Battery E, Fourth Artillery. Forsyth and his contingent arrived at 8:30 p.m., and the artillery soldiers labored into the wee hours to ready their armament on a low rise about three hundred feet south and directly overlooking the north side of the Sioux camp.

It is critical that readers of the following accounts comprehend the expanse and topography of the terrain where succeeding events played out. On the night of 28 December, the troops and American Indians occupied a gently undulating landscape extending from a moderate rise five hundred yards west of Wounded Knee Creek upon which the artillerymen toiled through the night emplacing their guns. Immediately east and northeast of the battery stood troop bivouac areas, while tents for Oglala scouts and an adjoining picket line for army mules sat to the south. Big Foot's tent was near the scout tents, beyond them a line of army supply wagons. From there, the open terrain that would play so critical a role in coming events gradually declined for six hundred yards to the deep ravine that trailed down to Wounded Knee Creek. On its north lip stood tipis, assorted wickiup shelters, and wagons comprising the Lakota camp, which took the form of a straggling crescent, its eastern end closer to the ravine than its north-trending western end. At the center of the camp, the people raised a white flag on a stick, denoting their peaceful intent, while their ponies and cattle grazed to the west across a path called Fast Horse Road. Troops closely guarded this road, which paralleled the north edge of the camp, through the night.

On the morning of 29 December, Forsyth and his officers designated a council area—a level space fronting near Big Foot's tent and situated well below the artillery contingent and troop bivouacs on the north rise and the Lakota camp on the south, altogether encompassing roughly an acre. It was here that the first shooting erupted. Soon after dawn—a clear, calm day—and following a breakfast of army rations distributed among the Lakotas, native criers circulated, calling on the men to assemble at the council area to hear Colonel Forsyth speak. The men, many wearing blankets and sheets, congregated as directed in groups and took seats on the grass. Despite the morning chill, no snow appeared on the ground. Big Foot, now extremely sick, declined to participate and remained in his tent. With Whitside, other officers, and interpreter Philip F. Wells at hand, Forsyth greeted the people. He spoke of the circumstances of the moment and announced that they would soon be departing for Pine Ridge Agency. He further called for the surrender of the band's weapons, explaining that they would be compensated for them. When no guns appeared to be forthcoming, he told them to return to their camp in groups, collect their guns, and bring them to the council area. He made no mention of the plan to remove the Lakotas east by train. After an extended period, the men returned to the council with but few guns, all outmoded and in derelict condition, which the sergeants and privates collected in piles west of the assembly. None of the firearms that the Miniconjous had visibly brandished the preceding day seemed to be included. Forsyth's men counted 120 warriors in the assembly, a figure that did not correlate with the relatively few guns relinquished.

Soldiers brought Big Foot forward from his tent and requested that he direct his followers to listen to Forsyth. The colonel ordered two companies (B and K) of the Seventh Cavalry to march along either side of the seated Lakotas and flank them on the south and west to keep the assembly in check. Two squads of soldiers from those companies then entered the camp to search for weapons. In discordant fashion, the troops disrupted the women and children, tossing their possessions about and leaving lodges and wickiups in disarray, thus further provoking the Lakotas. The soldiers seized perhaps four dozen guns, as well as bows, arrows, axes, knives, crowbars, and scissors—anything that might be construed as a weapon. Again, the guns were mostly damaged, derelict, and useless. Returning to the council, the troops tossed the retrieved weapons onto the piles. The Lakota men in the assembly meantime heard the repeated cries and wailing of upset women and children emanating from the camp, constituting yet another irritant.

Distrusting the Lakotas in the council area, Forsyth directed his soldiers to search the warriors individually, checking their blankets for not only guns but ammunition belts. At approximately 9:15 a.m., he instructed the Lakota men to return to their camp by passing between soldier details arranged at the southwest corner of the assembly, where each would be searched for guns and ammunition. Around the same time, a medicine man in the council area who had initiated earlier Ghost Dance movements began agitating and haranguing against the soldiers, repeatedly gathering up dirt in his hands and tossing it toward them. When the searches began, however, he argued loudly as he moved among the younger men seated in the rear of the assembly, now exhorting them to resist the troops. Forsyth at last induced the man to sit down, while Father Francis M. Craft, a Catholic prelate who had accompanied the soldiers from Pine Ridge, moved about with crucifix in hand trying to calm the people amid their surging anxiety.

As the searches commenced, some of the warriors vacillated while the older men assented and began filing south through the opening between the troops, giving up their arms and ammunition. As they did, the medicine man, suddenly back on his feet, recommenced his harangue and excitedly exhorted the younger men to resist. He at last raised his hands to the sun, declaring the soldiers' bullets would not harm them. Just as two soldiers struggled to yank a rifle from a young man, the medicine man bent down to scoop up and toss dirt skyward. A shot precipitously rang out, and as a sudden furor erupted, an officer was heard to scream above the rising din, "Look out! They've broken!" The shooting and killing that ensued, to include the imminent barrage of fire from the Hotchkiss guns north of the Indian camp, would result in at least 146 (and likely more than 200) Lakota dead, with many others wounded, while army losses totaled 46 men killed and 36 wounded. These are the essential prefatory details about Wounded Knee. What happened next is presented herein by Lakota survivors and collateral witnesses, who best tell the story from this point forward.

Note on Sources

The native participants' reflections on the tumult of 29 December 1890, both in their immediate and reminiscent statements, help to clarify the specifics of what happened on that horrific day. Most importantly, these participants present the tragedy faithfully and objectively, however poignantly. Most of the accounts have been derived from assorted reports, books, government documents, diaries, interviews, and other diverse sources containing native commentary on Wounded Knee.

Among the sources is a medical diary kept in the aftermath of the event that chronicles the treatment of the Lakota wounded. Newspaper descriptions—not only those appearing in the days, weeks, and months after Wounded Knee, but some from as late as the 1960s and 1970s—offer additional descriptions and provide evocative contributions by participants and their relatives. Still other sources appeared during internet searches of names, and some had to be obtained circuitously via descendants and extended families because so many adult males associated with Wounded Knee were killed there. In addition, this volume includes the memories of civilian personnel serving as government scouts and interpreters and nurses' aides, as well as accounts from mixed-blood witnesses who shared their knowledge of the events. Period rosters of tribal members who took part in the action are also included, as well as one listing of those who were not present. Ultimately, it is hoped that the selections provided here might together enhance not only Lakota family recollections and genealogical records for the ancestors who perished at Wounded Knee but also for the descendants of survivors.

By offering personal and family perspectives, the accounts herein dramatically personalize the events at Wounded Knee, imparting vital knowledge as well as a sense of how individuals and groups felt, reacted, interacted, perished, and endured. These perspectives augment and perhaps correct and otherwise balance conclusions found in government documents. One should keep in mind that, unlike their predecessors of the 1860s and 1870s in the wilds of early Dakota, Wyoming, and Montana, many in the Lakota generation who experienced Wounded Knee had known reservation life for more than two decades. Through education and day-to-day contact with whites, they had become increasingly conversant in English. Moreover, because of their closer proximity to whites, interviewers at the time sought and recorded their statements. Thus, native survivor accounts gathered and accumulated since the events at Wounded Knee have become ever greater in volume and richer in content. Taken together, they provide clear images of what happened from individual points of view. Redundancy of detail in these testimonies demonstrates honesty and tends to validate accuracy. Thus, these accounts provide dimension, extend empathetic value of the human experience, and give context and depth to what happened. It is essential to note that women informants—the wives and daughters of the men, some of whom stood outside of the council area that morning, near the edge of the Indian camp and behind the cordon of Seventh Cavalry soldiers—provide most of the Lakota recollections. Of all the Lakotas present that day, they predominantly survived.

Many of the selections presented herein repose among the Eli S. Ricker holdings of the Nebraska State Historical Society, and some have been previously published elsewhere, as indicated in the introductory remarks accompanying the selections. Others have been drawn from sundry manuscripts, books, or repositories as indicated. Principal institutions from which manuscript items have been collected (as cited herein) consist of the libraries and archives of the Nebraska State Historical Society, Lincoln; the South Dakota State Historical Society, Pierre; the Leland D. Case Library at Black Hills State University, Spearfish, South Dakota; the I. D. Weeks Library at the University of South Dakota, Vermillion; the George and Eleanor McGovern Library at Dakota Wesleyan University, Mitchell, South Dakota; the Brigham Young University Library, Provo, Utah; the Lilly Library at Indiana University, Bloomington; and the Denver Public Library. For further guidance regarding sources, readers might consult the inclusive bibliography in Jerome A. Greene, *American Carnage: Wounded Knee, 1890* (Norman: University of Oklahoma Press, 2014), pp. 535–73. Many of the accounts presented herein were assembled during the research for that book.

Accounts, Statements, Reports, and Interviews

In the following reminiscences, statements, and commentaries, readers will discern occasional repetition in the accountings of the events of 29 December 1890. Yet, such recurrence tends to accentuate and ratify the profound terror and distress the native people and their families endured on that altogether horrific and tragic day. In most cases, the accounts by different individuals reflect not only commonly shared perceptions of what happened at Wounded Knee, but also the unique individual perspectives of contributors. Occasionally, participants rendered more than one account of their remembrance of events. For example, Iron Hail, also known as Dewey Beard, throughout the course of his long life following Wounded Knee (he died in 1955) provided at least five or six descriptions of the event, possibly even more. Such multiple statements are presented herein chronologically, among all the others. Readers are encouraged to jump ahead as desired to seek out and compare their contents.

Most of the early accounts, that is, those given during the weeks and months directly following Wounded Knee, as well as in the immediately subsequent years, describe the sheer terror of Wounded Knee as the people individually witnessed family members and friends being injured, maimed, and killed—often in front of them—as they themselves struggled to survive. These elements also characterize statements that emerged in the decade or so following the massacre. During the early period of the twentieth century, however, amid discussion regarding government compensation for survivors—especially as congressional efforts advanced in the early 1930s—a rash of participant accounts from expectant and aging Lakota survivors of Wounded Knee emerged. With hopes thus raised, more of the people grew inclined to speak openly of, or in some cases to re-express, their remembrances. Although the anticipated compensation never materialized, many accounts generated during that period of expectancy reflected the Lakotas' urgent commitment not to forget what happened to them on that day. For them and succeeding generations, Wounded Knee thus serves as an exclamation point to the societal trauma they endured from the 1850s forward. Beyond symbolic, for them Wounded Knee was forever cataclysmic in a fundamentally personal and existential way.

Beyond the reflections of Lakota participants, this volume presents the accounts of government-employed American Indian scouts and interpreters as well as full- and mixed-blood Lakota observers who either partook directly in the events or witnessed and recorded the carnage and its aftermath. Included, too, are accounts from medical personnel chronicling the treatment of injured Lakotas in the days following the massacre, as well as a correspondent's description of the dedication of the Lakota-erected monument overlooking the field thirteen years later. Further, the volume includes fairly contemporary rosters of tribal members who took part in the action, as well as of others who did not.

The following selections embody a variety of little-known sources explaining what happened at Wounded Knee, encompassing early and later accounts by men, women, and grown children that appeared in official government reports, newspapers, and collected published reminiscences, including a few diary and published commentaries of non-Indian observers that bear directly on the subject. It must be restated that most of the adult men of warrior age who had attended the morning council at Wounded Knee died there. Other selections have been drawn from transcripts contributed by survivor participants, including American Indian government employees, that repose today in various public institutions. Comprehensive source information is provided for each of the entries. Editorial comments, corrections, and clarifications appear in brackets, and certain punctuation elements have been standardized for clarity and readability.

1. Lakotas wounded at Wounded Knee taken to Holy Cross Chapel, 1890–1891

The following list, written in the hand of Major Medical Director Dr. Dallas Bache, constitutes the first contemporary account of Indians hospitalized directly after the tumult on 29 December 1890 and, as it describes Lakotas' wounds and treatment, is the first document tied directly to the event to appear in its immediate aftermath. "Lakotas wounded at Wounded Knee taken to the Episcopal chapel of the Holy Cross, at Pine Ridge Agency[, 1890–1891,]" Pt. 1, Entry 3783, Letters and Telegrams Sent by the Medical Director's Office, Dec. 1890–Jan. 1891, Records of United States Army Continental Commands, 1821–1920, Record Group (RG) 393, National Archives (NA), Washington, D.C.

Wounded Indian prisoners from from [*sic*] action on Wounded Knee
Brought in

Date	Category		Count	Total
Dec. 29	Adult males		4	
	" females		9	
	Children	males	9	
	Females		4	
	Inf[ants?] [illeg.] not stated		2	
			28	28
Jan. 1st	Adult males		3	
	" females		1	
	" child		1	
			5	5
Jan. 4th	Adult males Dec[']d Jan. 6" a.m.		1	
	" females		1	
			2	2
			Total	35

Died

Jan 2	Adult males	2
	" females	1
" 3	" "	1
	Boy	1
" 4	Adult female (waiting burial)	1

Males–4 + 3 + 1 =   8
Females–9 + 1 + 1 =   11
Children   14

____

33 + 2 = 35

Dec'd [Deceased] Jan. 5 — His a day

Dec'd Jan. 6 – 8 a.m. Lost Man — brought in from field Jan. 4th.

2. Leather-bound journal notebook titled "Indians wounded in fight at 'Wounded Knee' South Dakota," 1890–1891

The people in the following list, including Mrs. Big Foot, were quartered for medical treatment in the Episcopal Church at Pine Ridge. Most of their locations in the "alcove" or "chancel" are indicated. Leather-bound journal notebook, 1890–1891, 7 ½" x 4 ½", titled in ink, "Indians wounded in fight at 'Wounded Knee' South Dakota, December 29, 1890. Treated by Frank J. Ives[,] Capt. & Asst. Surgeon, U.S.A." State Archives Collection, South Dakota State Historical Society Archives (SDSHS), Pierre.

No. 1 Has-a-dog [His-a-Day?] age 17
   Gunshot wound upper lobe of left lung—
   Jan. 5. Hemorrhage—died.
Alcove
No. 2—Frog [age?] 32
   Flesh wound gunshot: Entrance outer side of right thigh,
juncture middle & lower third—passed transversily [*sic*] through.
Exit—opposite—behind femur.
   Jan. 5. Suppuration set in. Bichloride dressing[.]
Alcove
No. 3 Help-'em-up
   1. Comp'd fracture, middle third right femur.
   2. Flesh wound left thigh lower third posteriorly[.]
   3. Comp'd fracture right radius upper third.
Alcove
No. 4 Looking Elk [age?] 38
   1. Flesh wound upper third right thigh bullet passed through
   2. Wound left thigh—lower outer side
   direction of ball upward & inward
   ball not found
Chancel

No. 5 Child—female—6
   "Holy-bone"
   Comp'd fracture upper third
   left thigh
Chancel
No[.] 6 Woman. "Puts-away-moccasins"
   Flesh wound upper third left thigh—ball passed through
Chancel
No. 7 Mrs[.] Big Foot—
   Two flesh wounds upper third left thigh [crossed out:] very near
groin.
   1 enters below middle of pouparts ligt. Exit over greater
trochanter & behind[.]
   2 low [?] ant. [anterior] inf. spinous process
   Exit two inches below first wound
   [Jan.?] 5 both suppurating
   [Jan.?] 13 Died of Pneumonia
No: 8. Squaw Ralthing [? illeg.] White Cow Woman
   Flesh wounds right thigh—
   Wound right side penetrating abdomen.
   Jan 10 Died Jan 10th. 6[:]45 a.m.
No[.] 9. Child—Swift boat
   Flesh wound right thigh
   Outer & upper aspect
[No.] 9 ½ Belly Woman
No. 10 Squaw. Yellow eyes
   1 Comp'd—comm-frac. right leg
   2 Severe flesh wound upper part right arm
   3 Gun shot flesh wound of buttocks
   4 " " " back
No. 11 "Long-holy-" Tall [crossed out: Tall, sound(?) boy]
   Flesh wound both shoulders
No. 12 Man—Shot many times
   1 Severe flesh wound right side
   fragment of shell.
   2 Wound right foot below joint
   3 Wound through left ankle joint or [illeg.] calcis [?]
   Jan. 5 Suppuration—Wound dressed

[Jan.] 6 Wound in side looking well; dressed

Other wounds dressed—looking well

[No.] 13 Girl—Deaf & dumb [?]—12 yrs.

1 Wound through right wrist

2 Flesh wound right side

Jan. 5 Suppuration both wounds doing well

[No.] 14 Squaw—"Sack woman" [Age?] 40

Flesh wound right hand, ball passed between 4 & 5 meta carpal.

[No.] 15 White-cow—boy 4 yrs—Son of 14

Flesh wound under [illeg.] middle third right forearm.

Jan. 5 Suppurating

[No.] 16 Pretty boy—6—

Burn left foot involving entire foot & ankle

[No.] 17 Boy Runs around the lodge 7

Com'd fracture radius upper third left arm

Jan. 5 Suppurating

[No.] 18 Baby—male—1 year with Mortur [illeg. Mother?]

1 Gunshot wound through left buttocks

2 Gunshot wound through scrotum

Both wounds made by same ball

Jan. 5 Suppuration in both. hernia left testicle Dressed

[Jan.] 9 Transferred to Indian Camp

[No.] 19 Squaw. "No name Woman"

Wounded through right hand between meta carpal bones

Jan. 5 No suppuration[,] doing well

[No.] 20 Yellow hair—10 yrs

Wound right ankle[,] D'g well

[Jan.] 9th Transferred to Indian Camp

[No.] 21 Fish—boy—8 [years]

Flesh wound right leg

[No.] 22 Squaw "Plain Voice"—21 [years]

1 Gun shot wound through pelvis—severe

2 Gun shot

[Jan.] 7th Died at 10 a.m.

[No.] 23 Last-Man 40 [years]

Gun shot wound through abdomen—lay on the field until the 5th [of] Jan.

Died Jan. 6—at 8 a.m.

[No.] 24 Knife Scabbard 68 [years]

1 Flesh wound[,] back[,] over centre of scapula running nine inches & emerging left side of spinous processes

2 Same as first—six inches below

[No.] 25 "Hunts-Alone" 50 [years]

1 Gunshot wound through knee joint—fracture of patella left leg—

2 Flesh wound outer side upper third left thigh

3 Gunshot wound entered upper lip—emerged at angle of jaw left side

[No.] 26 Squaw Holds-a-woman 16 [years]

1 Flesh wound left thigh[,] entrance front lower middle[,] exit outer side upper third

2 Gunshot wound through right knee by joint[,] entrance left of patella[,] exit in rear.

[No.] 27 Looks-back 18 [years]

Flesh wound left foot

[No.] 28 child "Liking" 7 [years] male

(1) Gun shot by one ball—flesh wound [illeg.] below middle of calf left leg.

(2) [no entry]

[No.] 29 Squaw Walking-buffalo 37 [years]

Flesh wound back lumbar region

[No.] 30 Squaw "Stands-a-showing"

Almost blind

Trachoma both eyes

[No.] 31 Child[,] 5, "Steals a running horse"

Gun shot injury over left scapular dorsum [dorsalis?], left side of neck & lower flow [floor?] of mouth carrying away part of inferior maxilla right side.

[No.] 33 Yellow Hair

Admitted Jan. 8th

Compound fracture middle third right humerus

[Jan.] 8 Proceeded to Indian camp

[No.] 34 Woman came in Jan. 8th

Comp'd fracture (gunshot) phalanges of little [illeg.] & lacerated wound middle finger of left hand.

Jan 9 Transferred to Indian camp

[No.] 35 Scout tent—19 [years]
   Jan[.] 9 1. Flesh wound calf right leg
   2. Flesh wound sole right foot.
   [Jan.] 13 Transferred to Indian camp
[No.] 36 Blue Hair—14 [years]
   Flesh wound post-aspect[,] left thigh—
   Wounded at fight on Wounded Knee.

3. Account of the scene at Wounded Knee on 1 January 1891, by Charles A. Eastman

Dr. Charles A. Eastman (Santee Dakota), a graduate of Boston University Medical School, offered this account of the scene at Wounded Knee on 1 January 1891, three days after the action there. At the time Eastman served as agency physician at Pine Ridge; the letter was written to a friend on 3 January. It appeared in the Cheyenne (Wyoming) Daily Leader *on 11 January 1891.*

Dear Mr. Wood—I will send you a short letter. Thursday morning [1 January 1891] I visited the field of battle, where all those Indians were killed on the Wounded Knee, last Monday. I went there to get the wounded, some who were left out. The soldiers brought with them about twenty-five, and I found eleven who were still living. Among them were two babies about 3 months old and an old woman, who is totally blind, who was left for dead [Stands-a-Showing?]. Four of them were found out in a field in the storm, which was very severe. They were half buried in the snow. It was a terrible and horrible sight to see women and children lying in groups, dead. I suppose they [each group] were of one family. Some of the young girls wrapped their heads with shawls and buried their faces in their hands. I suppose they did that so that they would not see the soldiers come up to shoot them. At one place there were two little children, one about 1 year old, the other about 3, lying on their faces, dead, and about thirty yards from them a woman lay on her face, dead. These were away from the camp about an eighth of a mile.

In front of the tents, which were in a semi-circle, lay dead most of the men. This was right by one of the soldiers['] tents. Those who were still living told me that that was where the Indians were ordered to hold a council with the soldiers. The accounts of the battle by the Indians were simple and confirmed one another, that the soldiers ordered them to go into camp, for they were moving them, and told them that they would give them provisions. Having done this they (the Indians) were asked to give up their arms, which was complied with by most of them, in fact all the old men, but many of the younger men did not comply, because they either had no arms or concealed them in their blankets. Then a[n] order was given to search their persons and their tents as well, and when a search was made of a wretch of an Indian, who was known as Good-for-Nothing, he fired the first shot, and killed one of the soldiers. They fired upon the Indians instantaneously. Shells were thrown among the women and children, so that they mutilated them most horribly. I tried to go to the field the next day [30 December] with some Indians, but I was not allowed to. I think it was a wise thing not to go so early. Even Thursday I thought I would be shot. Some of the Indians (friendly) found their relations lying dead. They waited and began to pull out their guns. My friend, Louis de Coteau, was with me, but left me when they acted in this manner. Before he left me the hostiles appeared. We did not take in all the wounded. Those we could not carry away we left in a log house and gave them food. I am busy in taking care of the wounded. I shall write in a day or so again. My love to all. Affectionately yours,

Chas. A. Eastman

4. Account of Zella Vespucia, January 1891, as published in the *St. Louis Post-Dispatch*

Zella Vespucia (Oglala), a mixed-blood Indian from Pine Ridge, was present at Wounded Knee. His personal account, recorded at Pine Ridge on 16 January 1891, was published in the St. Louis Post-Dispatch *four days later. The correspondent was Dent H. Robert.*

Zella Vespucia is the son of Wild Horse, an Ogallalla [*sic*] Sioux who went South many years ago and in his travels visited Mexico. Zella was born in Mexico during this visit, and a priest who did not like the name of Young Wolf, which would have been given him, presented him with the euphonius and aristocratic name of Zella Vespucia. Zella is a remarkably intelligent Indian and though too young to have acquired influence in his tribe, he is looked upon as the most intelligent man among them. He reads, writes and speaks both English and Indian and he is a firm friend of the white man. He was at the battle of Wounded Knee, and he was describing it to me the other day, showing the location of the troops. He paused in his recital and said: "That is a good story, but none of you newspaper men have told it yet. You don't know how. No white man knows how to tell of an Indian fight."

"Suppose you write it out for me?" I said.

"I will. I will tell how it happened."

He brought it to me to-day, and with a smile on his face.

"It took me a day and [a] half to do it," he said, "but here it is."

I send it exactly as he wrote it, without touching a pencil to it, and as an Indian's account of an Indian battle it is a rare curiosity.

[Ed. note: The following account contains numerous spelling and punctuation errors. Aside from correctly rendering and capitalizing proper names and punctuation to ensure clarity and accuracy, they have not otherwise been modified.]

PINE RIDGE AGENCY, S.D.

Indian battle of the fall of Dec. 29 in the year of 1890. . . . On Dec. 28 I was asked by [First] Lieutenant [William J.] Nickerlson

[Nicholson] of company I 7calvary commanded by Maj [Samuel M.] Whiteside [Whitside], to bring to them thier mail and one tent for them from Pine Ridge to wher they wer in campment at Wounded Knee, south Dakota as I thought there would not be any harm[.] I set out on my jouney the eavning of Dec 28, 1890 with a twenty mile drive over hills and throug deep canyons until I reached the command at sun down fealing very tierd. I drove up and dilevered my mesage and tent to capt vaumn [Varnum] of company B and 7 calvary . . . [illegible] . . . beaing one of the people of [illeg.] Reserve and my Little Log [illeg.—house?] being only 200, yards from camp [I] concluded to go there for my nights rest w[hen] to my surprise there were three reporters [illeg.] and at the waiting for big foots band of Indians who were on porcupine creek in camp. [The three reporters were Will Cressey, *Omaha Bee*; William F. Kelley, *Nebraska State Journal* (Lincoln); and Charles W. Allen, *Chadron Democrat*, who was a stringer for the *New York Herald*.]

It was a pleasant evening and I had a horse standing at my home[.] I thought it wise to go and catch him. I lit out for him a foot as it was close and my horses very tired and as a general thing Indian horses always range close where they are Left. I set out whistling, whith a piece of Dried beef in my hand as I really was very hungry.

I had just gone 150 yards when I looked westward towards Porcupine bute when my eyes full upon something very dark a mile or two a way which Looked Like a drove of Buffalo but I knew that there [were] no such things in the country in such Late days as this.

I knew it could not be any thing else but big foot's Band, which to be sure it was acompaid [accompanied] by the remains of custers Little 7 calvary, they came in very peaceful and camped near the soldiers camp not more than 50 yards. every thing went on very peaceful though the night and about midnight the rest of the calvary from Pine ridge came in for fear of danger from the red skins which the savages knew nothing of.

It was talked over by officers and scouts during the night to take their guns and amunition from them and give them lots of rations. Let them rest for a few days as thier horses was tierd then after that escort them in to Chief Red Clouds camp with the rest of their Band, of Sioux. during the night I felt very funy at times but did not Let it be known to any one as I am so acquanted with the Indians that I knew it best to keep my mouth shut.

I knew to take a gun from an Indian was almost dear Life, well I shall tell you my sight on the next morning.

I aroused bright and early to see all of the things in full trim. you can bet they were about as full as a goose. I mean mischief they were on it, yes, on it worse than a tag on good tobacco, you ought to bet they stayed on it I mean layed dead on the ground be fore night, well it was a scene that actress play on a ten cent stage in a dime musium.

they would shoot and shoot and got shot but not very bad as to consider the gang there were 5 soldiers to one Indian.

DISARMING THE BAND

but they needed them or they would have played a full house. at half past six on the 29 of dec. 1890, about half of the mounted soldiers mounted surounded the Indian village[.] then maj whiteside had the inturpretur to call all of the bucks out to hold a Little counsel and that they were a going to disarm them but did not entend to hurt any of them but after they had taken all of thier arms from them that he would send for some rations and give to them.

they all came out very nicely and set in a circle with their blankets on their backs. then the major gave command for three companies to be dismounted and form an angle around the bucks which was completed to comand them. He asked them

how many of you are willing to give up your guns?

when two steped forward and gave up their guns

then 19 more came to the front and said we havent any guns but if we had they would be for you if you want them.

In the meanwhile sevral Lieutenants and capt were going through their village taking guns arrows bows and war clubs, which was a very fine thing to most any ones eyes after they stoped fooling with the squaws and came back talking and making remarks about what nice guns and things they had in camps and returning to the dimond or triangle troops on foot they made a remark that we are all right now when one of the sergants said

are you not going to search the other gang who are going through those foolish motions.

They were just haveing a flying time with the medacine men at work. one said it wont take long to do a way with such few soldiers.

At that moment they began to search the other squad they began.

the first was a young man aged 17 named his dog [He's a Dog?]

they raised up his blanket to take his gun when he shot and threw up a handful of dust in his left hand

that means war

the soldiers said when the boy his dog [He's a Dog?], shot it was fowled by all of the rest of the Indians each bringing their man.

I was in between the soldiers & the reds & never got a scrach.

I had no gun or revolver but I did have a good belt full of morline cartrages.

I stayed like a Little boy stuck in tar.

I had to stay for I could not move.

I have heard people say that they have been so sceard that thier heart was in their mouth.

I really was so screard that I thought my whole stomache was in my mouth. when the ambulance team came wright straight in to the battle and up set the ambulance.

I heard people saying that they never Lost any Indians[,] you can bet I never Lost any bulets and I never got any either nor the worst of it was I dident want any either.

you can bet your gov. Boots.

Well the fight Lasted fully half an hour be fore the hotkiss [Hotch-kiss] guns comenced and when it did comence it threw Indians soldiers horses squaws and hard tack three miles from where they commenced.

but you must rember that the squaus were runing with their ponies and the soldiers after them just after eating hard tack crackers.

at about half-past 5 o'clock we all pull for Pine Ridge[,] what I mean by we all those who were Left a Live and some wounded.

the most preculiar case I ever saw was a priest by the name of father craft [Father Francis M. Craft.]

he was caring an Indian of[f] for rescue in his arms when his nobl arms man stab him in the shoulder and fled to get more blood but got Left,

well I am a catholic my self but what is the diference when a man is at wa[r?] especialy as young as I am and my nationality be sise [besides?] aught to be thought of well.

I will Leave my self out and stay with the battle.

we got home at midnight and when reaching the agency there was not an indian in the country [meaning at Pine Ridge Agency].

they had all Left for the ghost Dancers. . . .

I have been at Rev. C. [Charles] S. Cook Church since taking care of the Big foot's band of wounded which numbered about 60 in all but they have a great many of them died.

There is a woman by the name of Thankful who I think will Live[.] she is wounded 7 times with two compounds fractures. She won't alow them amutaded [amputated], they all seem to be doing very nicely, and for my self I am alright you may bet on that. I hope you will excuse my poor composition, but for a young wariors [this] sure is my best. I wish all my readers good Luck as my self, I am now [on] my way to Arizona. Yours truly,

Zella Vespucia.

[Postscript:] This is the story of the fatal encounters between the Indians and the soldiers, told with the similes of the frontier, the illustrations borrowed from poker, base ball and the hunt, and decked out here and there with a gem of the red man's natural eloquence. The letter is the result of the unaided labor of a day and a half—the story of the conduct of soldiers and Indians, and a sample of Indian sentiment which the Interior Department might profitably inspect with care.

Dent H. Robert [Staff Correspondent]

5. Edited version of Zella Vespucia's account, January 1891

This edited version of Zella Vespucia's account appeared in the Washington *(D.C.)* Evening Star *on 17 January 1891.*

[During] an evening of December, 1890, I was asked by an officer of the seventh cavalry to carry a tent and some mail out on Wounded Knee district for Major Whiteside [Whitside], who at that time was in command of a part of the same company [regiment] which was at that time looking for this man Big Foot. I, of course, as most all half-breeds, jumped at the offer just to say I was with soldiers. The next morning [28 December] at half-past 8 o'clock I made a break for the drive. I knew the road very well. When I had gotten about half way—it was only twenty miles distant from the agency to the scene of the Big Foot massacre, which happened after this time[—]I saw something coming along on top of a hill about 400 yards from the road. They were three Indians. They came up to me and one of them talked with me, but he said nothing at first to amount to anything, when he, all of a sudden, asked me where I was going. I sized him up to be a tough. I said in a very mild way in his own language that I was on my way home, for I only lived 200 yards from where the soldiers were camped. Then he asked me for some matches and also 25 cents. I gave him a few matches, but for the 25 cents I could not do anything for him, not as I did not wish to help him out, but because I had not a cent to my name. Money is a very hard thing to get in this country, if you believe me.

It was about a half an hour or more before they left. They talked of matters that are not to any one's benefit, therefore I will not mention them. When pulling out from my Indian friends I did feel very cheap, but made out that I was brave as any one of them. They turned and went back in the hills and I steered for my soldier friends. . . .

It was just about an hour and a quarter before reaching the camp. It was along in the day when I pulled in very tired. I drove up and inquired for the commander in charge, when Capt. Vaughn [Varnum?] spoke up and said "Son, I am left in charge of the camp, as the major [Whitside] has gone to Porcupine Tail creek to capture Big Foot's band, which was found by Little Bat [Garnier], a scout." I began to unload my little freight and tell the captain about my encounter. He immediately sent an Indian scout by the name of High Backbone after them, but he soon returned, stating that he saw something over on the divide going toward the agency, about ninc milcs from mc. [High Back Bone was ultimately killed at Wounded Knee.] In the meantime I drove over to the house of ours and put up my team. It was very lonesome at the house, as I walked back to the camp for company.

On reaching camp, Capt. Vaughn asked me to do a little interpreting for him from two Indians, who were found by the same scouts. The captain said to them: "Did you all catch sight of the buffalo soldiers [then operating north of Pine Ridge Agency]? The Indians call the negro soldiers buffaloes. One of the Indians spoke up and said: "If we should have laid our eyes on them we would have driven them out of the country." There were a great many teamsters standing around listening to the conversation, when they all broke into a roar of laughter. The Indians looked very savage, but I did not feel anyways afraid of them at the time. The name of one of them was Wi-Ya-Ka-Waste, which means in English Good Feather, and the other was named Tu-We-Wi-Ko-Ki-Pe-Ini, which is translated Afraid-Of-No-One. About that time the troops returned homeward with Big Foot's band. Si-Tan-Ka is the Indian name of the noble Big Foot. But in my opinion his feet were not any larger than the general run of Indians'. But he has taken a furlough to the happy hunting ground, from which, I think, he will not return very soon. You must not think he went alone, for he had with him a great many others. His wife did not go when he did, but about one week later she passed in her checks very quietly with a wound in the left thigh, but very severe. She had the pneumonia with the wound. It was a very heavy burden for her to take, but could not be helped, as the seventh cavalry wanted to get even. They did not tell me that, but the way they fought was enough to tell, and you can bet I was in the fight and witnessed it all the way through. . . .

I started to tell you about them coming in camp. They came in that evening and camped only across the road from the troops camp and the soldiers divided up their bedding with some of the Indians that night. In the meantime two soldiers and a scout made their way for the said agency, where they had the rest of their company of troops to come for help if there should be any trouble, as they were talking of taking the guns away from the Indians. They also ordered rations for the Indians and told them they were going to issue them to them tomorrow.

On the morning of the battle I rose early and said to one of my friends that "I will stay until you all go in and go with you all for company," but at 8:30 the ball began to roll, and they did roll for awhile—I mean cannon balls.

Then soldiers began to search the village and take the guns. They proceeded very nicely and quiet, going through the village, but when they got through collecting guns from the squaws and came back into the circle where the bucks were sitting down they proposed to search the men. There were about twenty-one on one side who gave up their guns very peacefully. . . .

When the soldiers stepped over to the next game and began to disarm them there was a young man by the name of His Dog, who had a gun and objected to give it up. He had been quite intimate with the medicine man. When His Dog refused to give up he fired a shot. Then all of the rest of the Indians fired a volley before the soldiers did anything. Then some of them said, "Look out!" several times. Then one buck, with a painted ghost shirt on, shot and Capt. Wallace staggered back. By that time an Indian came up behind him, and taking from his hand a war club and struck him several blows on the cranium until he fell dead on the ground, but that fellow got it plugged to him very near the same time he hit the captian [*sic*]. Friends, I don't say that from hearsay, but I was in the center of the fight without any arms to fight with, except a belt full of cartridges. Well, I shan't put anything of my particulars, as I am all right, but God was the one who saved me, or at least I have that idea. . . .

When they killed Capt. Wallace they did not cease shooting, but became all the worse. I heard a man, whom after the battle I found out was [First] Lieut. [William J.] Nicholson, say two or three times: "Don't shoot squaws," and after that several others repeated the same words. In my judgment, though[,] it could not be helped, as a deep ravine ran on one side of the battleground with the Hotchkiss guns pouring straight into the men who were at it and it was so close that the squaws could not be helped. In those twenty-one who first came out were some of our Oglala Sioux. I am acquainted with some of them. One is named Carol Heartman, aged sixteen years, badly wounded in left arm and thigh. He lives on Wounded Knee creek, a good young man. Last fall the rule came for them to cut the hair of the boys that attended school. He was a day school scholar and had been in our boarding school at the agency. His father comes to see him and is very sorry for his son's misfortune, but he told me that the boy deserved what he received, because he would not listen to him and ran off from home to keep from getting his hair cut.

6. Account of Help Them, January 1891

Help Them (Oglala Lakota) gave his "Statement of Help Them, son of Heart Man, living on Wounded Knee [Creek]," as translated by Philip F. Wells, on 7 January 1891, at Pine Ridge Agency. Copy in Folder 41, Drawer 6, Thomas Odell Collection, Leland D. Case Library for Western Historical Studies, E. Y. Berry Library–Learning Center, Black Hills State University, Spearfish, S.Dak.

I am an Oglala. I went on a visit to Big Foot's camp on Cheyenne River and, as I was on my way home, I came along with Big Foot's people.

When we were taken by the soldiers, we were treated kindly by them, and we were given provisions to eat. The only thing that didn't look friendly on the part of the soldiers was, they kept their guns in readiness for action, and when we came into camp they placed two cannons on a hill covering our camp. The men were not allowed to take the horses to water, so the watering of the horses was done by the little boys. To the best of my knowledge, the Indians had no intention of fighting.

The disarming of the Indians had begun peaceably by some of the men. I had given up my gun and had left the circle and was going towards our camp, where all of the women and children were.

For some time before that, the medicine man had been going around going through the maneuvers of the Ghost Dance. He stopped and turned around facing a crowd of young men who were standing together with their guns concealed under their blankets and spoke to them, but I could not hear what he said, though I heard all he spoke to answer, "How ["Yes"]."

Shortly after I heard a white man say something in excited tones, which I could not understand. I looked around and I saw some of the Indians throw off their blankets and raise their guns, and one of the Indians fired a shot. I did not recognize him. As I turned to run, I heard a few shots following the first. Then the firing began so fast I could not tell what happened after that.

The medicine man had been telling the other Indians all the way that the soldiers' bullets could not reach them (the Indians), no matter how the soldiers would shoot at them.

7. Account of Frog, January 1891

Frog (Miniconjou) gave his "Statement of Frog, of Big Foot's Band," as translated by Philip F. Wells, Colonel Forsyth's interpreter, circa 7 January 1891, within two weeks of Wounded Knee, at Pine Ridge Agency. Copy in Folder 41, Drawer 6, Odell Collection, Case Library.

I am a brother or [of] Big Foot. We left Cheyenne River where we . . . had been living, as Big Foot was tired of the bad treatment he had been getting at the hands of both Indians and white people, and be-sides[,] Big Foot and his band had been asked at different times during the summer by Red Cloud, Little Wound, [Young Man] Afraid-of-his-Horses[,] and No Water to come to Pine Ridge Agency and join them.

From the time we left home till we came to Pine Ridge Reservation, we had not been interfered with by soldiers or anyone else. When we were taken by the soldiers the day before the fight, they treated us with nothing but kindness and brought [us] to camp. The following morning the soldiers began blowing their bugles, and they began standing around us in ranks, but I thought nothing of it, as it was their natural custom to do so. And then we were told (all of us) to come out and sit down at a place near the door of Big Foot's tent, which we did. Then a lot of soldiers got in between us (men) and our camp, separating us (men) from the women and children. An officer told us then he wanted to take our guns, and as soon as we gave them up, he would give us provisions and we [could] go on our way. We, the older men, consented willingly and began giving them up. We had all given them up, as I thought, when I saw an Indian with a gun under his blanket. And the soldiers saw it at the same time, and they took it away from him. They (soldiers) commenced searching the Indians one at a time. The medicine man was going through the incantations of the Ghost Dance. [He] stopped and began speaking to the young men, but I paid no attention to what he said, as I had not the least fear of any trouble. So I pulled my blanket over my head and didn't see anything till I heard much talking in loud voices. I uncovered my head and I saw everyone had arisen on his feet. And

I heard a shot coming from where the young Indians stood. Shortly after that, I was shot down and I [lay] there as I fell. The firing was so fast and the smoke and dust so thick I did not see much more of the fight until it was over. I heard someone saying, "Indians, all of you who are yet alive, raise your hands. The white men do not wish to kill you." I raised my head and saw a man standing among the dead, and I asked him if he was the man they called Fox [interpreter Philip F. Wells], and he said he was. And I said, "Will you come to me?," and he came to my side. I then asked him, "Who is that man lying there half burnt?," and he said, "I understand it is the medicine man," and I threw at him (the medicine man) [in a five-fingered hand gesture] my bitterest hatred and contempt. I then said to Fox, "He has caused the death of all of our people."

8. Account of Hehakawanyakapi (Elk Saw Him), January 1891

Hehakawanyakapi (Elk Saw Him) (Oglala) gave the following undated account (probably 7 January 1891), which Reverend Charles Smith Cook and interpreter Philip F. Wells verified. Philip F. Wells materials, Folder 41, Drawer 6, Odell Collection, Case Library.

I am 38 years old, Hump's band. A ghost dancer. I came along with Big Foot's band by accident. We heard that Big Foot and his people were invited to come and live here with the Oglalas. I joined them, being myself an Oglala. The fifth day out we met the soldiers. We were just coming down the hills beyond Porcupine Tail Creek, when we were met by four scouts. I saw only one, Highback Bone. The others rode back rapidly to tell the soldiers of our coming. I asked the scout the object of his coming to us. He answered, "we heard you were coming and so we have come to meet you. Everything will be all right." We got into Porcupine Tail Creek and made coffee there. Then we came on, preceded by our horsemen. Presently it was said, "Soldiers are coming." I looked and saw them coming, making much dust. They finally halted at a given place not far from us. We still went toward them, preceded by our horsemen. On a little rise they placed two cannon covering us, having their other guns in readiness for firing. We went right on towards them and finally reached them, our people saying "They are only fooling us." We finally mingled together with them, and came on with them, some of the soldiers preceding us and the rest coming on behind. We reached the Wounded Knee, where we camped right by their side. Of course, we were guarded. It was a lonely coming. Rations were soon given us and everything seemed friendly. There being no bad intentions on our part, we entertained no sense of fear. There was no suspicion on our part towards the soldiers. We were simply coming this way because of the invitation from Red Cloud, Young Man-Afraid-of-His-Horses and other chiefs.

We did not ask for the usual passes because we knew we would be refused. At the Wounded Knee the men were not allowed to take the horses to water. The boys had charge of that. Even then I did not think that we were under suspicion. After breakfast that morning [29 December], I went to the place near Big Foot's tent, which was near the soldiers. The soldiers said they wanted all our guns. Many of the soldiers (cavalry) arranged themselves in positions, and the infantry [*sic*—dismounted cavalry troopers; there were no infantry troops at Wounded Knee] came on between us and the women and children. All the men were thus separated from the women. I heard an officer saying something. He must have given orders, because the soldiers began loading their guns and holding them in readiness for firing. I called out and said, "Let us give up every gun." I said this because I thought it was best to do so. Many were brought. I cannot say exactly how many, but I thought all were gathered up. Every man in the Indian party did not have a gun. I gave up my Winchester, which was all that I had. A man named Hose-Yanka (a rascally fellow) was at this juncture "making medicine," but I did not hear what he was saying. About this time a more rigid searching of the Indians was instituted. When soldiers came to me, I gave up my cartridge belt. A soldier took it and began taking off the cartridges, apparently to return to me the belt, so I stood by him waiting for it. Just then I heard the report of a gun and saw a man throwing off his sheet covering. Then followed firing from all sides. I threw myself on the ground. I then jumped up to run towards the Indian camp, but was then and there shot down. I was hit on my right leg and soon after was shot again on the other leg.

When the general firing ceased, I heard an interpreter calling out, saying the wounded would be kindly treated. I opened my eyes and looked about and saw the dead and wounded all around me. Five men and Mrs. Big Foot were near me, alive. My wife and younger child, I hear, were not killed, but my older sister is missing. . . . The young man who fired the first gun is the one who brought all this trouble upon us."

9. Account of Long Bull, January 1891

Long Bull gave this account of Wounded Knee. It was originally printed in the Washington Evening Star, *28 January 1891.*

Long Bull, a Minnecongue [Miniconjou] Sioux who escaped from the battle of Wounded Knee, told how the Big Foot band came to leave Cheyenne river. He said: "We did not like the way were treated at Cheyenne river. Our rations were poor and many hearts were bad. Red Cloud had sent to us to say that if we were not well treated we might come to Pine Ridge and live. We were at our homes when a white man came to us—I do not know his white name, but his Indian name is Red Beard [John Dunn]—and he said the soldiers were coming to fight, so we had better get out. Then we came to Wounded Knee and had that fight. We did not want to fight. The soldiers said we must give up our guns and some of us did. I had no gun. Then the soldiers went into the tepees and kicked the beds about and upset everything a great deal. Some Indians had guns under their blankets, hiding them, for an Indian thinks much of his gun. The soldiers used the Indians very roughly and made them mad, until by and by 'Sits Straight' (the medicine man) gave the signal to shoot. Big Foot did not want to fight; he was sick. We were prisoners all the night before and in our tepees we talked peace. Among ourselves we said we would give up all the guns, for we did not expect to fight. Indians much like white men. They get mad when a man hurts them and tears their clothes and pulls their guns away. That made us fight."

10. Account of Ellis Standing Bear, ca. January 1891

Luther Standing Bear gave this third-person account of his brother Ellis Standing Bear (Sicangu Lakota) circa January 1891. Ellis Standing Bear served the army as a scout and was present at Wounded Knee. Luther's rendition of this story appeared in his book My People the Sioux, *ed. E. A. Brininstool (Boston: Houghton Mifflin Co., 1928), pp. 231–33.*

My father and his wives were living at the [Pine Ridge] agency. . . . My brother Ellis was employed as a scout for the soldiers [at Pine Ridge Agency]. . . . He was present at the killing of all of Big Foot's band, and was a witness to everything that happened. Here is what he related to me:

The whole band of Big Foot had their tipis in a circle. They were quiet, but the soldiers surrounded their camp, on horseback, with their guns pointed right into the faces of the Indians. An officer gave the command to disarm all the Indians. Their guns and knives were to be taken away from them, leaving them without any weapons.

A few of the soldiers went forward to collect the weapons of the Indians as they stood and sat around. Among this band was one boy who was not as bright as he might have been, being somewhat half-witted, and hardly any one ever paid any attention to whatever he did or said. In times of a crisis such people are the sort to be watched.

He stood around with the rest of the Indians while the soldiers held them with covered guns. This fellow saw that the weapons of his people were being taken away without resistance. He kept saying in the Sioux tongue, "Don't give up your guns and knives; I am going to shoot." However, his talk made no impression on any one, as he had always been considered harmless and not accountable for his speech or actions.

As a soldier approached him for his gun, he did not hand it over, but suddenly raised it and emptied the full contents right into the soldier's face. The man dropped dead. Most of the weapons of the Indians had already been collected, and this half-witted youth was the only one who shot at that time. The next instant the command came from the officer in command of the troops, "Fire!" The soldiers were in a circle, surrounding the Indians, and when they began shooting, many of their bullets went across the circle and killed their own men.

When the shooting began, my brother Ellis knew there was no chance for the life of any one who remained within that circle, so he ran his horse at top speed to the highest point of a hill about a quarter of a mile away. There he was a witness to all that happened. The soldiers kept shooting until nothing stirred within the entire camp. Little babies were shot to death right in the carriers strapped to their mothers' backs. All the trouble was due to the foolish, uncalled-for act of one half-witted Indian!

In the white men's accounts of this slaughter, it states that many soldiers were shot. So they were, but they were killed by their own comrades, as there was not a gun among the Indians at the time the shooting began.

My brother Willard, who was a scout at the agency, then told me what happened after the slaughter was over. Some of the scouts ran their horses to the agency to let the people know what was happening. To many this meant great sorrow, as they had relatives among Big Foot's band. The Episcopal Church was immediately turned into an emergency hospital. Here the wounded [Indians] were taken to be cared for.

11. Statement of Elaine Goodale regarding wounded survivors, January 1891

Elaine Goodale, supervisor of education at Pine Ridge Agency, included this statement in her report to the Bureau of Indian Affairs on 12 January 1891. It was based on accounts derived from wounded Lakota survivors of Wounded Knee that she attended in the makeshift hospital at the Holy Cross Episcopal Church at Pine Ridge Agency, as well as others present on the field, and published in the Washington Post, *17 January 1891. See also Goodale's extended remarks in Elaine Goodale Eastman,* Sister to the Sioux: The Memoirs of Elaine Goodale Eastman, 1885–91, *ed. Kay Graber (Lincoln: University of Nebraska Press, 1978), pp. 163–68.*

I was not an eye-witness of the fight, and my information has been obtained chiefly from Indian prisoners who engaged in it and half-breeds who were present, and from parties who visited the battlefield several days after the encounter.

The testimony of the survivors of Big Foot's band is unanimous on one important point: namely, that the Indians did not deliberately plan a resistance. The party was not a war party according to their statements (which I believe to be true), but a party intending to visit the agency on the invitation of Red Cloud.

The Indians say that many of the men were unarmed. When they met the troops, they anticipated no trouble. There was constant friendly intercourse between the soldiers and the Indians, even women shaking hands with the officers and men. The demand for their arms was a surprise to the Indians but the great majority chose to submit quietly. The tepees had already been searched and a large number of guns, knives and hatchets confiscated when the searching of the persons of the men was begun. The women say that they, too, were searched and their knives (which they always carry for domestic purposes) taken from them. A number of the men had surrendered their rifles and cartridge belts when one young man (who is described by the Indians as a good-for-nothing young fellow) fired a single shot. This called forth a volley from the troops and the firing and confusion became general.

I do not credit the statement which has been made by some, that the women carried arms and participated actively in the fight. The weight of testimony is overwhelming against this supposition. . . . They were pursued up the ravines and shot down indiscriminately by the soldiers. . . . The killing of women and children was in part unavoidable, owing to the confusion, but I think there is no doubt that it was in many cases deliberate and intentional. The Seventh Cavalry, Custer's old command, had an old grudge to repay. [A common viewpoint circulated that the Seventh Cavalry held resentment against the Lakotas since their victory over Lieutenant Colonel George A. Custer's command at the Little Bighorn River fourteen years earlier in 1876.]

The party of scouts who buried the dead report eighty-four bodies of men and boys, forty-four of women and eighteen of young children. Some were carried off by the hostiles. A number of prisoners, chiefly women, have since died of their wounds, and more will soon follow. The party who visited the battlefield on January 1 to rescue any wounded who might have been abandoned, and brought in seven, report that nearly all the bodies of the men were lying close about Big Foot's tent, while the women and children were scattered along a distance of two miles from the scene of the encounter. . . . The irresponsible action of one hot-headed youth should not be the signal for a general and indiscriminate slaughter of the unarmed and helpless.

Respectfully,
Elaine Goodale.
Supervisor of Education.

12. White Buffalo's opinion on the Battle of Wounded Knee, February 1891

White Buffalo offered the following opinion on Wounded Knee, as published in the Kansas City Star *on 10 February 1891. He is listed as White Bull on "Copy of Muster Roll, Company A. Indian Scouts. November 27, 1890 to Apr. 30, 1891," Pine Ridge Agency, Folder 650, Box 657, General Records, Main Decimal Files, Records of the Bureau of Indian Affairs,* RG *75,* NA, *Kansas City, Mo.*

White Buffalo, the noted Sioux scout, who has been in the service of the United States for several years and who figured prominently during the recent Indian troubles in the Northwest, was in the city last evening on the way to Kingfisher, OK, performing a government mission. White Buffalo is above the average Indian in point of intelligence, and he speaks the English tongue plainly enough to be understood.

White Buffalo was at the battle of Wounded Knee. When asked by a reporter for THE STAR regarding the origin of the trouble which resulted in the death of Captain Wallace and several brave soldiers and scouts, not to mention the number of Sioux braves who were sent beyond the "great divide," he said the soldiers were plainly at fault, and that it was the insulting and overbearing conduct of a certain captain, whose name the scout refused to give, that precipitated the trouble.

There need have been no serious results from the surrender of the Indians, said White Buffalo, had Colonel Forsyth's orders been strictly observed by the subordinates. The Indians were subject to insults of the greatest character when they chose to come into camp and give themselves up.

"White man shoot Indian first," said White Buffalo[.] "Indian run for him gun and fight heap much. White man shoot Indian heap, too, and I shoot Indan [*sic*], too."

White Buffalo told how the Indian agents at Pine Ridge and Standing Rock had systematically swindled the Indians for years. The Sioux, he declared, were actually suffering for the want of food, which was furnished to the agents for them in sufficient quantities by the government, but the full amount of which never reached the Indians, owing to the dishonorable and disreputable methods resorted to by agents. There would never have been an uprising among the Sioux had they been well fed.

The Sioux, he thinks, will prosper and make rapid strides in advancement toward civilization if they are properly fed and the children continue to receive the instruction of the Indian schools and that which the missionaries give them.

13. "Account given of Indians of the fight at Wounded Knee," Washington, D.C., February 1891

The following extracts are from the verbatim stenographic report of councils held by delegations of Sioux with the Commissioner of Indian Affairs in Washington, D.C., on 11 February 1891. Originally printed as "Account given by Indians of the fight at Wounded Knee Creek, South Dakota, December 29, 1890," in U.S., Department of the Interior, Office of Indian Affairs, Sixteenth Annual Report of the Commissioner of Indian Affairs to the Secretary of the Interior, 1891, *vol. 1 (Washington, D.C.: Government Printing Office, 1891), pp. 179–81. It was reprinted in James Mooney, "The Ghost-Dance Religion and the Sioux Outbreak of 1890," in* Fourteenth Annual Report of the Bureau of Ethnology to the Smithsonian Institution, *1892–1893, pt. 2 (Washington, D.C.: Government Printing Office, 1896), pp. 884–86. (A slightly variant version, perhaps provided by another translator, also appeared in the* New York Times, *12 February 1891.) The delegations included fourteen representatives from the six Sioux reservations. Red Cloud did not attend. The council served to permit the chiefs in attendance to air concerns regarding recent appropriations, compensation for property losses in the wake of Wounded Knee, education, and reservation boundary matters. Note that several spellings of "Oglala" appear in this account; they have not been corrected.*

Turning Hawk, Pine Ridge (Mr. Cook [Rev. Charles S. Cook, prelate at the Holy Cross Episcopal Church at Pine Ridge and a Yankton Sioux], interpreter). My purpose to-day is to tell you what I know of the condition of affairs at the agency where I live. A certain falsehood came to our agency from the west which had the effect of a fire upon the Indians, and when this certain fire came upon our people those who had certain far-sightedness and could see into the matter, made up their minds to stand up against it and fight it. The reason we took this hostile attitude to this fire was because we believed that you your-self [i.e., Commissioner Thomas J. Morgan] would not be in favor of this particular mischief-making thing; but just as we expected, the people in authority did not like this thing and we were quietly told that we must give up or have nothing to do with this certain movement. Though this is the advice from our good friends in the East, there were, of course, many silly young men who were longing to become identified with the [Ghost Dance] movement, although they knew that there was nothing absolutely bad, nor did they know anything absolutely good in connection with the movement.

In the course of time we heard that the soldiers were moving towards the scene of trouble. After a while some of the soldiers finally reached our place and we heard that a number of them also reached our friends at Rosebud [Agency]. Of course, when a large body of soldiers is moving towards a certain direction they inspire a more or less amount of awe, and it is very natural that the women and children who see this large moving mass are made afraid of it and be put in a condition to make them run away. At first we thought that perhaps Pine Ridge and Rosebud were the only two agencies where soldiers were sent, but finally we heard that the other agencies fared likewise. We heard and saw that about half of our friends at Rosebud Agency, from fear at seeing the soldiers, began the move of running away from their agency towards ours (Pine Ridge), and when they had gotten inside of our reservation they there learned that right ahead of them at our agency was another large crowd of soldiers, and while the soldiers were there there was constantly a great deal of false rumor flying back and forth. The special rumor I have in mind is the threat that the soldiers had come there to disarm the Indians entirely and to take away all their horses from them. That was the oft-repeated story.

So constantly repeated was this story that our friends from Rosebud, instead of going to Pine Ridge, the place of their destination, veered off and went in some other direction, towards the "Bad Lands." We did not know definitely how many, but understood there were 300 lodges of them, about 1,700 people. Eagle Pipe, Turning Bear, High Hawk, Short Bull, Lance, No Flesh, Pine Bird, Crow Dog, Two Strike, and White Horse were the leaders.

Well, the people after veering off in this way, many of them who believe in peace and order at our own agency, were very anxious that some influence should be brought upon these people. In addition to our love of peace we remembered that many of these people were related by blood. So we sent out peace commissioners to the people who were thus running away from their agency. I understood at the time that they were simply going away from fear because of so many soldiers. So constant was the word of these good men from Pine Ridge Agency that finally they succeeded in getting away half of the party from Rosebud, from the place where they took refuge, and finally were brought to the agency at Pine Ridge. Young-man-afraid-of-his-horses, Little Wound, Fast Thunder, Louis Shangreau, John Grass, Jack Red Cloud, and myself were some of these peacemakers.

The remnant of the party from Rosebud not taken to the agency finally reached the wilds of the Bad Lands. Seeing that we had succeeded so well, once more we went to the same party in the Bad Lands and succeeded in bringing these very Indians out of the depths of the Bad Lands and were being brought towards the agency. When we were about a day's journey from our agency we heard that a certain party of Indians (Big Foot's band) from the Cheyenne River Agency was coming towards Pine Ridge in flight.

CAPT. SWORDS [Sword, who was not present at Wounded Knee]. Those who actually went off of the Cheyenne River Agency probably number 303, and there were a few from the Standing Rock Reserve with them, but as to their number I do not know. There were a number of Ogalallas, old men and several boys, coming back with that very same party, and one of the very seriously wounded boys was a member of the Ogallalla boarding school at Pine Ridge Agency. He was not on the war-path, but was simply returning home to his agency and to his school after a summer visit to relatives on the Cheyenne River.

TURNING HAWK [who was not present at Wounded Knee]. When we heard that these people were coming towards our agency we also heard this. These people were coming towards Pine Ridge Agency and when they were almost on the agency they were met by the soldiers and surrounded and finally taken to the Wounded Knee Creek, and there at a given time their guns were demanded. When they had delivered them up the men were separated from their families, from their tepees, and taken to a certain spot. When the guns were thus taken and the men thus separated there was a crazy man, a young man of very bad influence and in fact a nobody, among that bunch of Indians fired his gun, and of course the firing of a gun must have been the breaking of a military rule of some sort, because immediately the soldiers returned fire and indiscriminate killing followed.

SPOTTED HORSE. This man shot an officer in the Army; the first shot killed this officer. I was a voluntary scout at that encounter and I saw exactly what was done and that was what I noticed; that the first shot killed an officer. As soon as this shot was fired, the Indians immediately began drawing their knives and they were exhorted from all sides to desist, but this was not obeyed. Consequently, the firing began immediately on the part of the soldiers.

TURNING HAWK. All the men who were in a bunch were killed right there, and those who escaped that first fire got into the ravine and as they went along up the ravine for a long distance they were pursued on both sides by the soldiers and shot down, as the dead bodies showed afterwards. The women were standing off at a different place from where the men were stationed, and when the firing began those of the men who escaped the first onslaught went in one direction up the ravine, and then the women who were bunched together at another place went entirely in a different direction through an open field, and the women fared the same fate as the men who went up the deep ravine.

AMERICAN HORSE [who was not present]. The men were separated as has already been said from the women, and they were surrounded by the soldiers. Then came next the village of the Indians and that was entirely surrounded by the soldiers also. When the firing began, of course, the people who were standing immediately around the young man who fired the first shot were killed right together, and then they turned their guns, Hotchkiss guns, etc., upon the women who were in the lodges standing there under a flag of truce, and of course as soon as they were fired upon they fled, the men fleeing in one direction and the women running in two different directions. So that there were three general directions in which they took flight.

There was a woman with an infant in her arms who was killed as she almost touched the flag of truce, and the women and children of course were strewn all along the circular village until they were dispatched. Right near the flag of truce a mother was shot down with her infant; the child not knowing that its mother was dead was still nursing, and that was especially a very sad sight. The women as they were fleeing with their babes on their backs were killed together, shot right through, and the women who were very heavy with child were also killed. All the Indians fled in these three directions, and after most all of them had been killed a cry was made that all those who were not killed or wounded should come forth and they would be safe. Little boys who were not wounded came out of their places of refuge, and as soon as they came in sight a number of soldiers surrounded them and butchered them there.

Of course we all feel very sad about this affair. I stood very loyal to the Government all through those troublesome days, and believing so much in the Government and being so loyal to it, my disappointment was very strong, and I have come to Washington with a very great blame on my heart. Of course it would have been all right if only the men were killed; we would feel almost grateful for it. But the fact of the killing of the women, and more especially the killing of the young boys and girls who are to go to make up the future strength of the Indian people, is the saddest part of the whole affair and we feel it very sorely.

I was not there at the time before the burial of the bodies, but I did go there with some of the police and the Indian doctor [Charles A. Eastman] and a great many of the people, men from the agency, and we went through the battle field and saw where the bodies were from the track of the blood.

TURNING HAWK: I had just reached the point where I said that the women were killed. We heard, besides the killing of the men, of the onslaught also made upon the women and children and they were treated as roughly and indiscriminately as the men and boys were.

Of course this affair brought a great deal of distress upon all the people, but especially upon the minds of those who stood loyal to the Government and who did all that they were able to do in the matter of bringing about peace. They especially have suffered much distress and are very much hurt at heart. These peacemakers continued on in their good work, but there were a great many fickle young men who were ready to be moved by any change in the events there, and consequently, in spite of the great fire that was brought upon all, they were ready to assume an [*sic*] hostile attitude. These young men got themselves in readiness and went in the direction of the scene of battle so that they might be of service there. They got there and finally exchanged shots with the soldiers. This party of young men was made up from Rosebud, Ogalalla (Pine Ridge), and members of any other agencies that happened to be there at the time. While this was going on in the neighborhood of Wounded Knee—the Indians and soldiers exchanging shots—the agency, our home, was also fired into by the Indians. Matters went on in this strain until the evening came on, and then the Indians went off down by White Clay Creek. When the agency was fired upon by the Indians from the hillside, of course the shots were returned by the Indian police who were guarding the agency buildings.

Although fighting seemed to have been in the air, yet those who believed in peace were still constant at their work. Young-Man-Afraid-of-His-Horses, who had been on a visit to some other agency in the North or Northwest, returned, and immediately went out to the people living about White Clay Creek, on the border of the Bad Lands, and brought his people out. He succeeded in obtaining the consent of the people to come out of their place of refuge and return to the agency. Thus the remaining portion of the Indians who started from Rosebud were brought back into the agency.

Mr. Commissioner, during the days of the great whirlwind out there these good men tried to hold up a counteracting power, and that was "Peace." We have now come to realize that peace has prevailed and won the day. While we were engaged in bringing about peace our property was left behind, of course, and most of us have lost everything; even down to the matter of guns with which to kill ducks, rabbits, etc., shotguns, and guns of that order. When Young-Man-Afraid brought the people in and their guns were asked for, both men who were called hostiles and men who stood loyal to the Government delivered up their guns.

14. **Variant account of Washington, D.C., meeting, 11 February 1891**

*A variant description of the Washington, D.C., meeting on
11 February 1891 appeared as follows in Edward S. Ellis,* The Indian
Wars of the United States from the First Settlement at Jamestown,
in 1607, to the Close of the Great Uprising of 1890–91 *(Chicago:
J. D. Kenyon & Co., 1902), pp. 452–55.*

Frightened at the approach of the soldiers, and hearing all manner of rumors as to what the soldiers were going to do with them, they [Big Foot's people] fled into the Bad Lands. [While they were heading to Pine Ridge,] and when they had almost reached the agency, they were met by the soldiers and surrounded and finally taken to the Wounded Knee Creek, and there, at a given time, their guns were demanded, and when they had delivered them up the men were separated from their families, from their tepees, and taken to a certain spot, their guns having been given up. When the guns were thus taken and the men thus separated, there was a crazy man, a young man of very bad influence, and in fact a nobody among that bunch of Indians, fired his gun; and, of course, the firing of a gun must have been the breaking of a military rule of some sort, for immediately the soldiers returned the fire, and the indiscriminate killing followed.

The Commissioner [Thomas J. Morgan]: Did this man fire at the soldiers, or did he simply shoot in the air?

Spotted Horse: He shot an officer in the army. The first shot killed this officer. I was a voluntary scout at that encounter and I had just asserted that I saw exactly what was done, and that was what I noticed—that the first shot killed an officer.

The Commissioner: Did the soldiers return the fire immediately, or did the Indians keep up their firing?

Spotted Horse: As soon as the first shot was fired, the Indians immediately began drawing their knives, and they were exhorted from all sides to desist, but this was not obeyed; consequently the firing began immediately on the part of the soldiers.

Turning Hawk: All the men who were in the bunch were killed right there, and those who escaped that first fire got into the ravine, and as they went along up the ravine for a long distance they were pursued on both sides by the soldiers, and shot down, as the dead bodies showed afterward.

The Commissioner: In this fight did the women take any part?

Turning Hawk: They had no firearms to fight with.

The Commissioner: The statement has been made in the public press that the women fought with butcher knives, and this has been given as a reason why the women were shot.

Turning Hawk: When the men were separated and were bunched together at a given place, of course only the men were there; the women were at a different place entirely, some distance off.

The Commissioner: Was it possible for a soldier to tell the difference between an Indian man and an Indian woman? The statement has been made in the public press that the soldiers shot the women because they dressed in such a way that they could not tell they were women.

Turning Hawk: I think a man would be very blind if he could not tell the difference between a man and a woman. I have told you that the women were standing off at a different place from that where the men were stationed, and when the firing began those of the men who escaped the first onslaught went in one direction up the ravine, and then the women, who were bunched together at another place, went entirely in a different direction through an open field, and the women fared the same fate as the men who went up the deep ravine.

The Commissioner (to the interpreter): Tell these men that are present that I would like if he (Turning Hawk) makes any statement which they do not accept, that they will correct it. I want to get at the truth.

American Horse: The men were separated, as has already been said, from the women, and they were surrounded by the soldiers, who then came next [to] the village of the Indians, and that was entirely surrounded by the soldiers also. When the firing began, of course the people who were standing immediately around the young man who fired the first shot were killed right together, and then they turned their guns—Hotchkiss guns, etc.—upon the women, who were in the lodges, standing there under a flag of truce, and, of course, as soon as they were fired upon they fled, the men fleeing in one direction and the women running in two different directions. So that there were three general directions in which they took flight.

The Commissioner: Do you mean to say that there was a white flag in sight over the women when they were fired upon? [The white flag was further confirmed elsewhere.]

American Horse: Yes, sir; they were fired upon, and there was a woman with her infant in her arms who was killed as she almost touched the flag of truce, and the women and children, of course, were strewn all along the circular village until they were dispatched. Right near the flag of truce another was shot down with her infant. The child, not knowing that its mother was dead, was still nursing, and that was especially a very sad sight. The women, as they were fleeing with their babes on their backs, were killed together, shot right through, and the women who were very heavy with child were also killed. All the Indians fled in these three directions. After most of them had all been killed, a cry was made that all those who were not killed or wounded should come forth and they would be safe, and little boys who were not wounded came out of their places of refuge, and as soon as they came in sight a number of soldiers surrounded them and butchered them there.

The Commissioner (to the interpreter): I wish you would say to him that these are very serious charges to make against the United States Army. I do not want any statements made that are not absolutely true, and I want anyone here that feels that the statements are too strong to correct them.

American Horse: Of course we all feel very sad about this affair. I stood very loyal to the Government all through these troublesome days, and believing so much in the Government and being so loyal to it, my disappointment was very strong, and I have come to Washington with a very great blame against the Government, on my heart. Of course it would have been all right if only the men were killed; we would feel almost grateful for it. But the fact of the killing of the women, and more especially the killing of the young boys and girls, who are to go to make up the future strength of the Indian people— those being killed is the saddest part of the whole affair, and we feel it very sorely. This is all I know about that part of the story, and my good friend here [pointing to Turning Hawk] will continue his narrative.

The Commissioner: Does American Horse know these things of his own knowledge, or has he been told them?

American Horse: I was not there at the time before the burial of the bodies, but I did go there with some of the police, and the Indian doctor, and a great many of the people, men from the agency, and we went through the battlefield and saw where the bodies were from the track of the blood.

The Rev. Mr. Cook, a Sioux half-breed, pastor of an Episcopal church at Pine Ridge, who had at times acted as interpreter during the conference, rose, and, among other things, said:

"Much has been said about the good spirit with which the members of the Seventh Cavalry went to that scene of action. It has been said that the desire to avenge Custer's death was entirely absent from their minds. In coming toward Chicago in company with General Miles, I talked with one of his scouts, who was almost killed because he was compelled to fly with the Indians, being fired upon by the men whom he tried to serve and help. He told me that after he recovered from his flight, and succeeded in getting among the soldiers after they all got in from killing the Indians, an officer of high rank, he did not know who, came to him and said, with much gluttonous thought in his voice: 'Now we have avenged Custer's death,' and this scout said to him: 'Yes, but you had every chance to fight for your lives that day; these poor Indian people did not have that opportunity to protect and fight for themselves.' If that is an indication of the spirit of a number of the men in that company, I am sure the Seventh Cavalry cannot be free from any charge of going there with the kindest of motive simply to bring these poor people back."

After several others had spoken, the Commissioner declared the conference at an end.

15. Descriptive report of Lakota impressions of Wounded Knee, February 1891

This descriptive report reflecting Lakota impressions of Wounded Knee appeared in the Black Hills Weekly Journal *(Rapid City) on 20 February 1891. It references the dispersal of Lakota bodies in the area, as observed by an unidentified Pine Ridge informant conversant with the Oglalas. Part of this statement was later reprinted in Thomas A. Bland,* A Brief History of the Late Military Invasion of the Home of the Sioux *(Washington, D.C.: National Indian Defense Association, 1891), pp. 17–18.*

A Journal reporter yesterday enjoyed a conversation with a gentleman who, though seldom quoted on Indian matters, is remarkably well informed concerning them. He has been at or about Pine Ridge agency in an official or semi-official capacity for a number of years, is a close observer and has many means of information denied to most people. This gentleman says that so far as the Indians are concerned they do not manifest much feeling over the recent disturbances, excepting some hostility to the soldiers. [Regarding Wounded Knee,] they say it was all right for the troops to shoot down the warriors who brought on the fight, but that they were not warranted in killing defenseless women and children. They point to the fact that bodies of women and children were found miles away from the scene of the battle, to indicate that there was unnecessary slaughter. The fact that women and children were killed far from where the fight commenced was stated in the report of the court of inquiry in Colonel Forsythe's [*sic*] case, and endorsed by General Miles. The Journal's informant states that the bodies of one squaw, two little girls and a little boy were found five miles from the scene of the fight a week or more after that event. The bodies were evidently those of fugitives who had found their way from the battle field into the hills where they had subsisted several days on whatever they could gather. Their condition indicated they had not been dead longer than a day or two when found. Whether they were killed by soldiers or Cheyenne scouts was not known.[1] One or two of the faces were powder burned, indicating that whoever did the killing did it at short range. At one spot near the battle field were found the bodies of five girls, probably from nine to nineteen years of age. All had their blankets drawn over their faces, evidently to shut out the sight of the soldiers as they advanced to fire upon them. One little boy nine or ten years old told a pitiful story as he lay wounded in the [Episcopal church] hospital [at Pine Ridge Agency]. He was in Big Foot's camp when the fight commenced and hand in hand with another little fellow of about the same age he started out at the head of the gully so often referred to as the scene of greatest carnage. They ran to the top of the hill, when a soldier came in pursuit riding a white horse. When the trooper rode nearly up to them he dismounted, dropped on one knee and shot the narrator's companion through the head. "He then," continued the little sufferer, "fired again, the ball striking me in the leg. I fell, and the soldier got on his horse and rode away." Such incidents as these are responsible for what bitterness of feeling the Indians now display toward the troops.

1. Reference is to the killings at White Horse Creek, about five miles northwest of Wounded Knee and within hours of the fighting there, by a detachment of Seventh Cavalry under Captain Edward S. Godfrey. The dead included an Oglala woman, Walks Carrying the Red, and her three children, ages seven, nine, and twelve. They were buried at the site. *See* Jerome A. Greene, *American Carnage: Wounded Knee, 1890* (Norman: University of Oklahoma Press, 2014), pp. 240, 333–35.

16. Commentary of trader
Charles P. Jordan, March 1891

*In this letter, dated 11 March 1891, Charles P. Jordan, a trader at
Rosebud Agency, South Dakota, relates the experience of former
mixed-blood agency clerk Charles Tackett. The name of the recipient
is not known. Jordan to "Dear Doctor," vol. 1 [ledger], File Box 043,
Charles Percival Jordan Papers, H74-42, State Archives Collection,
SDSHS.*

[After Wounded Knee,] Chas Tackett guided the [army] command
from here [Rosebud Agency] to Pine Ridge [Agency], which while
enroute there, was ordered to bury the dead Indians at Wounded
Knee. He interviewed several wounded survivors—who laid all the
blame upon two young Indians who fired the first shots, [and] that
caused the other armed Indians to open upon the soldiers, the Indians then mingling among their women & children and continued
the fire upon the troops. One Indian who struck for a tent—just va-
cated by two half breed scouts, where they had left their guns, took
the latter and killed five soldiers before he was located and quitted
by a Hotchkiss. Such close fighting & continuous firing must have
produced a dense smoke, which rendered it difficult to distinguish
men from women, and in a group of dead, photographed, I saw a full
grown squaw who had on a catridge [*sic*] belt full of cartridges. . . .

Several times during my "short and *eventful*" career I have gotten
into trouble for telling the truth, and I generally have the reputation of resorting to nothing else. I might inform you of many easily
unsubstantiated facts, which would be of interest but might be the
cause of making it too interesting for myself. Your views and mine
as to certain matters regarding the management and control of the
Sioux, very naturally disagree, and I hope before you publish your
history of the Wounded Knee affair & the cause of the disaffection
of the Sioux, you will consult other persons for facts than (hearsay
evidence furnished by) "*instructed delegates*" to Washington.

17. Account of Philip F. Wells, May 1891

*Philip F. Wells (1850–1947), of mixed white and Santee Dakota
ancestry, was born in Minnesota and served as interpreter for
Colonel Forsyth at Wounded Knee on 29 December 1890. Wells
worked as an army guide at Fort Laramie and Camp Robinson in
1876–1877, and later as a scout. He was an interpreter on the Pine
Ridge, Cheyenne River, and Rosebud reservations, and subsequently
ranched near Kadoka, South Dakota. His statement herein
regarding recent enlistees among the Seventh Cavalry is accurate.
This early interview with Wells regarding Wounded Knee took place
in Sioux City, Iowa, and appeared in the* Sioux City Journal *on
5 May 1891.*

"[Wells] was willing to talk freely on Indian affairs. He was of the
opinion that the trouble of last fall and winter had been overcome
and that another uprising was improbable so long as the authorities
use due precaution in dealing with the Indians. . . .

[Question:] What do you know about the origin of the Wounded
Knee fight?

I was acting as interpreter for Col. Forsythe [*sic*], who commanded
the troops engaged in the fight. The Indians were drawn up in line
to be disarmed. I stood in front of them, trying to persuade them to
give up the guns that we knew were under their blankets. This they
refused to do. While I was talking a medicine man was addressing
the warriors. He told them that he had been assured that the bullets
of the white men could not pierce them and in his way, he was urging
them to fight. I knew what it meant and turned to tell the colonel that
we were to have a fight.

Just as I turned I heard a shot from the line of Indians, and turning about was in time to see a soldier fall and the Indians throw their
blankets aside and commence shooting. Then I heard some one coming up behind me, and looking about saw an Indian striking at me
with a knife. I threw my gun over my head as a guard and dropped to
the ground, but the fellow's knife caught the end of my nose and cut
it nearly off. This is the scar.

["]What became of the Indian?"

Oh, I got him. I struck him with the butt of my gun across the neck and he backed away from me and fell to the ground to avoid my shot, but I waited until he squatted and shot him through the heart. He is a good Indian now.

"Why were so many squaws killed?

Well, that is easily explained. The warriors, as soon as they fired, broke into the ranks of the squaws. The soldiers were mostly new recruits who could not tell squaws from bucks, and consequently shot them both. I defy any man to pick the squaws from among the bucks in a group of Indians, at a distance of 100 feet, who has not had considerable experience among them.

18. Statement of former agent Valentine T. McGillycuddy, 1891

Former Pine Ridge agent Valentine T. McGillycuddy, who visited Pine Ridge Agency within days of Wounded Knee, was quoted making the following statements in Stanley Vestal, New Sources of Indian History, 1850–1891 *(Norman: University of Oklahoma Press, 1934), p. 85. He cites an unnamed former agency policeman and Oglala army scout who had been present and injured at Wounded Knee. McGillycuddy served as agent at Pine Ridge from 1879 to 1886.*

I was intercepted by a party of blanket Indians on a cross road in a wagon, and one of them accosted me in these words, "Little Beard [McGillycuddy's Indian name], eleven years ago [1879] we made an agreement and promise with you that if we would give you fifty of our young men to act as police, you would have the white soldiers taken away, the police would control, and we would have a home government. We kept our promise, and you kept yours." Then he threw his blanket off, and showed me a bullet hole through the left arm, received that day [of Wounded Knee] and from which the blood was trickling, remarking, "I was one of your police. Who brought back the soldiers, and what were they brought for?" Very reluctantly I had to reply, "I am sorry, my friend, but I am no longer your agent."

19. Account of Iron Hail (Dewey Beard), transcribed by James R. Walker, 1896–1914

*Physician and ethnologist James R. Walker transcribed this
account by Iron Hail (Dewey Beard) during his tenure at the
Pine Ridge reservation from 1896 to 1914. As a young man, Beard
was known as Iron Hail and had fought at the Battle of the Little
Bighorn in 1876. Beard, who was born circa 1856 and died in
1955, was perhaps thirty-four years old at the time of Wounded
Knee. His long and fascinating life is well chronicled in Philip
Burnham,* Song of Dewey Beard, Last Survivor of the Little
Bighorn *(Lincoln: University of Nebraska Press, 2014). Walker's
transcription is excerpted here from James R. Walker,* Lakota
Society, *ed. Raymond J. DeMallie (Lincoln: University of Nebraska
Press, 1982), pp. 157–68. Some elements of Beard's rendering in
this statement appear out of sequence when compared to his other
accounts herein. Nonetheless, they are presented as he apparently
explained them to Dr. Walker.*

[En route south from their camp at Cheyenne River,] Big Foot was
sick and bleeding from the nose, but we moved on to what is now
called Big Foot springs. The next day we moved to Red Water Creek.
Big Foot was so sick he could go no farther, and we stayed there two
days and two nights. All the time the young men were watching the
soldiers [searching the countryside for the Indians], and saw them
come up on the north side of the White River and get farther away
from us, and we felt safe from them.

Then Big Foot said, "We will try to get to Red Cloud's camp [at
the agency] before I die," and at sundown we broke camp and moved
all night and camped on American Horse Creek . . . and stayed there
all day. The next day we moved up Yellow Thunder Creek and when
we came opposite to Porcupine Butte we crossed over to Porcupine
Creek and stopped for dinner, when we saw four Indian scouts. We
called for them to come to us but they ran away as fast as their horses
could go.

After noon we hitched up and started towards Porcupine Butte,
and when near there, to the northeast of the butte, we saw soldiers

coming to the northwest of the butte, and they had pack mules. Big Foot said, "Go and meet the soldiers." The soldiers formed in a line and set a cannon pointing at us, and it looked as if they were about to shoot at us. Then Big Foot said he would go ahead and meet the soldiers and tell them we only wanted to go to Red Cloud's camp at the agency.

Big Foot was so sick that he could not ride on a horse and he had been lying in a wagon ever since we left the Red Water. He had the wagon driven towards the soldiers, and the officer came to meet the wagon. I rode by the wagon with Big Foot and when the officer came near I said, "Do not shoot. We don't want to fight. We want to go to the agency."

The officer said, "Which is Big Foot?" An Indian said, "He is [in] that wagon. He is sick." The officer asked, "Is he able to talk?" The officer ran up to the wagon and pulled the blanket off of Big Foot's head and said, "Can you talk?" Big Foot said, "Yes." The officer said, "Where are you going?" Big Foot said, "We are going to our friends and relations at the Pine Ridge Agency." The officer said, "You will have to lay down your arms, Big Foot."

Big Foot said, "Yes. I am friendly and I will give up my arms. But I am afraid something will happen to me after I do this. Will you not wait until we get to the agency? I will go with you to the agency and my people will give you all their guns when we get to the agency. When we get there we will have a council with the General [Brooke] and we will understand everything. But now I do not understand and I am afraid something will happen to my people if they give up their arms now. I am sick, and I do not want to have any trouble."

The officer said, "Oh, I am glad to hear this. I have a good wagon here with four mules to draw it and I will put you in it." Big Foot said, "Yes, I will go in your wagon and you may do with me as you wish, but I put my people in your hands, and I wish you would see that no trouble comes to them."

The soldiers brought a sick wagon (ambulance), and four soldiers put Big Foot on two gray blankets like the soldiers have and they carried him and put him in the sick wagon. I was then afraid for Big Foot, for the officers laughed when they put Big Foot in the wagon. Then the soldiers moved back towards Wounded Knee Creek with a guard around Big Foot and all the Indians followed.

I said to the medicine man, "My friend, you would better stop and dance the ghost dance for I am afraid there will trouble come to Big Foot.["]

One Indian wanted to shoot the officer but my father [Horned Cloud] told him that that would do no good as the soldiers would only shoot at all the Indians and kill the women and children. Beside[s], it would only be worse for Big Foot.

I rode close to the soldiers with an Indian who could understand English, for I was troubled at the way the soldiers acted and I wanted to know what they said. We came to Wounded Knee Creek and the soldiers camped. They put Big Foot in a tent and kept him there with guards around him and all the Indians came up and put their tipis close to the camps of the soldiers. When the Indians put up their tipis an under-officer came with soldiers and put them as guards around the Indians.

My father said, "Why do you put guards around us? We would not have followed you if we had wished to run away." But the soldiers only laughed at us. Then my father called me and my brothers and said, "My sons, I am thinking some trouble will come to us. Whatever the soldiers tell you to do, I want you to do it, and do not do anything that will give the soldiers an excuse to do you any harm."

Then some of the Indians wanted to come on to the agency but the guards turned them back. This made all the Indians very uneasy so that they could not sleep. The guards were changed very often and a fast-shooting cannon [Hotchkiss gun] was put on a hill nearby and pointed at the camp with the Indians in it. The soldiers were working about this gun and we were afraid they were getting ready to fire on us.

In the night many more soldiers came and with the soldiers were some Indian scouts, but the soldiers would not let the scouts come to us and this made us very much afraid. About midnight, some of the Indians tried to get away to go to the General [Brooke] at the agency, but they found that a great many more guards were placed around us and they could not slip away. When we were told this, we felt that we were prisoners. Some of the soldiers told an Indian who could understand that we were to be disarmed and taken to the railroad and sent far away to the south where the ocean would be all around us.

Nobody in the Indian camp slept much that night except the children, for we were going from tipi to tipi talking about our situation. All agreed to give up their guns if they were asked to do so, but I intended to hide my gun and come and get it again. Some of the young men who had good guns, magazine guns that they had bought, would not say they would or they would not give them up.

Then my father asked the medicine man what he could do and told him that if his Messiah was of any account, now was the time to get his help. But the medicine man was sullen and would only say he would bring help when the time came for it.

When it was coming light the bugles sounded and we all came out and stood watching what the soldiers would do. Then the bugles sounded again and the soldiers surrounded the Indian camp. Some soldiers were on foot and they were nearest the Indians, and some were on horses and they were further away, out around the others. A half-breed named Phillip Wells interpreted for the officer and said, "All the Indians get in a ring and there will be a council." Then all the Indians sat in a ring except four men and the women and children and Big Foot, who was still in the tent under guard.

Then the soldiers came up close around the Indians on three sides and the soldiers on the horses were farther away across a deep ditch. Some of the soldiers were about the cannon on the hill nearby and some were in a line by the camp of the soldiers. Then the interpreter said that the officer wanted the Indians to give up all their arms. An Indian asked what Big Foot said about this and the interpreter said that Big Foot said for the Indians to give up their guns to the officer.

Then the Indians all went into their tipis. I dug a hole in the ground and buried my gun, and when I came out a great many guns were piled nearby where the Indians were sitting. When I sat down there were soldiers behind me and soldiers on both sides of me. I was looking towards the hill at the cannon so I did not feel afraid. Then the officer said, "You have twenty-five more guns and I want you to bring them out. I know that you have more guns for we counted them yesterday. You have plenty of cartridges and knives and I want you to give them all up." But the Indians had piled nearly all their guns in the pile and not more than four or five had hidden their guns.

My father asked the officer if the Great Father [President] would feed the Indians after he took all the guns away from them. The officer said, "I don't know anything about that. All I know is that I am going to get all the guns, and they are not all in that pile." But the Indians would not bring any more guns.

Then one of the four Indians who would not come into the circle at first came and sat down with the rest. The other three were the medicine man and the two young men named Black Fox [also known as Coyote] and Yellow Turtle. Black Fox and Yellow Turtle said they would not give up their guns and they held them in their hands. They told the officer they would give up all their cartridges and could carry their guns empty. But the officer said they must give up their guns and that he would go into the tipis and get all the rest of the guns. He went into a tipi and came out and went into another. While he was doing this an under-officer and four soldiers went towards Black Fox and Yellow Turtle who were standing by the tipis. There were soldiers behind them, and they began to walk away from the tipis towards the creek. The medicine man came and stood between the tipis and the Indians and my father said to him, "Give up your gun. Your ghost shirt will be all you need." The medicine man said, "My friend, I am afraid."

Then Philip Wells came and said, "When the soldiers have all your guns, you Indians will all march past them and they will hold out their guns towards you. He meant they would hold their guns in front of them, but the Indians thought they would point their guns and take aim at them. My brother said, "When they point their guns at us they will shoot us." Then my brother said to the medicine man, "You told us your Messiah could protect us from the white man's bullets. They will aim their guns at us. See now if he can protect us. You stand there like an old woman."

The officer was talking very excitedly to the soldiers and the medicine man began to sing a prayer to the Great Spirit. Then an under-officer and two soldiers started towards Black Fox and Yellow Turtle. Yellow Turtle said to the soldiers, "My friends, do not come to me in that way for I do not want to hurt you." Then he said to Black Fox, "Now you will see if I am brave. Do not give up your gun." Black Fox said to the soldiers, "Keep away from me. I will die before I will let you have my gun, and if I die I will take some of you with me."

Then some of the Indians said, "They are going to shoot us. Let us get our guns and get to that ditch and get away." Then I looked away from the two young men and an old Indian said, "No, do not do that. It is the interpreter who is making all this trouble. If he brings trouble I will kill him with my knife."

My father said to the medicine man, "Now is the time for help. Now do your best." Then the medicine man stopped his singing and began to cry to the Great Spirit, and gathered up a handful of dust [dirt] and through [threw] it towards the sky and waved his blanket under the dust, as they did in the ghost dance when they call for the Messiah. Just then the officer came out of a tipi with a gun in his hand, and I was looking at it for I thought it was my gun, and I heard a soldier cry out, "Look out! Look out!" And someone cried out in Indian, "Stop! Don't shoot!"

I turned and looked towards Black Fox and Yellow Turtle. They were holding their guns in their hands as if ready to raise them to shoot and were laughing at the under-officer and the two soldiers who were walking away from them very fast and looking back at them as if they were afraid. I was looking down the ditch [ravine] towards the creek. I heard a gun fire behind me and up the ditch from where the two young men were, and the two soldiers and the under-officer were walking away from the ditch, and not towards where the gun was fired. Immediately, both Black Fox and Yellow Turtle turned and raised their guns and fired toward where I heard the first gunfire.

Then all the Indians jumped up. Some cried that we would all be killed and some cried "Get your guns and get away!" Several shots were fired by the soldiers on both sides of us, and both Black Fox and Yellow Turtle fell. Yellow Turtle began to sing his death song and, raised on his elbow, shot at the soldiers. It appeared to me that all the soldiers began to shoot and I saw Indians falling all around me. I was not expecting anything like this. It was like when a wagon wheel breaks in the road.

An Indian shouted in my ear, "Get your gun!" I was very much frightened and started to run. I saw some soldiers running, and I ran that way. I ran into smoke so thick that I could not see anything. While I was running I took my knife out. The first thing I saw in the smoke was the brass buttons on a soldier's coat. A gun was thrust towards me and fired, and it was so close that it burnt my hair. I grabbed the gun and stabbed at the soldier with my knife. I stabbed him three times and he let go the gun. I tripped and fell and when I got up I found that I was among the soldiers aiming at me and I felt something hit me in the shoulder and I fell down.

I raised my head and saw a soldier aiming at me, but he missed me. I aimed at him with the gun I had taken from the soldier and snapped it, but I had forgotten to load it, so I quickly began to load it, and the soldier ran away. I began to breathe very hard and every breath hurt me very much. I got up and tried to run but could not, so I walked. I was strangling with something warm in my throat and mouth. I spit it out and looked at it, and it was blood, so I knew that I was shot.

Before I got to the ditch I saw some soldiers coming towards me and I charged towards them, for I thought I was dead anyway. They ran back into the smoke. I went on towards the ditch and came to a dead soldier and I stopped and cut off his belt of cartridges, for the cartridges I had would not fit the gun I had taken from the soldier. I tried to take his gun also, but I was too weak to carry it.

When I started for the ditch again I thought I stepped into a prairie dog hole for I fell, but when I tried to get up I could not do so, and I found that I was shot through the leg. So I sat there and loaded and fired towards the soldiers as fast as I could. When my cartridges were nearly gone I broke a cartridge in the gun and could not use it any more. I then began to hop towards the ditch, and I could see nothing but dead women and children and dead soldiers were among them.

I got into the ditch and an Indian gave me a carbine he had taken from a dead soldier. Then the fast-firing cannon (Hotchkiss) began to fire and I began to crawl up the ditch. I met White Face, my wife, coming down the ditch. She was shot, the ball passing through her chin and shoulder. She said to me, "Let me go, you go on. We will die soon. I will get my mother. That is her body at the top of the bank." She went up to her mother's body and took it under the arms to lift it up when she fell dead, shot again. I came up on the bank for I thought I would as well die quickly.

Just as I got to the top of the bank, an Indian pulled me back, and as I fell back he was shot through the head. I took his cartridges, as they suited the carbine I had, and I started up the ditch again. I saw a woman coming towards me with a revolver in her hand. It looked like a soldier's revolver and I think she took it from a soldier, for she was very bloody. I started towards her and I saw some soldiers peep over the bank and shoot her. I shot at them and they ran back. I crawled up the ditch as fast as I could and I came to White Lance, my brother. He was sitting against the bank and another brother, Pursued [William Horn Cloud], was lying by him. They were both wounded and Pursued was almost dead. He said, "My brothers, we will all be dead soon. But you must kill as many as you can before you die." They had three belts of cartridges taken from soldiers. When we saw that Pursued was dead, we went behind a little knoll where the ditch turns and where we could see the soldiers, and we fired at the soldiers. I looked and saw the Hotchkiss aiming at us. White Lance and I lay down close behind the knoll and the dirt and gravel scattered over us, thrown up by the Hotchkiss cannon. I got very sick and weak and thirsty and could shoot no more.

I could hear the soldiers coming close by me, and I saw a soldier peep over the bank. I fired at him, but I was too weak to take aim. The soldiers ran back and they fired the Hotchkiss again, and a shot from it cut Hawk Feather almost in two. Some soldiers were on a hill not far from the cannon, and they shot at me also. One of their bullets struck so near me that it threw the gravel in my face and I thought I was shot again. I lay very still and after a little while all quit shooting at me.

White Lance had gone on up the ditch and after a while I crawled on up the ditch to look for him. While I was crawling an Indian scout shot at me, and then ran away. I felt very sick and wanted to die as I crawled on top of the bank and shot at some soldiers, but I was too weak to stand up. They fired the Hotchkiss gun at me again and the balls passed very close to me so that I could almost feel the wind from the balls lift me from the ground. But I was too sick to stand up, so I lay very still. After a long time all the firing stopped. I crawled over the top of the hill and my brother [Joseph Horn Cloud], Yell at Them, and Jack LaPlant came to me with a horse, but I could not ride so they put their arms around me and took me away. But I was so sick I told my brother to go and leave me, but he said, "We have started for the agency and we will go there together or we will die together."

Then some of the Oglala Sioux came to us and they told us that all the Indians had gone from the agency to the hostiles' camp with Short Bull. So I went to Short Bull's camp, but when I got there I found that the Indians were not all there. But I was so badly wounded I could be taken no farther then. I learned while there that my father, whose named [sic] was Horn Cloud, my mother, whose name was Yellow Leaf, my wife, whose name was Pursued [also known as Wears Eagle], and my sister, whose name was Her Horses[,] had all been killed in the fight, and that my two brothers, White Lance and Enemy, were wounded.

When Big Foot was in the badlands we were very much closer to the camp of the hostile Indians than we were to the agency, and I sometimes think that if we had all gone and joined the hostiles instead of trying to go to the agency, my people would not have been shot down like wolves. But I remembered my father's words, and as soon as I could be hauled without danger to my life I was taken from Short Bull's camp and finally came to the [Pine Ridge] agency.

20. Reminiscent account of the massacre scene by Charles A. Eastman, 1900

Dr. Charles A. Eastman provided this reminiscent account of viewing the scene at Wounded Knee within days of the massacre. Eastman, the Pine Ridge Agency physician, accompanied the first party to visit the site three days after the massacre when the snowstorms had passed. Eastman's description here is from his memoir, From the Deep Woods to Civilization *(Boston: Little, Brown, & Co., 1916), pp. 111–14.*

On . . . [1 January 1890] it cleared, and the ground was covered with an inch or two of fresh snow. We had feared that some of the Indian wounded might have been left on the field, and a number of us volunteered to go and see. I was placed in charge of the expedition of about a hundred civilians, ten or fifteen of whom were white men. We were supplied with wagons in which to convey any whom we might find still alive. Of course, a photographer and several reporters were of the party.

Fully three miles from the scene of the massacre we found the body of a woman completely covered with a blanket of snow, and from this point on we found them scattered along as they had been relentlessly hunted down and slaughtered while fleeing for their lives. Some of our people discovered relatives or friends among the dead, and there was much wailing and mourning. When we reached the spot where the Indian camp had stood, among the fragments of burned tents and other belongings we saw the frozen bodies lying close together or piled upon one another. I counted eighty bodies of men who had been in the council and who were almost as helpless as the women and babes when the firing began, for nearly all their guns had been taken from them. A reckless and desperate young Indian had fired the first shot when the search for weapons was well under way. Immediately the troops opened fire from all sides, killing not only unarmed men, women, and children but their own comrades who stood opposite them, for the camp was entirely surrounded.

It took all of my nerve to keep my composure in the face of this spectacle and of the excitement and grief of my Indian companions, nearly every one of whom was crying aloud or singing his death song. The white men became very nervous, but I set them to examining and uncovering every body to see if any were living. Although they had been lying untended in the snow and cold for two days and nights, a number had survived. Among them I found a baby of about a year old warmly wrapped and entirely unhurt. I brought her in, and she was afterward adopted and educated by an army officer. One man who was severely wounded begged me to fill his pipe. When we brought him into the chapel [make-do hospital at Pine Ridge Agency], he was welcomed by his wife and daughters with cries of joy, but he died a day or two later.

Under a wagon I discovered an old woman, totally blind and entirely helpless. A few had managed to crawl away to some place of shelter, and we found in a log store nearby several who were badly hurt and others who had died after reaching there. After we had dispatched several wagonloads to the agency, we observed groups of warriors watching us from adjacent buttes; probably friends of the victims, who had come there for the same purpose. A majority of our party, fearing an attack, insisted that someone ride back to the agency for an escort of soldiers, and as mine was the best horse, it fell to me to go. I covered the eighteen miles in quick time and was not interfered with in any way, although if the Indians had meant mischief, they could easily have picked me off from any of the ravines and gulches.

21. Newspaper report on monument to Lakota dead at Wounded Knee, 1903

*This description of the dedication of a monument to the
Lakota dead at Wounded Knee on 28 May 1903 appeared in
the* Minneapolis Journal, *6 June 1903.*

"Indians Erect and Dedicate a Monument. . . ."
    Special to The Journal.
"Wounded Knee Battlefield, Pine Ridge, Indian Reservation, S.D.,
    June 4.

Five thousand Sioux Indians—the greatest gathering of red men
of modern times—gathered around a lit[t]le knoll in the lonely valley of the Wounded Knee, on the apex of which in one huge grave lie
buried hundreds [*sic*] of red warriors, was the curious sight which
the few whites who were at the dedication of the "Big Foot" monument saw on May 28.

Patterning after the whites who called the battle on the Little Big
Horn the "Custer massacre," and builded [*sic*] a monument in memo-
riam to the slain, the Sioux have erected a tall marble shaft to their
fathers and brothers who were killed at Wounded Knee and term the
battle which occurred at that place the "Big Foot massacre," after the
chief under whom they fought. Many of the warriors who are buried
at Wounded Knee rode in that whirlwind of death which engulfed
Custer, and many more were among the crowd of sullen red men who
gathered to see the monument erected and dedicated.

Where these children of the plains, the Dakotas [*sic*—Lakotas],
got their dramatic instinct can only be surmised, but it was a master
dramatist who arranged the opening details of these exercises, and
the effect produced on these half-wild people of savage instinct cannot be described.

The little knoll, 100 feet high, by the side of and overlooking the
battlefield, was covered on all sides by gaudily dressed Indians, whose
love of brilliant coloring is well known. The green of the surrounding
hills formed a splendid background to the gaily bedecked Indians,
who silently watched the monument as piece by piece it reared its
head under the hands of the workmen.

A large band of squaws had pushed themselves nearest to the little iron fence which inclosed the one huge grave, and stood with stolid faces gazing at the mound. . . .

Suddenly, as the last stone of the monument was put in place, up from the battlefield in the distance came a strange, shrill, mourning cry. Not an Indian moved a muscle, but the few whites present looked with interest in the direction from whence the cry came, and saw an old squaw, bent with age, dressed in the proverbial blanket, slowly emerge from "Bloody Gulch," where so many women and children were killed during the battle, and slowly climb the side of the hill towards the grave.

During the ten minutes required for the ancient squaw to mount the knoll, her wierd [*sic*] cry continued to ring out—the cry of the Dakotas [*sic*—Lakotas] mourning for the dead.

Arriving at the apex[,] the mourning squaw took her stand at the head of the grave wherein lay her father, husband, brothers and sons, and continued her lament, representing in her person a century of persecution and death of the one[-]time powerful owners of the entire northwest.

Standing at the foot of the grave, throwing her arms from side to side, the old woman shrieked out her weird song. The surrounding squaws became excited. Here and there one joined in the song for a moment and then ceased, as tho afraid. Then one summoned courage to continue—and another—and still others. And then the whole bunch broke into the most weird, blood-cu[r]dling song imaginable. But thru the whole awful noises the sobbing of the women could be heard with distinction.

While the lamentations were at their height, the old war cry broke out from a few braves—but only for a moment. The lamenting was left to the women, and any resentment against the whites which the memories might have aroused, remained unshown.

Gradually the shrieking of the women subsided into crooning and[,] covering their heads and bodies with their blankets[,] the crooning subsided into soft sobbing while the leader of the women cast bright-colored clothes over the grave. . . .

This impromptu exhibition over, the real ceremonies begun [*sic*]. Rev. W[illiam] J. Cleveland, [Episcopal] chaplain at the agency, stepped forward and resting one hand on the monument, delivered a short address on "God Made of Men One Nation," speaking in the Dakota language.

Then Joe Horn Cloud, prime mover in erecting the monument, stepped out and with that eloquence possessed by savage tribes, said:

"Standing by the grave wherein lies my father and my brother, and gazing upon the battlefield where they died, as did many of my people, I have only good feeling towards the whites and hope we will always be friendly."

Fire Lightning, an old chief, said: "For many, many years I have been friends with the white people; I helped make the treaty with them; I have never broken that treaty and I wish to end my days a friend to them."

After a prayer in Sioux, the whole lot joined in and sang "America" in the Indian language, but it is doubtful if "My Country, 'tis of Thee," meant much to the Sioux, who are virtually prisoners in a large yard.

After the exercises were finished, the Indians filed past the monument and those who could read English, read to the others this inscription: "This Monument is Erected by Surviving Relatives and other Ogallala and Cheyenne River Sioux Indians in Memory of the Chief Big Foot Massacre, Dec. 29, 1890, Colonel Forsythe [*sic*] in Command of U.S. Troops[.] Big Foot was a great chief of the Sioux Indians. He often said: 'I will stand in peace till my last day comes.' He did good and brave deeds for the white man and for the red man. Many innocent women and children who knew no wrong, died here."

22. Account of Philip F. Wells, recorded by Eli S. Ricker, October 1906

Philip F. Wells was again interviewed by Judge Eli S. Ricker at Pine Ridge Agency on 2 October 1906. The interview has been excerpted from Tablet 4, pp. 24–30, Eli S. Ricker Papers, RG 1227, Nebraska State Historical Society, Lincoln. Statements that appeared in parentheses and brackets in the original are all rendered in parentheses here. See also *Richard E. Jensen, ed.,* Voices of the American West, *vol. 1,* The Indian Interviews of Eli S. Ricker, 1903–1919 *(Lincoln: University of Nebraska Press, 2005), pp. 127–30, 155–60; Donald F. Danker, ed., "The Wounded Knee Interviews of Eli S. Ricker,"* Nebraska History *62 (Summer 1981): 205–10. Wells also made nearly verbatim observations in "Ninety-Six Years among the Indians of the North West," as told to Thomas E. Odell in* North Dakota History *15 (Oct, 1948): 265–312, and in* Chicago Westerners Brand Book *3 (Feb. 1947): 84–85.*

On the 28th the scouts located Big Foot at Porcupine Butte. A courier was sent to Major Whiteside [Whitside] at Wounded Knee, who had been out there two or three days. Whiteside marched with the Cavalry to Big Foot and found his men drawn up in line, but after a parley it was agreed that they should come in with the soldiers and camp at W.K.

Mr. Wells spent the night before the battle about half a mile down the road leading to the Agency, with a troop of Capt. [Charles W.] Taylor's scouts. These came out the night before [the action] with Col. Forsyth and arrived about 11 p.m. In the morning after taking breakfast where they had camped that night, he could see that the soldiers were drawn up between the Indians and the Wounded Knee Creek. . . .

Colonel Forsyth turned away while Mr. Wells was watching and listening to the medicine man on the west side of the circle, who was facing to the west and holding up his hands and praying for protection. The Colonel asked Mr. W. what the man was saying. "It is nothing but a harmless prayer that he is saying, Colonel; but don't disturb me, for I must pay very close attention to catch all he means; however, I will let you know just as soon as he says anything you should know." "All right," answered the Colonel, and he walked away. Then the medicine man stopped praying, and stooping down took some dirt and rose up facing the west, raised his two hands, and still facing the west cast the dirt with a circular motion of his hand toward the soldiers in rear. Then he walked round the circle, and when he got back to the starting point on the west side he stopped and uttered exclamations which in Sioux signify regret, and that he has decided on a desperate course; for instance if he has submitted to abuse, insult, or wrong with patience and fortitude but has made up his mind to retaliate or take revenge upon the offender, he exclaims: "Haha! Haha! I have lived long enough" (which means in Sioux that he is ready to give his life for this purpose)... [soon after,] Colonel Forsyth spoke to Big Foot through me as follows: "You tell Big Foot that he tells me that his Indians had no arms, when yesterday at time of surrender they were all well[-]armed. I am sure that he is deceiving me. Tell him, Big Foot, that he need have no fear in giving up his arms, as I wish to treat you with nothing but kindness. [Forsyth told him:] "Have I not done enough for you to convince you that I intend nothing but kindness? Did I not [through Major Whitside] put you into an ambulance and treat you kindly, and put you into a good tent [here], and put a stove into it to keep you warm and comfortable, and I have sent off to get provisions for your people which I expect here before long so that I can feed you well, and I have had my doctors taking care of you." Then Big Foot answered: "They have no guns only such as you have found. (Which I, the interpreter, saw was about a dozen old rifles, tied up with strings, different old-fashioned rifles, not a decent one in the lot.) I gathered up all my guns at the Cheyenne River Agency and turned them in and they were all burned up." Then General [*sic*—Colonel] Forsyth answered: "You are lying to me in return for all my kindness to you." Big Foot answered in substance as before. At this time the soldiers were searching again. During this time a medicine man all painted up and fantastically dressed, was going on with a silent ghost dance, or rather the maneuvers of the ghost dance worship, throwing up his hands and occasionally picking up dust and throwing it towards the soldiers who were standing in ranks around; then he turned toward the young bucks who were standing together, and said "do not be afraid and let your hearts be strong to meet what is before you; we are all well aware that there are lots of soldiers about us and that they have lots of bullets; but I have received assurance that their bullets cannot penetrate us. The prairie is large and the bullet[s] will not go toward you but over the large prairies, and if they do go towards you they will not penetrate you. (To go in Mr. Wells' Statement: This should be added to the medicine man's words after the final ones[:] "they (the bullets) will not penetrate you:" "As you saw me throw up the dust and it floated away, so will the bullets float away harmlessly over the prairies.") Mr. W. does not want the word "buck" used. He did not and never does use it.

Mr. Wells then stepped to Big Foot's brother-in-law to talk with him and get him to try to quiet and pacify the Indians. This brother-in-law impressed Mr. W. by his better dress and his generally intelligent appearance as a man of more than average parts—as a rather superior Indian. Just then Colonel Forsyth called out to him saying that he better get out of there, for it was beginning to look dangerous. Mr. W. answered, "In a minute, Colonel. I want to see if I cannot get this fellow to quiet them." Then he addressed the Indian and said: "Friend, go in among the young men and quiet them, and talk to them as a man of your age should.["] This was said to him in a low tone so that the others should not hear. He replied very loud so that all the Indians could hear his words: "Why, friend, your heart seems to beat. Why, who's talking of trouble or fighting?" "Yes, friend, my heart beats when I see so many helpless women and children if anything should happen,["] replied Mr. Wells. "Friend, it is unnecessary that your heart should beat," again said in a loud voice by the Indian. After the Indian's first reply to Wells a powerfully built young man stepped out of the circle and came around to where these two were standing and talking. He kept taking steps slowly as though he intended to get behind Mr. Wells without his observing what he was doing. But Mr. Wells suspected his purpose and was watching him, and as the young Indian moved around, he kept turning his own body so that he did not get in rear of him; at the same time, seeing that he could not persuade the old Indian, he continued to talk attempting to change the subject. He held his rifle with both hands at the muzzle, the butt resting on the ground. The young Indian had no gun under his blanket, but Mr. Wells could not tell but he had a revolver or a knife concealed, and he was reflecting on the different modes of attack which this Indian might be contemplating—whether he would grapple and try to overpower him—whether he would strike him with a club or knife—whether he would shoot with a revolver—or wha[t]ever else he would attempt to dispose of Mr. Wells and get his gun; for one of his main objects was to obtain that, as Mr. Wells saw from the way he was eyeing it. He dared not turn his back on the Indian, but began to move backwards with the intention that when he got far enough from him to walk away with safety he would get out of the circle. By this time Mr. Wells was convinced that a clash was coming. On that instant he heard the cry to his rear and left, coming from the direction of the soldiers, "Look out! look out![”] Wells threw his gun into position of "port" and turned his head quickly to the left and rear for a look at the Indians standing in a circle; one Indian near the center of the circle stood facing the soldiers with his gun pointing at an upward angle—in the last position in which a hunter holds his piece before placing it to his shoulder to fire; still holding his gun so, it was discharged, the contents going into the air, over the soldiers' heads, as the smoke indicated. At that instant 5 or 6 young warriors behind him threw off their blankets and drew their guns. Mr. Wells says that when this first shot was fired and the Indians dropped their blankets and drew their guns, he heard the command which sounded like Colonel Forsyth's voice: "Fire! Fire on them!" Mr. Wells having the Indian near him in his thought, turned toward him, both movements occupying only an instant of time, [but?] the Indian was already upon him with an upraised long butcher knife ground to a sharp point, in the act of dealing a deadly blow. A man of surprising agility, Mr. Wells dropped on one knee, at the same time throwing up his gun with both hands as a guard, and ducking his head to avoid a blow in his face. The Indian's wrist struck the gun, but the knife was long enough to reach his nose which was nearly severed, and hung down over his mouth, held by the skin. Before Mr. Wells could rise[,] the Indian renewed the attack, standing over him with the same knife uplifted and trying to grasp his gun with his left hand. It was a desperate play between life and death and lasted but a moment. Mr. Wells, holding the gun above his head kept it in swift motion as a guard against the knife; the Indian now summoned all his strength to break down the guard with a furious blow and the weight of his body, and raising his blade higher in the air for the mighty stroke he opened his own guard and Wells gave him a blow on the ear with the muzzle of his gun which . . . stunned him. This gave Wells time to regain his feet. The Indian staggered back a step or two. Wells sprang backwards. Now they are three paces apart. Wells leveled his piece at his breast; the Indian was glaring into his eyes; to escape the shot that he thought could not be withheld he turned a quarter round and dropped on his hands and knees. Wells had saved his fire; like a flash the muzzle of the gun went down and the bullet entered the Indian's side below the arm; he pitched forward on his face dead. Then a corporal rushed up to the prostrate body, placed the muzzle of his own gun between the shoulders and fired. About the same instant a bullet struck him inflicting a mortal wound from which he died in a day or two in the hospital at the Agency. Having vanquished his foe Wells started for shelter behind the wagon close by in which some of the guns taken from the Indians had been placed. While running he slipped on the grass and nearly fell; a young brave who it was afterwards learned, was following him, dealt a blow with his knife from behind, intending to stab between neck and shoulder, overreached and left a cut in the front of Wells' coat.

(This wagon is the one of which [Peter] McFarland speaks as being . . . overturned by the mules swinging round. Mr. Wells describes the incident. As he was running towards it a bullet hit one of the leaders and the animals plunged and swung round, upset the wagon, and mules and wagon were tangled up. Some of the men disengaged them.)

Mr. Wells remained in the action until the main part was over; when he was taking aim with his gun the piece of his nose suspended by the skin was in the way and once he tried to pull it off but could not, and it is well . . . for him that it would not yield, for it was replaced by the surgeon and he has had many years' use of it since and it has performed its . . . functions, including that of good appearance, down to the present time. Lieut. Preston saw him in the fight covered with blood, and came up and asked if he was badly hurt, and seeing his condition led him away to the surgeon. Preston was the second in command of the Taylor scouts. . . .

After the action he [Wells] stood by the dead body of Big Foot's brother-in-law, and after Indian custom addressed the dead man "Haha!" the Indian exclamation of regret. "Friend, I tried to save you but you would not obey me, and now you have destroyed yourself." At that the wounded Indians lying within hearing uttered their approval of what he said, by the usual "How." They had heard him in conversation with this man before the battle and knew from the Indian's answers that Wells was pleading with him to pacify the people. . . .

In the battle Father Francis M.J. Craft was wounded. . . . [Wells] says the Rev. Father Craft was the bravest of the brave, most earnest, enthusiastic and sincere in his duty. . . . Mr. Wells says that when the main part of the action was over at W. K. he [Forsyth] sent by Lieut. Preston, who went with his dispatch from Forsyth to the agency about 9.a.m., for protection to be furnished for his [Wells's] wife and children. Preston found that they were safe. A little later Wells sent an Indian scout, one of Taylor's named White Deer, and on his way to the Agency he met some Indian relatives who told him that the Indian women had removed them to the Mission, and he returned to W.K.

[The following by Wells appears here in the Danker transcription: "Captain Wallace was killed in the rear of his troop K. He was struck by a bullet in the upper part of his forehead and it tore through the top of his skull.

Mr. Wells confirms what (Teamster Peter) McFarland has said about the Indians falling back up the ravine and when ever [*sic*] the place where one was hidden was discovered a Hotchkiss shell was thrown there.

The first dispatch from the battlefield to the Agency announcing what had taken place was borne by (Second) Lieutenant Guy (H.) Preston, accompanied by a soldier of the Seventh Cavalry."]

When Wells reached the Agency the night of the battle about 10 or 11 o'clock P.M. he went to the hospital inside the Agency inclosure [*sic*], in hospital tents and saw 30 or 40 wounded soldiers and the surgeons very busy. He stepped in and was shown by a doctor a place in another tent where he could lie down, there being plenty of robes. He rested there till daylight [30 December].

[Again, from Danker's transcription: "I (Ricker) asked Mr. Wells his opinion as to the intention of Big Foot of giving the whites battle, and he said:

'I do not believe they had any intention of fighting, and for these reasons:

First, when Major Whiteside [Whitside] met Big Foot at Porcupine Butte, Big Foot was drawn up in battle array and was perhaps equal to Whiteside in numbers, or nearly so. Second, the ground was in his favor, being adapted to the Indian style of fighting; whereas, the soldiers would have had, for awhile [*sic*] at least to operate on the open plain. Third, after the Indians knew they were discovered and the troops were coming, the Indians had ample time for defensive preparations and did not improve the opportunity to make themselves more impregnable.

When Whiteside met them, he formed his troops in line of battle. While in these positions, a long parley took place. If the Indians had not been willing to yield, they could have safely retreated with the landscape favoring their movements and their rear guard fighting. Fourth, but the Indians surrendered. This was where the actual surrender was. When they came to Wounded Knee, they were prisoners in possession of their arms. The battle there was over the question of giving up the guns. Big Foot admitted the principle which Forsyth contended; namely, that the Indians should surrender their weapons, but used evasion to avoid doing so. The Indians had delivered before the action only some inferior pieces.'"]

23. Account of Joseph Horn Cloud, recorded by Eli S. Ricker, October 1906

Joseph Horn Cloud gave the following account to Judge Eli S. Ricker on 23 October 1906. Excerpted from Tablet 12, pp. 52–81, Ricker Papers. See also Jensen, ed., Indian Interviews of Eli S. Ricker, *pp. 196–203; and Danker, ed., "Wounded Knee Interviews of Eli S. Ricker," pp. 164–76.*

[Big Foot's people departed Cheyenne River for Pine Ridge Agency on 23 December, and moved along steadily, as stated previously.] On the 27th they moved about noon and at supper time arrived at Medicine Root Creek about where Kyle now is. Here Big Foot said he wanted to see the chiefs and urged his people to move on. They drove five miles farther to American Horse Creek where there was a log school house, and where there is now the regulation Day School No. 17. Big Foot was unable to proceed any farther, being a very sick man. On the 28th the camp was astir early and began the march up Yellow Thunder Creek toward Porcupine Creek. By noon they had proceeded fifteen miles, and as they reached the hills skirting Porcupine on the east four Indian scouts were discovered watering their horses in the stream. A few Indians made a dash upon them and captured two. . . . The other two made their escape. After the capture of these scouts they all halted on the Porcupine for dinner. The Indians did not learn from their captives of the soldiers being on Wounded Knee. On the passage from White River to Porcupine, while they passed a number of hours no person was seen except Francis Mayock, a crazy Irishman [who was husband to an Oglala woman and] who was guarding a house belonging to [local resident] Condelario Benavidez. He told them all the Indians had gone to the Agency to get annuities or to do fighting.

About 2:00 o'clock p.m. they hitched up their teams and started for Wounded Knee. Having crossed the Porcupine and raised up to the top of the hills on the other side, they saw a cloud of dust rising and when they had descended on the other side the soldiers had also come over the hills from the west, and the two columns met there on Pine Creek, the soldiers crossing it and taking position in line of battle facing the approaching Indians who had hoisted a white flag. Four [*sic*—two] Hotchkiss cannon had been run out a few yards in front of the line of soldiers. Pine Creek is a dry creek two miles east of Porcupine butte. . . .

[A] white-haired officer with an interpreter . . . [Ricker's comment: I suppose Major Whiteside (Whitside) and Little Bat] asked for Big Foot, and the wagon in which he lay was pointed out. They went up and the officer asked: "What is your name? "My name is Big Foot." "Where are you going?" Big Foot answered: ["]I am going to Pine Ridge to see the people." "Why do you go to Pine Ridge?" Big Foot replied: "I am going because they sent for me." "Do you want peace or to fight?" . . . inquired the officer. "No," said the chief, "My great fathers were all friendly to the white people and died in peace, and I want to die the same." The officer then said, "If you are telling me the truth I want you to give me 25 guns." Big Foot answered: "I am willing to give you the 25 guns; but if I do I am afraid you will do some harm to my people. Wait till we get to the Agency and we will decide as we please. I will give you all you ask and I will return to my home." Big Foot's strength was failing; he spoke slowly and in faltering accents. The officer said, "All right," and extending his arm, the two shook hands. Big Foot continuing, said: "I am going to see the Pine Ridge people to make a peace for them and the white people; and if I make a peace I will get a hundred horses for a reward."

The officer spoke to the people and said that Big Foot was in a bad place, and said that he should be put into his ambulance, at the same time motioning to some of his men to bring up the ambulance. Big Foot was then taken out of his own wagon in a blanket and removed to the officer's conveyance. The Indians and soldiers now started for Wounded Knee about five miles away, the Indians being ahead and the ambulance containing Big Foot being in the lead. This was flanked on either side by a sergeant and a soldier mounted. There were about 40 Indians on horseback; they were flanked on each side by a line of cavalry soldiers. The rest of the soldiers were in the rear of the column. On this movement from the Cheyenne [River] the Indians had ridden either in wagons or on horseback. It was nearly sunset when this motley procession reached the camp on Wounded Knee.

When they crossed W.K. Creek on the bridge they passed by the door of the trader's store and some of the Indians went in and bought candles, sugar, coffee, bacon, etc. The store was kept by George E. Bartlett. Now they moved to the soldiers' camp. The Indians were placed just north of the ravine. . . . The soldiers' tents were already pitched on the east side of the camp. They had been here before and had marched out that morning to intercept Big Foot. . . . The tent in which Big Foot slept is just in front of the soldier's tents. Bull Eagle lived in a house on Cemetery Hill. Down at the foot of this hill the guards were stationed during the night, and from this place the reliefs were sent out. Horn Cloud saw for the first time the Cavalry in a light valley west of Cemetery Hill, . . . when the council was formed. The Hotchkiss cannon were in front of the guards at the foot of the hill. . . .

Colonel Forsyth came out from the Agency at night, arriving about 11 p.m. with Capt. Taylor's scouts and some wagons. The first thing after the guard had been changed in the morning, an old Indian named Wounded Hand harangued the camp telling the people that there was going to be a council with the soldiers [Wounded Hand was among those killed at Wounded Knee]. Then all the young men came forward and sat down in the circle with the old men in front of where Big Foot had slept the night before. Then Big Foot was by direction of an officer brought out on a blanket and laid down near the eastern extremity of the half or three-quarters circle or council. On his left was his brother, on his right was Horned Cloud, father of Joseph Horn Cloud. Just behind Big Foot stood old man Wounded Hand. The Indians sat quietly in the circle looking at the officers. Capt. Wallace was standing just behind Horned Cloud and John Shangrau, interpreter[,] was in the group. Capt. Wallace thinking from the costume of Joseph Horn Cloud who was in citizen[']s clothes that perhaps he belonged to the Pine Ridge Indians[,] asked John Shangrau who he was. Shangrau said, "You ask him; he talks English." Wallace asked Joseph his name and he replied, "Joseph Horned Cloud." "Where is your father?" continued the Captain. Joseph pointed out his father near him in the section on the east side (and north of the eastern end of the council). Horned Cloud was sitting at Big Foot's right, with a fur cap on his head. He was smoking and passing his pipe to Wounded Hand who was standing behind him. The Captain asked Joseph if he was sure that he belonged to this outfit, meaning Big

Foot's band. Joseph said "Yes." An officer spoke up (it must have been Major Whitside) and said to Big Foot, "Big Foot, I want 25 guns. Yesterday everybody had a gun. I want 25 of them."

Big Foot said, "All right." He said to the people, "Bring 25 guns. If I was able to talk I would talk for you, but I cannot talk." Blood was flowing from his nose, he was stiff and weak.

The young men went to their quarters and brought out 25 guns and laid them down in the center of the circle. The officer then said, "I want five more." The young men went again and brought forward five more guns. Then the officer demanded five more, and added, "I want them all." Big Foot said: "Bring them all, boys." They answered back to Big Foot, "There are no more guns." Then the officer said, "What have you done with all the guns? I will send the soldiers to get the guns themselves." Big Foot said, "All right, let them do it." Speaking to his followers he said, "Boys, do not be mad; let them do it." The soldiers went back into the Indian camp, took sacks out of wagons and emptied them on the ground; went into tents, and everywhere examining, picked up some old shot guns, knives, tomahawks, arrows and awls; and they searched the persons of the women.

While this was going on the same officer said to the Indians, "I want you all to stand in a rank before the officers." There were 125 in the council, including Joseph Horn Cloud. Continuing he said, "I want the same number of soldiers to stand in front of the Indians and take their cartridges out of their guns and cock them and aim at their foreheads and pull the triggers. After this you will be free. Afterwards you will go to the Agency and I will give you nine beeves." Some of the Indians were getting wild at such talk, and some said, "Now he sees that we have nothing in our hands so he talks this way." Others said, "We are not children to be talked to like this." A man cried out: "Take courage! Take courage!" Big Foot spoke up: "Yes, take courage! There are too many children and old people," meaning in these words addressed to his people, that they should be calm; because there were so many old men and women and little children that they must keep their patience and take no risk and bring on no danger.

Two or three times Big Foot was raised to a sitting posture by his brother Iron Eyes on one side and Horned Cloud on the other; he wanted to address his followers and encourage them to be patient and remain cool and do nothing to bring on trouble, but he could not sit up but a moment and had to be laid down to rest.

The maudlin talk of the officer set all the Indians to murmuring. Capt. Wallace spoke to Joseph Horn Cloud and said, "Joseph, you better go over to the women and tell them to let the wagons go and saddle up their horses to be ready to skip, for there is going to be trouble; for that officer is half shot." Joseph started and when he came to the guards they would not let him pass, but Captain Wallace seeing this motioned to the guards to let him through, and he went on. Joseph told the women to saddle the horses and be ready to run. He went to catch his own horse which was just in the rear of this Indian camp but in front of the line of guards. They helped him to catch the horse; then he brought him in and hitched [him] to a wagon. Then he returned to the council. He went through the ranks of soldiers immediately in rear of the council, and then he saw the deaf man making a big cigarette out of fag [i.e., cigarette] paper. He was standing and three cavalry sergeants (they each had three yellow stripes or chevrons on [their] arms) were moving toward him from behind. They seized him before he knew they were there, two taking hold of his arms, the others trying to take the gun away from him. Before the sergeants had come up, this man who was deaf, had been holding up his gun in both hands over his head and telling the Indians that this was his own gun, that it had cost him a good deal of money, that if anybody wanted it he must pay for it, for he would not give it up without pay. As soon as this was said the three sergeants approached him from behind as above stated. Just as the struggle between him and the sergeants began someone cried: "Look out! look [*sic*] out!" These words were scarcely uttered when the gun went off elevated in the air at an angle of about 45 degrees and pointing eastwardly. Instantly there was a volley from the soldiers standing around the circle. These shot the men in the back.

Before this point was reached I should have said that the searching party was going around on the inside of the circle or council and taking the guns, and had got pretty well around toward the east extremity of the circle when the firing broke loose. There were a few of the warriors at this end who had not been searched and still had guns. They were near the deaf man who was gesticulating and talking about his gun.

Another omission: Just before Capt. Wallace sent Joseph to tell the women to saddle up, the Medicine Man was swinging his arms and singing ghost songs and marched around inside the circle. He was a Rosebud Indian named Good Thunder. (He was wounded. Afterwards he was an Episcopal preacher on the Rosebud Reservation for awhile; then he quit & has done nothing since.)

Shakes the Bird went round on the outside of the council singing ghost songs. When the shooting began the women ran to the ravine. The shooting was in every direction. Soldiers shot into one another. Many of the Indians in the circle were killed. Many of them mingled with the soldiers behind them, picking up guns from dead soldiers and taking cartridge belts. They took guns they had turned over and the cartridge belts that they had turned over with them. Many Indians broke into the ravine; some ran up the ravine and to favorable positions for defense.

[Dewey] Beard (who is a brother of Joseph Horn Cloud, but is not called Horn Cloud, called *Beard* only); and William Horn Cloud, Daniel Horn Cloud, who is now called White Lance, and is a brother of Joseph; and George Shoot the Bear and Long Bull both cousins of Joseph; and two old men, one of whom belonged to Big Foot's band and the other to Sitting Bull's band; and a woman Helena Long Bull and a little son, these all took refuge in the pocket in the ravine, and here William Horn Cloud was killed, and here Beard killed four soldiers, one being stabbed with a knife (a sergeant), the others he shot. White Lance received three wounds in his right leg and one slight [wound] on top of his head; he was borne from here up the ravine by George Shoot the Bear and Peter Stand.

Some cannon were moved to the bank of the ravine & some were planted on Cemetery Hill.

When the firing began there was soon so much smoke enveloping the scene that nobody could be seen with distinctness. There was no wind to clear it away. It hung like a pall over the field. Through rifts in the smoke heads and feet would be visible. Women were killed in the beginning of the fight just the same as the men were killed. Women who were wounded and had babies digged hollow places in the bank and placed the little things in them for safety; some women made places for themselves and crawled into them for protection; some women were found lying dead with dead infants on their breasts; one mother lay dead; her breast covered with blood from her wound, and her little child was standing by her and nursing.

Before the burying party came out from the Agency [five days later] the Indians had been over the field, especially was this true of Short Bull who belonged to the Rosebud Reservation. Short Bull who was with the hostiles came on to the field from the Agency and gathered up his relatives who were in the fight.

The soldiers shot women the same as they shot men. Beard was wounded while in the pocket first in his shoulder close to where the collar bone joins the shoulder, and the bullet ranged down his back nearly the whole length of his body; he was wounded the second time in his right leg. Men, women and children, boys and girls fled in a stream [of people] up the road and around the northeast corner of the big field and within close range of the cavalry. A great many women and boys and girls were killed along here. Some turned off into the field to get out of reach of the cavalry fire and a number were killed in this field. Joseph Horn Cloud passed up this road and went around the field and crossed over south of the canyon or ravine and went into it, and then out of it again, following the road on the north side of the field back into the fight where the cavalry was; then he soon went to a lot of horses that had collected from all quarters, some with harness, some with saddles on--all a little way northwest of the cavalry; and here he caught three horses, first one, then a second, and then a third, all of which were successively wounded; then he got two more and [with] these he went up to the hill a few hundred yards from the cavalry and northwest of the field; he heard a woman behind him call him "Brother, come and help me!" He turned back to her. She had a baby on her back. She was crying. The horses were unmanageable; they were hard on the bit and the best he could do was to circle around her in a wide circuit. At last I [*sic*—he] got up to her, and he jumped off his horse and told her to get on, this horse had a saddle on, but she could not mount, as the horse kept turning; while she was trying to mount and while her foot was in the stirrup she was knocked to the ground by bullets; the infant was strapped to her back all the time; she arose and [with] Joseph still assisting her she succeeded in getting into the saddle; Joseph threw the saddle from his own horse, which was rearing in the air, but catching [it] by the mane he seated himself on his back, then went over to the band of horses again and caught two more; he gave one of these to Chief Dog, a policeman at the Agency, who was a cousin to Joseph and wounded in the face; the other horse he gave to a Pine Ridge Indian; then Joseph came back again to the fight; this was afternoon; he came back behind the cavalry this time; when down here the cavalry moved up west to the top of the hills . . . and crossed and went down west and crossed Fast Horse Creek. Joseph followed far to the right out of reach of their bullets; the cavalry came back in a few minutes and Joseph fell in behind and followed; the cavalry resumed its old position; Joseph went over to the head of the ravine or one branch of it; here he heard the Pine Ridge Indians who had come; some soldiers had advanced up the north side of the ravine and turned the head of it and got around some of the Indians who had streamed up there; these Pine Ridge Indians coming at this moment released the prisoners, as the soldiers fell back; these released Indians went with the Pine Ridge Indians back to Pine Ridge. Joseph stayed around about an hour. In the meantime he went up toward the pine hills and over to the head of the ravine; here he saw his brother Beard coming out of the ravine, he was the last to leave it, the firing all ceased and the battle was at an end. Joseph offered Beard a horse but he could not ride on account of his wounds. So he walked to Fast Horse Creek. Some Indians came. Here an Indian with a saddled horse let Beard have it, as he could ride this; then Joseph gave the Indian his horse and he was left afoot; then Joseph and Beard and five other Indians all went to the Holy Rosary Mission, and then off north to the hostile camp at the big white gap on the White Clay, just above the commissary. Here the Indians were exhibiting all kinds of emotions—some crying, some singing the death song, some singing the ghost song and dancing.

Here he saw the Indian woman and baby that he furnished a horse to; she gave the horse back to him; she had seven bullets through her clothing, one also passing through the wrappings around the ankles of the infant, but none of these made a single wound; the woman remained in that neighborhood a few years, then returned to the mouth of Cherry Creek on Cheyenne River, her old home, and died there of consumption.

When the Pine Ridge Indians came up and released the captives these latter ran for the ravine to avoid the shots of the soldiers, but the latter killed three[,] . . . an old man, a Cheyenne woman, and a girl, and a Pine Ridge man was wounded in the right arm, his name was Yellow Hair; these were killed and wounded on top of the hills while running to reach the ravine. There were also two Indians killed near the top of the hills by some soldiers who were concealed in a hollow or ravine.

Joseph had his brother Sherman killed in the Council, also his father; and his mother and his sister Pretty Enemy were killed in the ravine back of the Indian camp; and . . . brother William . . . killed in the pocket. . . . Beard's wife and son Tommy were killed in the camp.

24. Account of Louis Mousseau, recorded by Eli S. Ricker, November 1906

Louis Mousseau offered this account in an interview with Eli S. Ricker on 2 November 1906. Mousseau, of French-Santee Dakota descent, owned the trader's store directly northeast of the Wounded Knee engagement site. Some of the Seventh Cavalry officers frequented and socialized at Mousseau's store during their brief occupation of the area preceding the capture of Big Foot's people. Tablet 26, pp. 51–60, Ricker Papers, Microfilm RF1227. See also Jensen, ed., Indian Interviews of Eli S. Ricker, *pp. 227–31, and Danker, ed., "Wounded Knee Interviews of Eli S. Ricker," pp. 228–33.*

The officers who had come out with [Major Samuel M.] Whiteside [Whitside] occupied Louis Mousseau's house behind the Commissary [trader's store]. He reserved the kitchen and bedroom. They put goods into his cellar. They played cards, gambled for money and drank some. He saw these things. He saw Captain George D. Wallace gamble. He [Louis] had $800 or $900 worth of goods, four wagon loads, just put in. When everybody was ordered into the [Pine Ridge] Agency [earlier] by the agent, he went in for fear of the Indians. On Dec. 26, 1890, the first troops came out from the Agency to W.K., 4 companies came commanded, he thought, by Capt. Wallace, as he was the one who was doing everything & giving orders around there next morning. Louis came out with these troops. After the battle he locked up his store and went into the Agency with the command. Short Bull's people were around the battle ground that night after the battle, and Louie's store was broken into and his goods destroyed and taken. He got only 2 sacks of flour[,] 4 sides of bacon and 45 pounds of Baking Powder. Afterwards Govt paid him $407 for loss. This was all he got out of $1200 worth in his store.

On the night of Dec. 28 after Big Foot was brought in[,] Louie was sent into [Pine Ridge] Agency by Capt. Wallace, as he was the one who was doing everything and giving orders around there. He [Louis] came right back with a message from Gen. Brooke. [Colonel] Forsyth came out that night [28–29 December] with four companies . . . after he [Mousseau] had returned to W.K.

Big Foot was found this way: On the morning of Dec. 28 Little Bat [Baptiste Garnier] came to his room [at Mousseau's store] early in the morning, before light. . . . He wanted salt and some sardines. Louis asked him what he was doing out there, in Louie's kitchen. He was after salt and sardines. He answered that he was going out after Big Foot. He said, "You fellows have been out here a week and cannot find him, and I am going out." He [Little Bat] went out and came back a little after sunrise and said he discovered them just as they were moving camp from Porcupine. Now one-half [of] the soldiers in camp were sent out, the others remaining in camp. Bat and other scouts went out too. The first time Bat went alone. Louis doesn't know what took place out there. Louie says the council circle [on the morning of December 29th] was filled clear round and the only opening was a small one at the southwest side.

Louie saw early in the game—when the disarming began—that there was going to be trouble; so he went to his house and stripped off some extra clothing so as to be free to move. Louis was at this time employed by [Will] Cressy of the *Omaha Bee* at $5 a day as interpreter. Not till the next spring did he go into the Govt. service, when he enlisted as a scout. . . . Capt. Wallace began by saying the Great Father wanted them to give them their arms. He said that in the past when Indians gave up their guns they were not paid for them, but in this case they would be paid, that the Govt. did not want trouble—wanted only what was right and he told them to tag their guns. In a little while two old guns were brought forward—an old Spencer and a Hawkins [Hawken].

As the guns were not produced[,] he told them again that if the guns were not brought out he would have to take them by force. None were brought in response to this. He waited a little while and as no more were brought he had a bugle call and ordered the soldiers to disarm them. They went around & lifted the Indian tents right up. The women went to crying. (He says the Hotchkiss cannon were first planted near the top of the hill. When the first soldiers [under Whitside] went out 2 cannon were taken out, and when Forsyth came, he brought 2 more.)

One pile of guns was up at the foot of Cemetery Hill—12 in this pile, the other pile, 57 in this[,] was down near the council and not far from the scouts['] tents. An officer at the pile of 12 (and Louis was right there then) called to the one down where 57 were and asked how many he had & he answered 57, and the officer at the pile of 57 asked the other how many he had and he said 12. At this time three Indians with blankets were standing inside the circle at abt. [about] the north & east side. Somebody went up to them (he thinks it was Captain Wallacc, and a couple of orderlies and an interpreter with him)[.] He opened the blanket of one who had a Winchester and the Indian turned it over to him; the second one didn't have any gun that Louie saw; when he went to the third he would not give his up, but he brought it up to "arms port" [port arms] and Wallace had hold of it, and they swung it first one end up & then the other, and when the muzzle was up it was discharged. Everybody went to hollering "Look out! Look out!" and there was quite a stampede. A wire fence was close by & many, both whites and Indians, went through it. The horses tied at the northeast corner of the camp to ropes when the firing began got to pitching and jumping. After this gun was discharged there was a pause of perhaps half a minute, may be [*sic*] not so long, two more shots were fired and he saw Wallace and the Indian fall. Then the Indians broke for the guns in the piles. Then the soldiers fired a sudden volley, that is, the dismounted cavalrymen. There was no infantry there. This dismounted cavalry must be what some speak of as infantry. He does not think that the mounted cavalry fired, their horses were jumping and charging. After this volley the firing was continuous and the field soon enveloped in smoke. Little Bat was at the upper end of the camp up the ravine with a party who were disarming. There were two parties disarming at same time—both started together. After the fight was about over the cannon were moved down but were not fired after the removal. He tells about building breastworks with sacks of oats &c and says the soldiers piled some up around his store.

He tells of a woman close to the road crossing of the ravine; he and Little Bat heard some hollering (after the battle was over) down by the ravine—heard words like these, "Shoot him again!" A wounded woman [was] lying in a washout right in the road and at her feet was a little baby swathed as is their custom, and it was alive; somebody took it (he thinks [it] was the one that went east or was the one [local trader] Charley Marivall's [Marivale's] mother took) and it was saved; a little boy about two years old was lying up against the bank half sitting as though it was yet alive, and four soldiers were standing right above it. Louie & Bat went down, drawn by what they had heard and found the woman and asked if she was hurt much & if she could get up. She did not want to be moved, and said "Those soldiers just now killed my two children (she thought both were dead) and I want to lie here and die with them." Bat went up to them and in his forcible way gave them a berating and made them go away.

He says as Horn Cloud does that the soldiers encircling the council fired toward the center at the Indians inside, and they surely shot one another.

He says it was a bungle and botch—no need of anybody being injured if it had been properly managed. He talked with Big Foot that morning and B.F. said he did not want any fight—no trouble. He said it was surprising that they should come out with cannon to meet him. He told his people to give up everything even to a jackknife, for they did not want trouble. Louie heard this. If there had been no attempt to disarm there would have been no trouble. Louis has been over all this summer (1906) on Cheyenne River Agency and the people over there say Big Foot was moving over to stay at Pine Ridge, that he had been receiving requests by Red Cloud & others to come over.

Louie says that another party of Indians belonging to Big Foot's [*sic*—Sitting Bull's] band were following and that Standing Soldier and Red Shirt piloted them in a wide circuit to avoid W.K. and they got into the Agency the next morning after the battle and went into the friendly camp north of the Agency. Thinks 367 Indians were killed. . . .

Father Croft [Craft] came out to W.K. with Forsyth the night before the battle. When Louie got up next morning in his house he found Father Croft in his bed on one side and Little Bat on the other side of him.

Louie Mousseau brought out a dispatch from General Brooke the night before the battle. Probably this contained an order to disarm the Indians. Possibly when Col. Forsyth went out a little later the same night he had orders to that effect.

25. Account of John Shangrau, recorded by Eli S. Ricker, November 1906

John Shangrau was three-quarters Lakota and served as an army scout in 1890. He accompanied Major Whitside's troops in the search for Big Foot and camped with troops overseeing Big Foot's captured followers at Wounded Knee Creek the night of 28 December 1890. His statement regarding the engagement the next day follows as recorded by Judge Ricker on 5 November 1906, at Allen, South Dakota. Excerpted from Tablet 3, pp. 12–24, Ricker Papers. See also *transcription in Jensen, ed.,* Indian Interviews of Eli S. Ricker, *pp. 256–71.*

John Shangrau says: He and two Indian soldiers guided Major Whiteside [Whitside] and about six troops of the 7th Cavalry out from the Agency to W.K. John was chief of scouts at this time. On the morning of the 28th Little Bat and Hand, a half-brother of Bat[,] and two other scouts went out early and about noon John was looking up the road towards Porcupine & he saw a mounted man coming fast, and it was Hand. He arrived & said, "We have discovered Big Foot. They are camped on Porcupine." He said that the Indians said they were going to come to the camp. John went and told Major Whiteside. He ordered the troops to saddle up right early. John said to him: "Major, Big Foot told the men that he was going to come to the camp & we may as well stay here till they come." He replied, "There are other soldiers over in there & they might shoot into them & I will go over to protect them & bring them back here." So the command went to Porcupine. Before they got there another scout came back & he reported that the Indians were moving toward W. K. So John told the Major. He answered, "We will go on and meet them." The command got right up under Porcupine Butte when they saw the Indians coming on the ridge from Porcupine. Little Bat and the other scout came back. John asked Bat how it was with those Indians. He said, "They look pretty tough. We are liable to catch it today." They came up on the hill and saw the column and stopped. John looked through a glass & saw them going forward and back & were tying up their horses['] tails as they do when they go to war. The soldiers then continued to advance & they to advance likewise. When they all got close together the soldiers formed in line on a little ridge, with the cannon right out in front of the soldiers. Two footmen were coming ahead of the Indians' wagons. John told the Major he was going to meet them. The Major said "All right, go on." John started toward them. When he got up to the two footmen he shook hands with them & said "Where is Big Foot? An Indian said "He is in the wagon sick." John went up and said to Big Foot, "How, Cola[,]" and shook hands with Big Foot. He said to Big Foot: "Partner come with me & see the commanding officer." Big Foot told his driver to drive on. The major came up and shook hands with Big Foot. All the warriors were scattered out round. Major said: "Big Foot, I want you to come to the camp with me." "All right," said Big Foot, "I am going there." Major said to Shangrau: "John, I want the horses and guns." John answered: "Look here, Major, if you do that there is liable to be a fight here; and if there is you will kill all these women and children and the men will get away from you." "But," he says, "I have an order to do that wherever I catch them." "Well," John said, "That might be it, but we better take them to camp & then take their horses away from them and their guns." He says, "All Right; you tell Big Foot to move down to camp at W.K." John told him & he replied, "All right, I am going down to camp; that is where I am going." So they all went down to the camp that day.

Next morning, the 29th, of December, a company of Indian soldiers pulled in that morning from Pine Ridge. These were Taylor's scouts. John says they were Regular soldiers, enlisted men. (They came in the night.) The Major sent for John & told him to tell all the Indian men to come in front of Big Foot's tent. John told them & they came and took position in a circle which was complete with an opening in the southwest side. The Major said to John to tell them he wanted their guns. John told them. Some of the Indians talking among themselves said to one another, said "You go and see Big Foot; whatever he says we will do." There were two Indians went into B.F.'s tent, & John followed them in. One of the Indians said to B.F., "The soldiers want our guns, but we came over to ask you, and whatever you say, we will do." B.F. said, "This is the third time they are going to take their guns away from me; but, I will tell you [to] give them some of the bad guns, but keep the good ones." John then told Big Foot: "You better give up the guns; if you give the guns, you can get guns again—you can buy guns, but if you lose a man you cannot replace him." Big Foot said: "No, we will keep the good guns." These two Indians came out & John followed. When they got back the two Indians reported what Big Foot had said, & then there were 7 or 8 poor guns given up. Then they would not give up any more. Philip Wells then came and he took Shangrau's place, & the latter was ordered with ten soldiers into the Indian camp to search for guns. This composed one of the two parties. Little Bat was also ordered with ten other soldiers to do the same thing. This was the second party. While they were searching the camp Lieutenant [Guy] Preston and Charley [Charles W.] Allen were in the camp; this was the first John saw them.

Shangrau got about nine guns; Bat also got some. Shangrau started in with his party at the end of the camp toward W.K. Creek. Bat started at the other end. Meantime an Indian with a ghost shirt on was outside the circle swinging his arms and saying ha, ha, ha. When Shangrau and Bat met, . . . a woman came up to Shangrau & said these soldiers are taking our knives from us, and he saw a soldier with an armful of knives. Shangrau took all the knives from him & gave them to the woman & told her to give them to their owners. As soon as he gave her the knives he turned to Bat to talk to him, [and] he heard a gun fired. He heard one of the women say: "There is a fight!" As soon as this was said he heard a volley. Bat then ran down to the ravine with Big Foot's people; they all stampeded. Shangrau went on a trot toward the cannon which were right close to the top of the hill. An Indian followed him, but was shot down before he reached John who was wondering what the Indian would do. When John got up on the hill he met a lieutenant who said to John: "Scout, we've got our revenge now."

And John said, "What revenge?" "Why, don't you know, the Custer massacre?" John said: "Look here, Lieutenant, Custer had all the guns to protect himself with, but they massacred him; and here you take all the guns away from them and then massacre them; you ought to be ashamed of yourself for saying such a thing!" Shangrau now went over towards his tent to try to get his gun. As he got to his door a soldier said to him: "You better get away from there; an Indian is in there shooting." So John did not go in. A soldier ran up to the tent and ripped it down with his knife and with both hands opened it and looked in; at the same instant the Indian within shot him in the breast. Then the soldiers poured a volley into the tent and a cannon sent a shell into it. A soldier got some hay, fired it, and threw it on the tent and it was burned up. John walked down where the circle of Indians was & they were piled up horribly and indiscriminately.

I should have said that the soldiers [previously] surrounded the Indian circle in two ranks. When John was coming out from among the dead he saw Father Craft sitting on the ground with his arms extended and his hands on the ground supporting himself. John spoke to him and said: "Father, are you shot?" He said: "Yes." [Shangrau asked,] "Can I help you?" "Yes." With the assistance [of] another . . . [he] helped move [Craft] a little distance away. A stretcher was brought and he was taken off the field. When he was lifted on to the stretcher John saw that he [Father Craft] was stabbed on one side of the spine between the shoulders. John said to him: "Father, you are not shot; you are stabbed." He answered: "I don't believe an Indian did that to me, I believe it was a white man." After this there was an Indian . . . in a pocket in the ravine shooting with deadly effect. The cannon was pitching shells over at him but failed to get him, and had to give it up. When John went over where the fight started . . . there he saw women and boys and girls lying dead, and some were wounded, some sitting up and some lying down (the injured men were mostly in the circle). After it was all over [they collected?] all the Indian and white wounded and placed them in wagons and the troops marched to the Agency arriving about 11 p.m. . . . When the fight began [First Lieutenant Charles W.] Taylor's Indian scouts broke and ran and took shelter under the bank of W.K. Creek. . . . Mr. Shangrau did not hear anyone say: "Remember Custer."

26. Account of Standing Soldier No. 1, recorded by Eli S. Ricker, November 1906

Standing Soldier No. 1, an Oglala Indian scout at the time of Wounded Knee, gave this account in an interview with Eli S. Ricker at Pine Ridge on 20 November 1906. Standing Soldier served at Wounded Knee in the detachment of scouts commanded by First Lieutenant Charles W. Taylor, Ninth Cavalry, who is erroneously referenced here as a captain. Tablet 3, pp. 12–24, and Tablet 4, pp. 56–70, Ricker Papers. See also Jensen, ed., Indian Interviews of Eli S. Ricker, *pp. 242–45.*

He says he was a First Sergeant of Indian Scouts under Captain Taylor during the troubles of 1890. Just before the Battle of W.K. the scouts were camping just southwest of the hospital at the [Pine Ridge] Agency, near the 7th Cavalry. While here Sitting Bull was killed [on the Standing Rock Reservation on 15 December 1890]. Capt. Taylor told him [Standing Soldier] that Sitting Bull's band and Big Foot's had left their Reserves and were marching this way and he thought they would come along Bear Creek, and he wanted Standing Soldier No. 1 to go and intercept them. He started next morning in charge of fifteen scouts. Red Shirt was not with him at this beginning. First night he camped on Porcupine Creek & 2nd night on the East fork of the Medicine Root. The third day he got up abt. 5 o'clock in the morning & went up on a hill & was taking in the country with a glass & saw the cattle running in every direction. He thought there might be some men around & he watched the place closely, and saw two Indians come out of a canyon & were going toward [the] northeast. They went up on a high hill & sat there awhile & then went out of sight. Standing Soldier & the scouts then went over to where the Indians had been but could not find anything of them. From there they turned & went eastward down to Bear Creek & there they found a trail of a band of Indians going south of the main Bear Creek. They followed the trail & at the head of Corn Creek this trail turned N.W., [and] from there it turned north & went down to the head of Medicine Root Creek. There they first met the band of Indians. These Indians on seeing these scouts took their guns as if to fight and he saw that they were not Oglalas, and he asked them who they were. They answered that they were a part of Sitting Bull's band. These Indians told him that some of these had taken part in the fight when Sitting Bull was killed, & that the widows of those who were then killed were here among these. One of the women showed Standing Soldier where she had been shot in the shoulder at the time of the killing of Sitting Bull. After they had finished talking Standing Soldier told them that he was an Oglala and a scout and that these scouts had been sent out to meet them and that he was glad to meet them. He told them that he had no soldiers with him; that he had been sent out to meet them & that they need not be afraid & that he was going to take them to Pine Ridge Agency where they would be protected. After he got through telling them, they told him they had nothing to eat & were about starved to death; so he sent two of his scouts out to take up two cattle belonging to the Indians, & these were killed & divided up among the Indians. These Indians did not have any tobacco, so the scouts gave them what they had. The hides of the beeves were put up on a house there. These cattle belonged to Black Prairie Chicken, & the Govt. paid him for these cattle killed. After these Indians had had a good feast he counted the guns which numbered 28; there were 73 persons—men, women & children—they had 31 head of horses and a span of oxen. The oxen belonged to the Indians & they used them to haul the luggage of the camp.

After he had counted what the Inds. had, they gave up to him all their guns. They were perfectly willing to surrender themselves to him. They stayed there that night, [and] next day they started & reached the second branch of Medicine Root Creek. There they struck Big Foot's trail coming this way. So he sent two of his scouts ahead to tell Big Foot to wait for him till he could come up with him, and they would all come in together to General Brooke. He told his scouts to tell Big Foot that Gen. Brooke was at the Agency & that Gen. Brooke and the Agent would protect them. He sent his scouts forward in the morning, and that night Standing Soldier and his Indians camped on the third branch of the Medicine Root Creek. Early the next morning one of his scouts returned & told him that the soldiers & Big Foot's band had met opposite Porcupine Butte & that they had gone on together to W.K., and that the next morning the Indians were all killed off by the soldiers. The scout told him that the soldiers slaughtered everything that was in sight. This scout told him that one of Standing Soldier[']s scouts had been killed at W.K. (Harback) [*sic*—High Back Bone] and that the scout interpreter had his nose cut off in the fight (Philip Well[s]), and that Capt. Taylor had sent him back to tell him about these things & that the soldiers had gone to the Agency. Standing Soldier asked [t]his scout what had become of the other two scouts whom he sent out with him, & the reply was that they both got scared & went right on to the Agency. This scout was with Capt. Taylor in the fight at W.K. He told Standing Soldier that [at Wounded Knee] Taylor's scouts were strung around on the outside south of the ravine, & when the firing began the shots came among these scouts. [The scouts then sought shelter in the ravine.]

Marshal[l] Hand who is also present at this interview [1906] and was [a bugler and] one of Lieutenant Taylor's Indian scouts in this battle says that the [gun]fire was warm, and one-half of the scouts broke toward W.K. Creek & the other half up the ravine toward the hills, leaving Taylor standing alone; the latter when the fire got too hot advanced down into the ravine for shelter. After the battle his scout was sent back to Standing Soldier by Capt. Taylor with news of the catastrophe, and with orders from Taylor to break up the Indians' guns which he had taken. This he refused to do, saying that he would bring them in to the Agency and turn them over to Gen. Brooke. He then sent a scout back with a letter written by himself to Capt. [*sic*—First Lieutenant] Taylor and Philip Wells informing them that the Indians needed something to eat and were out of tobacco. Their next day's march brought them to W.K. Creek. These Indians heard the firing of guns and cannon at W.K.; they were singing and crying. They were marching in the morning and sometime before noon camped on the head of the west, or third, branch of Medicine Root Creek. Some of these Indians were marching on foot. These Indians thought the soldiers were fighting some other band and they were excited and afraid. He himself knew that these outnumbered his scouts, and to calm them and to prevent them from attacking his scouts he told them that it was a custom of the soldiers to salute their officers and that this was what they were doing. He thus deceived them for the sake of safety to himself & scouts and the success of his errand.

They stayed at this place where they heard the firing over night. Next morning they started and went by the head of Porcupine Creek & head of Stinking Water and arrived at the W.K. crossing about sundown. This was the upper W.K. crossing where I crossed on my way to Allen. The lower W.K. crossing is at the battleground. They came right on and after they had crossed W.K. they met Chief Red Shirt with 30 scouts bearing provisions and tobacco. After they arrived at Wolf Creek, three miles east of the Agency, he dispatched Chief Red Shirt ahead to notify Capt. Taylor and Gen. Brooke that he was coming with the Indians. When within half a mile of the Agency he told the men to turn their guns over to the women and to form themselves in line. I should here correct something that has gone before. He did not take the guns from the Indians for fear they would suspicion something wrong, but left them in their hands, though they were willing he should have them.

He formed his line with ten scouts on each flank and ten in rear & they started to enter the Agency. He stopped close to the Agency. In front of the Indians he placed himself and raised his right hand saying "God, our Father, help us that we may make peace and friendship with the Oglalas tonight." Then turning toward the Indians he said: that away back in the treaties the . . . Great Father told the Indians that they must be friendly with the white people and have no more war with them. That was why he had gone to the great trouble to go away down there to meet and bring them safely to the Agency. Then they marched right on into the Agency, stopping in front of the Agent's office, arriving towards midnight, while everybody was yet up. Here Captain Taylor came to them & he allowed nobody to come near these Indians. (It should have been said that when Standing Soldier's scout brought word to him of the disaster at W.K. he instructed all his scouts to keep this painful information strictly to themselves and not let it be known to the Indians.)

Capt. Taylor went round and shook hands with all of the Indians. Just then a scout approached the Captain and told him that Gen. Brooke wanted to see him with two of these Indians. So he took two of the best and went over to Brooke's. When they entered Brooke's house the General asked Standing Soldier what two Indians he had with him. He told Brooke that they were members of Sitting Bull's band. Brooke asked the two Indians if they were willing to give up their guns and they said they were & that they had already delivered them to Standing Soldier. Brooke told them he was glad that they had done that & he shook hands with them & then wrote out an order to the quartermaster to issue rations to those Indians. They then went back to the Indians who gave up their arms to Captain Taylor and received rations.

Capt. Taylor encamped them where he had his scouts and they were there awhile. These Indians remained on Pine Ridge Reservation after the settlement of the troubles and are recognized as Oglalas.[2]

The reason why he took the Indians away round the circuitous route he did was because he remembered the treaty of 1868 in which the Great Father said they should have no more fighting with the whites, and he was afraid if the Indians smelled the blood of W.K. they would break out fighting.

Standing Soldier says if he had succeeded in reaching Big Foot he should have brought his band round as he did the others and they would not have been killed. The day he met the Indians was on the 29th of Dec. and moved to the west branch of Medicine Root where they heard the firing.

2. This group consisted of refugee Hunkpapa Lakotas from Standing Rock Agency who had fled during the emergency following Sitting Bull's death on 15 December. *See* Greene, *American Carnage*, p. 311.

27. Account of Dewey Beard (Iron Hail), recorded by Eli S. Ricker, February 1907

This account by Dewey Beard (Iron Hail) was drawn from his interview with Judge Eli S. Ricker on 20 February 1907 and interpreted by his brother, Joseph Horn Cloud, as Beard did not speak English. In the following narrative, Beard—or his translator—occasionally alternates between first and third person in referencing himself. Excerpted from Tablet 30, pp. 12–24, Ricker Papers. See also *transcriptions in Jensen, ed.,* Indian Interviews of Eli S. Ricker, *pp. 215–26, and Danker, ed.,* "Wounded Knee Interviews of Eli S. Ricker," *pp. 188–200.*

While on the ridge between the Medicine Root and Porcupine Creeks, [Big Foot's people] . . . discovered a lot of [Indian] scouts in front of them. These retreated with great precipitation. The young Indians chased them to find out who these scouts were, and discovered that they were scouts. White Lance [Dewey Beard's brother] and others went down into a ravine and up the next hill, and on the summit met scouts coming toward them. The Indians said, "How! How!" but the white scouts did not answer them but retreated hastily. . . . The Indian Scouts chased the others down the hill and caught one and held him by the bridle rein. When he was caught he told the Indians that there was nothing wrong at all; that the soldiers were camping on Porcupine Cr.; still two of the scouts had run towards W.K. [Creek]. By this time the Indian column had caught up with these advance scouts. Here the Indns. [*sic*] stopped for dinner; when that was over they went right on. Before they got up on the ridge, some Indian scouts in service of the Gov't came in among them[.] There was one, High Back, [who] was in the Indian column ahead of the others, but it is not known how he got there. When we got up on top of this ridge we saw some soldiers coming at the foot of Porcupine Butte, [and] also saw some pack mules. We agreed together that we would not be afraid to go in among the soldiers—we agreed together that way. At the foot of Porcupine Butte is a dry creek or ravine; and lots of pines there. Drawn up in line we found the soldiers on the east side of the creek, & in front of them were 2 Hotchkiss cannon that he saw. The Indians feared from the position and actions of the soldiers that the latter was going to fire on them; but Big Foot had told them to go right up to the soldiers calmly and confidently showing no fear, and they did so. The soldiers aimed their guns toward the Inds, and some of the soldiers laid down to be ready to fire. Their guns were clicking as if cartridges were being injected into barrels. All the Indians were all frightened and thought they were going to be killed. Beard dismounted by a Hotchkiss gun, and shoved his hand into it because he was anxious to die. While he was doing this he heard the wagons coming. He saw Big Foot coming in a light wagon driven by Big Foot's nephew; a pole was up at the front end and a white flag was floating from it. Big Foot's wagon was driven right down in front of the line of soldiers and stopped there. Dewey was on foot at this moment. He saw an officer go up to Big Foot's wagon & he went up & listened to the officer talking.

Big Foot was lying in his wagon, his nose bleeding all the time, [and] the blood had run in the wagon & the officer was standing & looking at the blood. The officer opened the blanket to see Big Foot's face and spoke: "Can't you talk[?]; ain't you able to talk?" Big Foot said, "How," & put his hand out to shake. The officer said: "How" too. "I heard that you came out from the Cheyenne River Agency, that you came fearful as a war party; I have been looking for you; now I see you today," said the officer. The officer continued: "Now I want you to tell me where you expect you are going to."

Big Foot answered: "I am going to see me [my] people over on the White Clay & come to the agency. The officer said: "I heard you were coming hostile; but now I see you today, & I am very glad to see you & you [to] see me too." Then both shook hands.

The officer said "I am very glad to see you are peaceable. Therefore I want you to give me 25 guns."

Big Foot said: "All right; but I am afraid; if I give you the 25 guns I am afraid you are going to do harm to my people in such a country. . . . I am willing to give you the 25 guns; but wait till we get to the Agency, and I will give you whatever you ask—the 25 guns, knives and horses."

The officer said, "I am glad you speak frankly to me; I had heard that you were hostile; but they have lied about you;" and he shook hands again with Big Foot. The officer continued: "I see you are in a hard wagon, and it is pretty hard for you in here; I want you to ride to our camp in an easier one," and he caused an ambulance to come up. Some soldiers put Big Foot into blankets and carried him & placed him in the ambulance. (Beard says he forgot to say that when the officer demanded the 25 guns Big Foot replied that he was that kind of a man.)

When B.F. was put into the ambulance they all then went over to W.K. in a friendly manner. When they arrived at W.K. soldiers were stationed who showed us where to camp in a circle. And they gave us some provisions. While the rations were being distributed, soldiers were putting up 5 tents for those who had no shelter to sleep in. Right in front of where the scouts were camped a small tent was put up large enough to hold four persons. Big Foot was put into it. During the supper & the putting of B.F. into the tent, some soldiers planted the Hotchkiss cannon on the [later] cemetery hill & brought up ammunition for them.

When B. Foot was put into the tent a physician went to attend to him, and Little Bat was there as interpreter. After this and late in the night, some scouts (Indian) arrived. The scouts camped just over on the other side of the ravine and these called across to the B.F. Indians about some relatives they had in his camp. The scouts had a camp-fire. The two lots were not allowed to pass & repass. An interpreter came into their camp & told them that soldiers were coming that night from the Agency.

I will now tell you my own part in what followed — what I saw and heard. I did not sleep that night — did not lie down till morning — was afraid — could not rest or be quiet or easy. There was great uneasiness among the Indians all night; they were up most of the night — were fearful that they were to be killed — were in doubt, did not know what was to happen. The soldiers were stationed all around them, and this was a feature that added to their alarm. That night and all the day ending in that night he had no appetite; was impressed with fear and foreboding, could not & did not eat; could not help thinking of the infants & children & what might befall them[.] He trembled[,] & he could not sleep or be easy. Before the sun rose his father came from B.F's tent & says, "I will give you advice — all my sons — therefore, I have come. They say it is peace, but I am sure there is going to be fighting to-day. I have been in war all my life, and I know when my heart is growing bitter that there was going to be a fight; so I know we are going to have a fight, and I have come to tell you — all my sons, what I want you to do. If one or two Indians go to start trouble, I don't want you to go with them; don't join them. Besides this, if the white people start trouble first, then you can do what you want to—you can die among your own relations in defending them. All you, my dear sons, stand together & keep yourselves sober, & all of you, if you die at once, among your relations defending them, I will be satisfied. Try to die in the front of your relations, the old folks and the little ones, & I will be satisfied if you die trying to help them. Don't get excited. When one or two under the Govt. laws, start trouble they are arrested & taken into court & put in jail, but I don't want any of you to get into such trouble, but to stand back until all the whites assail us, and then defend our people. I have come to tell you this as advice before the trouble begins. I want you to heed my warnings."

When he was done he [Dewey Beard's father] went to B.F.'s tent. At this[,] an Indian called & harangued all the men to come into a council. The haranguer said as soon as the council is through you are going right on to the Agency, & they want you to hurry up. The haranguer said that while the council was going on the women should hitch up the teams to be ready to go.

All the Inds. came to the center for the Council. Two lines of foot soldiers [i.e., cavalrymen on foot] stood immediately around the Inds. Another two ranks of soldiers encircled the Indian camp, the last rank being mounted. There was a council. I stayed inside my lodge—did not go to the council; had a notion to start with the wagons. While I was in my tent my mother came & looked in & said, ["]My son, some soldiers are coming & gathering all the guns & powder, & axes & knives, & bows and arrows, & they are coming this way.["] When I looked out I saw soldiers coming loaded with guns, knives, axes, crowbars, war clubs, bows & arrows. I saw all this with my own eyes. I went inside & took my carbine gun & dug a little hole & laid my gun in & covered some dirt over it, & threw the quilts & blankets over to the other side of the lodge (not over the covered gun)[.] A soldier came & looked in & told him to come to the Council. Before doing so he [Dewey] took some cartridges and buried them outside his lodge, in front of the door, covering them with manure, so that if while at council trouble started he would know where to find ammunition. While I was going to the Council with the soldier I passed my brother Joseph who was leaving the council, & I asked Joe what he was coming out of the Council for, & he replied that he was going after water—that Capt. Wallace had sent him out. I went into the council & saw ten young men standing a little to one side; these had given up their guns, & belts & knives.

While I was sitting in the council my father came to me & admonished me to remember what he had said this morning. Then he asked Dewey where his other brothers were, & the latter replied, ["]Two of them are standing over among those ten young men." And the father added that they ought all to stay together.

Then one of the interpreters said: "This officer asked yesterday for 25 guns, but you did not give them; now he will get them, he will take them himself; so he will pick them himself, & you better give those you have in your blankets, & your knives & belts & it will be all right. When you give all the guns & knives you will stand in one rank right along the edge of this bank (meaning the ravine), and the same number of soldiers will stand in front of you and aim the guns at your foreheads, but the guns are unloaded; they will pull the trigger, but the guns are not loaded.["] Joe explains that the Indians were to submit to this in the nature of penance, admitting thereby that in not turning over the guns the day before they had done wrong and would submit to this nonsense in order to wipe away their fault. (Forsyth must have been drunk!)

The Indians did not understand [the] soldiers' orders. They could not comprehend this foolishness. But this offended and angered them, and they reasoned among themselves and said they were human beings and not cattle to be used that way. They said they did not want to be killed like dogs. ["]We are people in this world."

Most of the Indians had given up their arms; there were a few standing with their guns, but the soldiers had not been to them. The knives were piled up in the center of the council; some of the young men had their guns & knives, but they had not been asked yet for them.

There was a deaf Indian named Black Coyote who did not want to give up his gun; he did not understand what they were giving up their arms for; the Indians agreed among themselves that they would explain to him what the disarming meant, & then they would take his gun away from him. The Indians who had so agreed wanted to tell the officer of their plans, but the interpreter was gone just then & Horned Cloud asked where the interpreter was. The people were getting excited. Nobody said anything in answer to Horned Cloud.

The people grew wild. The deaf man heard what was said about having guns pointed at their foreheads, & he said he did not want to be killed; he was a man & was raised in this world.

While the deaf man held his gun up, Beard could not hear all that was said on account of the confusion; but some soldiers came behind him and tried to take his gun from him; all the sergeants stepped back and said, "Look out! Look out! And held their guns toward the deaf man.

While two or three sergeants came to the deaf man and were struggling with him for the possession of the gun, Dewey heard something on the west side & looked that way & saw the Indians were all exited and afraid, their faces changed as if they were wild with fear; he saw that the guns of the soldiers were pointing at the Council, a part of whom were sitting down and a few were standing up. The old people had wrapped their blankets around their legs and were smoking. The struggle for the gun was short, the muzzle pointed upward toward the east & the gun was discharged. In an instant a volley followed as one shot, and the people began falling. He saw everybody was rolling and kicking on the ground. He looked southeastward & he did not know what he was going to do. He has only one knife. He looked eastward & saw the soldiers were firing on the Indians & stepping backwards & firing. His thought was to rush on the soldiers and take a gun from one of them. He rushed toward them on the west to get a gun. While he was running he could see nothing for smoke; through the rifts he could see the brass buttons of the uniforms; he rushed up to a soldier whose gun rested over Dewey's shoulder & was discharged when the muzzle was near his ear, & it deafened him for a while. Then he grabbed the gun and wrenched it away from the soldier. When he got the gun he drew his knife and stabbed the soldier in the breast, but the knife did not enter deep, & the soldier was trying to seize Dewey by the throat and by his buckskin coat about the breast; as the soldier raised his left arm, Dewey stabbed him again, this time in the side close to the heart. When the soldier fell down he still kept struggling & tried to rise, but Dewey got astraddle of his body and held his head down & then stabbed him by the kidneys till he died. The soldier was crying loud as he could. While Dewey was on this soldier, some soldiers were shooting at him but missed him & killed soldiers on the other side. When he got up he ran right through the soldiers toward the ravine; and he was the last Indian to go to the ravine; the soldiers were shooting at him from nearly all directions, and they shot him down. He fell down on his right arm; he began to rise up, and as he did so, he saw a soldier a few yards in front of him. The soldier began snapping his gun at him, but he was excited, & probably his gun was not loaded, as it did not go off. Dewey Beard at length raised to his knees to shoot the soldier; he snapped but he too had been in too much of a hurry & had not loaded his gun. The soldier was crying out as loud as he could. Soldiers were running all around him about this time.

Dewey tried to get to the ravine and succeeded in getting on his feet; as he was going he met a soldier coming up out of the ravine; the soldier tried to go around him but could not, and Dewey shot him in the breast & killed him. After the soldier fell he was kicking & Dewey jumped over his feet to go on. Right on the edge of the ravine on the south side were soldiers shooting at the Indians who were running down into the ravine, the soldiers' shots sounded like firecrackers and hail in a storm; a great many Indians were killed and wounded down in there. While he was going down into the ravine he was shot again, this time in one leg just above the knees [*sic*]; as he expresses it, "in the lap." He then sat down, got out his cartridges, and shot at the soldiers right at the edge of the bank; [he] doesn't know how many times he shot, but a good many. While shooting, a shell got stuck in his gun so he could not shoot it any more. Then he ran a little farther up the ravine.

When he went to the bottom of the ravine he saw many little children lying dead in the ravine. He was now pretty weak from his wounds. Now when I [he] saw all those little infants lying there dead in their blood his feeling that even if he eat [ate] one of the soldiers it would not appease his anger. He went farther up the ravine, and he came to an old Indian who had a gun which he was holding up, & he said to the old man, "Give me that gun, & you take this one," and they exchanged. When he got this gun he made another rush at the soldiers, accompanied by two other Indians who got killed on the flat on the south side of the ravine. He now returned [to the] ravine alone. Just before he got to the edge of the ravine to go down into it, he met what at first he thought was a soldier, but it proved to be an Indian scout; the two shot at each other, but both missed his man. Just before he started down into the ravine, but after shooting at the Ind. scout, one of Big Foot's men grabbed him by his buckskin coat

& swung himself behind Beard. The soldiers shot at the two men but missed Beard and killed the other man. The Indians all knew that Dewey was wounded, but those in the ravine wanted him to help them; and so he fought with his life to defend his own people. He took his courage to do that. I was pretty weak and now fell down. A man who was wounded by being shot through the lower jaw, had a belt of cartridges which he offered Beard and asked him to try to help them again. When he gave me the cartridges I told him I was badly wounded & pretty weak too. While I was lying on my back I looked down the ravine & saw a lot of women coming up & crying. When I saw these women, girls and little girls & boys coming up, I saw soldiers on both sides of the ravine shoot at them till they had killed every one of them. He saw a young woman among them coming & crying and calling, "Mother! Mother!" She was wounded under her chin close to her throat & the bullet had passed through a braid of her hair & carried some of it into the wound, & the bullet had entered the front side of her shoulder & passed out the back side. Her mother had been shot down behind her. Dewey was sitting up, and he called to her to come to him. When she came close to him she fell to the ground. He caught her by the dress and drew her to him & across his legs. When the women that the soldiers were shooting at got a little past him, he told this girl to follow them on the run, & she went up the ravine. He got himself up and followed up the ravine. He saw many dead men, women & children lying in the ravine. When he went a little way up, he heard singing; going a little farther he came upon his mother who was moving slowly, being badly wounded. She had a soldier's revolver in her hand, swinging it as she went. Dewey does not know how she got it. When he caught up to her she said: "My son, pass by me; I am going to fall down now." As she went up the soldiers on both sides of the ravine shot at her and killed her. I returned fire upon them, defending my mother. When I shot at the soldiers in a northern direction, I looked back at my mother & she had already fallen down. I passed right on from my dead mother. I met a man coming down the ravine who was wounded in the knee. Now these two men were the targets for many rifles on each side of the ravine. Hundreds of bullets threw the dust & dirt around them. This wounded man had a Winchester rifle and he offered it to Beard and asked him to kill as many as he could, but Beard did not take the Winchester. A little while before this he had got rid of the disabled gun in which a shell stuck; he had given it to White Lance's partner and taken one from him; these guns were some taken from soldiers. We didn't have any guns of our own; all these guns we were using we had taken from soldiers to defend ourselves with. We take the guns not from dead soldiers, but from living ones; all of us young men took them (*sic*) [as in original copy].

Afterwards, having used all the cartridges for the carbine he had, he now took the Winchester from the old man who said there were a good many cartridges inside of it. When he took this he heard more noise of shooting up the ravine. He heard someone say that White Lance was killed. Dewey was wounded so that his right arm was disabled; he placed the thumb of his right hand between his teeth, and carried his Winchester on his left shoulder, and then he ran towards where he had heard that White Lance was killed. As he ran he saw lots of women and children lying along the ravine, some alive and some dead. He saw some young men just above, and these he addressed saying to them to take courage and do all they could to defend the women. I have, he said, a bad wound and am not able to defend them; I could not aim the gun, and so told the young men this way. It was now in the ravine just like a prairie fire when it reaches brush and tall grass and rages with new power; it was like hail coming down; an awful fire was concentrated on them now and nothing could be seen for the smoke. In the bottom of the ravine the bullets raised more dust than there was smoke, so that they could not see one another.

When Dewey came up into the "pit" he saw White Lance up on top of the bank, & [he] was rolling on the ground towards the brink to get down into the ravine; he was badly wounded, and at first was half dead, but later revived from his injuries. When Dewey went into the "pit" he found his brother William Horn Cloud lying or sitting against the bank shot through the . . . breast, but yet alive, but he died that night. Just when I saw my wounded brother William, I saw White Lance slide down the bank and stand by William. Then William said to White Lance: "Shake hands with me, I am dizzy now." While they had this conversation Dewey said: "My Dear brothers, be men and take courage. A few minutes ago, our father told us this way, and you heard it. Our father told us that all people in the world born of the same father and mother, when any great danger or tragedy comes, it is better that all of them die together than that they should die separately at different times—one by one;" meaning that it is better for all of the same family to die at one time in front of their relations, between them and the enemy; it looks better for their bones to be piled altogether in defense of their own people—better than for the family to die separately, leaving some behind to mourn for those who had died or been killed singly and alone; I think this statement has the martyr spirit—the spirit of patriotism where a family give themselves all on the altar of their country in a single desperate struggle.

White Lance and William shook hands. Then White Lance and Dewey lifted their brother up and stood him on his feet; then they placed him on White Lance's shoulder[s]. White Lance was wounded in several places and weak from loss of blood, but he succeeded in bearing William to the bottom of the ravine; there he was put down upon the ground, leaning against the bank (says White Lance).

Dewey says we now heard the Hotchkiss or Gatling guns [*sic*—no Gatling guns were present] shooting at us along the bank. Now there went up from these dying people a medley of death songs that would make the hardest heart weep. Each one sings a different death song if he chooses. The death song is expressive of their wish to die. It is also a requiem for the dead. It expresses that the singer is anxious to die too. At this time I am unable to do anything more; and I took a rest, telling my brothers to keep up courage. The cannon were pouring in their shots and breaking down the banks which were giving protection to the fighting Indians. The warriors had before this been shooting at the cannon on the hill and driving back the gunners. The soldiers were pretty close to the edge of the bank and these kept up a continual fire on the Indians. Even if there was no more shooting, the smoke was so thick that the wounded could not live for it; it was suffocating. The Hotchkiss had been shooting rapidly and one Indians had got killed by it. His body was penetrated in the pit of the stomach by a Hotchkiss shell, which tore a hole through his body six inches in diameter. The man was insensible but breathed for an hour when he expired. At the same time this man was shot, a young woman close to Dewey was shot through between the shoulders, [and] the bullet came near hitting him. He heard a laugh and looked at her and she was smiling, all unconscious that she was wounded. The next moment a young man was shot down right in front of this woman. When the man fell, his bow and arrows fell all around on the ground. Dewey told some of the young men there to gather up the bow and arrows and use them again[.] Dewey said to them: "Get the bow and arrows and shoot at them; the white people are afraid of arrows."

Just at this trying moment Dewey's reason and recollection seemed to resume possession of him, and the sight of this wounded young woman recalled his thoughts to his own dear wife and little boy (25 days old) and his parents, not knowing their fate. He went up the ravine in search of them. He came on to a number of women and children hovering in a little pit for shelter from the infuriated soldiers who were all around shooting at them. When he arrived there they were nearly all wounded but were yet alive. In this same place was a young woman with a pole in hand and a black blanket on it. When she would raise it up the soldiers would whistle and yell and pour volleys into it. One woman here spoke to Beard and told him to come in among them and help them. He answered that he would stay where he was and make a fight for them; and that he did not care if he got killed, for the infants were all killed now, and he would like to die among the infants. When he was saying this the soldiers were shooting furiously. He had now regained some strength so that he could hold his gun. He was peeping out for the soldiers who were lying down on their breasts. There was one within a short distance, and him he shot and killed. Dewey now laid down again in a little hollow on his breast. When he raised up for another view of the soldiers, they were approaching; he took a shot at one and brought him down wounded, and two other soldiers took hold of the fallen man to drag him away. (After the trouble was passed, Dewey heard in the talking of the fight, some soldiers say that this wounded soldier begged them to take him back to the Indians, so they might kill him.)

Dewey laid down again in the same little hollow and reloaded his gun. The soldiers across from him were shooting at him while he was loading. While he was loading he heard a horseman coming along the brink of the ravine—could hear the footfalls. This man as he came along, gave orders to the men which he supposed were to fire on the women in the pit, for a fusillade was instantly opened on them. Dewey raised himself for a look at this horseman, and he was not sure that he had on a sword, but he had something swinging. Dewey took a shot at the man and he fell from his horse. This man was the one who had driven the soldiers up close to the bank. Dewey saw him hanging down from his horse after he was shot, and the soldiers were fleeing back when they saw this officer was shot. I was wanting to see how the officer fell; so he was raising up to look, when a bullet swept close to his ear, having first struck the ground and threw dirt in his [Dewey's] eyes so as to blind him. The battle was at this juncture very hot. But for being blinded by the dirt, he could have now picked off a number of soldiers, as they were standing on the level ground & he was behind the bank in the hollow. A good many shots were now directed at him, and he went down and moved along the ravine, thinking he was going down, but he was going up the ravine. The sun was going down; it was pretty near sundown. He saw lots of dead persons in the bottom as he passed on up the ravine. As he was going up hill in the ravine, all the cavalry were coming down the hill; they saw him and began shooting at him. There was an Indian scout pretty close who shot at Dewey, and the latter shot several times at him. Dewey climbed up the hill farther in a south-westerly direction. While going he looked back down on [what was to be called] Cemetery hill and saw something shining like a glass, and several shots were taken at him, going clear over his head and raising little clouds of dust ahead of him. While this was doing he saw five (5) Oglala Sioux on horseback. He called to them, but they were afraid and ran away. But he kept on calling and going till they all stood still and he came up to them. He went on with them a little way and soon met his brother Joseph coming toward them on horseback. Dewey asked: "Where are you going?" Joe answered: "All my brothers and parents are dead and I have to go in and be killed too; therefore I have come back."

Dewey said: "You better come with us; don't go there; they are all killed there," and the five Oglalas joined with Beard in the same appeal. Now the Oglalas left these two brothers. Then Joe got off his horse and told Dewey to get on. Dewey was covered with blood. He mounted the horse and Joe walked along slowly. After a little [while] a mounted Indian relation came up behind them. The three went together over to White Clay Cr[eek] below the mission and into the hostile camp . . . [and] camped there on both sides of the creek. When these arrived the Indians all flocked about them to look at them and to shake hands with them; they were crying and singing death songs; they did not speak with these three. When the people were done shaking hands with them, they were told that their two youngest brothers had been brought over there, and now these youngest brothers were brought to Dewey and Joe. These were Frank and Ernest. When

Dewey saw these two youngest brothers, he was now more sorry than he was over at Wounded Knee. He was wondering how these two youngest ones got out of their trouble and reached White Clay. Seven of us were saved from Wounded Knee—five brothers, one sister, & Dewey's little infant.

Seven of the family were lost, viz., Horned Cloud, Sr. & wife; two brothers, William & Sherman; Dewey's wife Wears Eagle; Good or Pretty Enemy (woman who lived with the Horned Clouds & was one of the family, and was a cousin of Dewey); Ernest was young and ran many miles and by over exertion and exposure contracted consumption and died twelve years afterwards, was never well again; Dewey's little infant, Wet Feet, died afterwards in [the] next March. This child was nursing its dead mother who was shot in the breast; it swallowed blood, & from this vomited and was never well—was always sick till it died.

When the fighting began at W. Knee the sun was just a little above the hills.

He has never before made so complete a statement of this affair to any person. He (Dewey) says he was at this time twenty-five years old.

28. Account of Frank Feather, recorded by Eli S. Ricker, March 1907

Frank Feather gave this account to Judge Eli S. Ricker on 4 March 1907, at Kyle, South Dakota. Excerpted from Tablet 3, pp. 12–24, Ricker Papers. See also *Jensen, ed.,* Indian Interviews of Eli S. Ricker, *pp. 239–40.*

Frank Feather says: The three living babies found on W.K. field by him and others next day [30 December] were under one year old. There were about 100 Indians and a few white men in the visiting party. Young Bull Bear, living on Medicine Root Cr., took one of these babies; Charging Bear, living on Pass Creek took one; and some Indian took the other, these babies were first taken into the Agency before they were taken by these foster parents. These were friendly Indians who came up from the Agency—the 100 who came. They picked up also the wounded & living. An Inspector, Harry Manns (he says) came out with them. This Manns [or Mauns] was a special agent. George E. Bartlett came over with them; he and Manns were the leading white men; just a few other white men were with these, the clerk of the special agent was along also; a photographer ([George] Trager), a little man, was along taking pictures; the additional Farmer [of the Wounded Knee District] (Clem Davis) came out also.

The wounded taken up were taken to the Agency in wagons. They took in seven wounded Indians, both men & women; one of these was not wounded, he was a man, he was scared & was found in hiding on the creek & was taken. They did not get all the wounded, for the hostile Indians were coming and the Indians at work on the field took the alarm & fled. Frank Feather remained behind on the field and was the last to leave it; he saw the hostiles and beckoned to them to come on to the field, but they did not come; they were approaching from abt. [about] the direction of the Day School, or more from the northwest. Frank Feather was a policeman from the Agency & was ordered out by his superior with this party. This was the day that Clem Davis fled; & Frank passed his abandoned wagon when he himself went in. Dr. Eastman was one of the party that visited the field that day.

Frank Feather is positive that this party went out to the battlefield the *next* day after the fight. He says the babies would not have been living if they had not done so. He says that it started in raining the night after the fight and turned to snow, and there were about three inches on the ground when they arrive[d] on the field at noon. They had their dinner there on arrival; he took his near where Big Foot lay. Big Foot and he were related.

The photographer was trying to get a picture of Big Foot. He set his camera, but Shot in Hand was lying dead next to it; Big Foot was lying farther back, and Feathers does not know whether [George E.] Trager got a picture of Big Foot; he did not tell him which was Big Foot, and he says the photographer did not know which he was.

29. Account of Paddy Starr, recorded by Eli S. Ricker, August 1907

Paddy Starr, a mixed-blood Oglala Indian scout who took part in the action at Wounded Knee, was interviewed by Eli S. Ricker on 20 August 1907. His account also appears in Jensen, ed., Indian Interviews of Eli S. Ricker, *pp. 237–39; and Danker, ed., "Wounded Knee Interviews of Eli S. Ricker," pp. 222–24.*

Paddy Starr says that he was at the battle of Wounded Knee. He was standing across the ravine among the scouts; he was a scout.

Before sunrise he was up. The women had the rations that had been issued to the Indians, and they were feeling happy and singing & it seemed as though they did not suspect any evil or danger. The trouble began about sunrise. The first Paddy noticed was a single shot where quite a lot of people were standing. He looked and saw the smoke of the gun rising above this assemblage. As soon as he looked there was another shot in the same place. As soon as he heard this he saw the swords of officers waving above their heads, and the glinting of the sunbeams from the rising sun. The morning was still and voices could be heard a long way off. Then came to his ears these words: "Look out!" then more prolonged and drawled out was the repetition "Look out!"

Then broke forth the thunderous peal of guns in a volley. John Shangrau was issuing crackers to the women. It seemed as though the fire was poured into these helpless creatures. All the soldiery joined in the fusil[l]ade, and the cannon rang out with fierce spirit. There were soldiers behind the scouts who were south of the ravine and about 400 yards from the headquarters & southwest from the headquarters. These soldiers fired also, and the scouts were obliged to run mounted south to escape the cross fire of the soldiers.

The fine line on Starr's map [not included] shows where the scouts fled. When they reached the X they halted, and at this point they were fired on by the soldiers, and then they moved again around behind the hill near where a Hotchkiss cannon stood.

Firing was in all directions; it was wild and reckless; all was confusion.

After the battle was over (it did not last till noon) he and others went down along the ravine and cried to the Indians that if any were living to sit up and be saved.

He saw a few women sit up, all badly wounded. He looked into the ravine and saw men and women and children, horses and wagons piled up dead and dying.

When the firing began he saw men and women and children fleeing to the ravine, some falling as shots took effect.

He saw, after the word had been given for them to sit up and be saved, one wounded man who raised up as well as he could, bracing himself with his hands behind himself, and was shot dead by some soldiers who were coming down the ravine from above. Perhaps these soldiers had not heard the cry to sit up and be saved; nevertheless they were killing everything clean as they went.

He says there were 30 or 40 taken prisoner, mostly wounded; these were taken to the Agency.

When Paddy Star[r] who had the contract to bury the dead at W.K. went out to bury the dead [five days later], his party found 7 living—5 grown and two little children, infants. One of the latter was badly frozen. Thinks it lived; he handed it over to Jim Harrison, a Mexican, & told him to take it over to Red Bear's house (log house) which stood abt. 30 yards in front of the commissary. In Red Bear's house he found an old decrepit squaw sitting by the door; she was blind and deaf and was holding a baby in her arms. This old woman was the mother of Crazy Bear who was himself insane. (He [Starr] says nobody went to the battlefield before his own party; I [Ricker] doubt this; for I think that the party that went for the wounded was ahead of him.) He was two days [3–4 January] burying the Indians. He went out with one company of the 7th Cav. (he thinks) and one wagon of working tools and two wagons of provisions for the burial party and about 30 laborers. When he went there were soldiers already out there entrenched on the ridge above the battlefield where I [Ricker] saw the pits.

He tells of Mary Thomas being found on the field when Zit-ka-la-nuni was found. Mary's Indian name is Niglicu win . . . , meaning "comes out alive."

He made his contract with Gen. Miles & was paid $2 for every body interred. Says 168 were put into the grave. Three women who were killed were pregnant. One boy about 10 years old, he remembers, had his left arm and shoulder and left breast torn away by a cannon shot. One woman had her entire abdomen shot away by a Hotchkiss shell.

Paddy Starr having the contract to bury & a price for each body would know better than [mixed-blood William] Peano how many dead were buried.

30. American Indian viewpoint at Wounded Knee as recorded by Walter M. Camp, 1910

Walter M. Camp, an editor and researcher known for conducting interviews with survivors of the Indian Wars, recorded this American Indian viewpoint of Wounded Knee in "Data on monument and notes of Battle field & fight from Indian side (1910)." Envelope 89, Walter M. Camp Manuscripts, Manuscript Department, Lilly Library, Indiana University, Bloomington.

The Inds say that, as a whole, they were not inclined to resist giving up guns. When the soldiers were disarming, just before firing began, it was the intention generally to give up the guns & they were doing so. There were, however, among them two discontented Inds who kept up an agitation to resist, but they had no sympathy from the rest of the Inds, and several times *they* were told to keep still. Nevertheless those two kept declaring that they would not surrender their arms and they were very bitter to see that the rest were doing so, and they could not be made to keep still[.] One of them kept calling out in a loud voice (the one whom the white men took for a medicine man) and throwing dirt on his shoulders. He had a gun cocked under his blanket and a knife, and when, at length, a soldier came up to search him, he drew his gun and shot the soldier through, and began cutting with his knife. The fight then started generally. These two loud Inds were both wild from ghost dancing, and the one who fired the shot was known to be temporarily insane if not permanently so. The Inds blame no one but themselves for starting the fight. The two Inds referred to were the cause of it. They blame the soldiers for much wanton killing. The gatling [*sic*—Hotchkiss] gun on the hill was turned on the lodges, killing women and children, who were entirely innocent and knew nothing of what was taking place where the disarming was going on. As soon as the firing commenced they tried to get away and many were killed on the flat south of the battlefield while driving off in wagons. A squaw with a baby on her back was killed on the hills on the road to the agency 1¼ miles from the battlefield.

More women and children were killed than men (this will bear investigation). In Pine Ridge a Christmas tree was cleared out of a church and hay strewn on the floor to receive wounded Indians who were brought in that night by the soldiers. . . . Where the monument now stands commanding both the bend in the ravine & the village, . . . it is reported that [a] gatling [Hotchkiss] gun was turned on the village[.] Inds were killed all along up the gully which forks and runs in three directions. Big Foot was killed at a point southeast of the monument and about half way between it and the ravine on the flat ground. Above information given me 7/12/1910 by Mrs. [Sidney] Keith, wife of the teacher at the battlefield, who has lived here 20 years & was living here then but was at the agency that day.

31. Excerpt from Joseph Horn Cloud's account, as told to Melvin R. Gilmore, 1913

This excerpt from Joseph Horn Cloud's account of the "Slaughter of Wounded Knee," is printed as it appeared in American Indian Magazine *5 (Oct.–Dec. 1917): 242–48. Horn Cloud gave this account to Melvin R. Gilmore, curator of the Nebraska State Historical Society Museum, near Pine Ridge Agency, on 24 October 1913. It was published in the* Lincoln (Nebraska) Daily Star *on 25 January 1914.*

That evening they [Big Foot's people] came to camp at the head of Pass creek. Next day we came through the Bad Lands north of White river and camped at the White River. That evening Big Foot began to be sick with pneumonia. We moved next day and camped at a spring now [1913] called Big Foot Spring, about six miles from White River. Then we moved to Red Water creek. . . . We stayed there a day and a half. We started from there to go direct to the [Pine Ridge] agency and camped by No. 17 Day School [location as of 1913] at American Horse creek. [On 28 December] we met four United States scouts on a divide between American Horse creek and Porcupine creek and we had dinner at noon on Porcupine creek. Some of the scouts went ahead of us and some of them ate with us. After dinner we came about three miles and met soldiers east of Porcupine Butte at Dry creek. The soldiers had two or three Gatling [*sic*—Hotchkiss] guns. They were formed in order, the gunners by the guns.

We came up facing the [Hotchkiss] guns and most of the soldiers went a little way back of the guns, only two or three soldiers standing by each gun. We had a white flag on the wagons all the time. So we stood right in front of the guns and saw the inside of them. Colonel Whiteside [*sic*—Major Whitside] came to Big Foot and asked him where he was going. Big Foot replied, "I am going to Pine Ridge agency, where my people are." Then the Colonel asked him why he was going there. Big Foot said that he heard there was a fire likely to break out there so he as going there to try to put out the fire, he was there to make peace. Colonel Whiteside said, "Big Foot, do you want to fight or have peace?" Big Foot said, "I want peace. My forefathers always had peace, and I will do the same." And the Colonel said again, "I have heard of you, and that you have become hostile and want to fight and have left Cheyenne agency to come to Pine Ridge. So ever since I have watched you on every hill, and now I see you today, and I find that you are not a hostile but a friendly Indian." Then they shook hands. Colonel Whiteside said, "What is the matter, Big Foot, you seem to be sick?" Big Foot said, "Yes, I have pneumonia and I am pretty sick today on account of my jolting wagons." The Colonel answered, "That is too bad. Now if you want to ride in my ambulance you may. That will be better for you than the rough wagon." Big Foot said, "If you please, I will ride in the ambulance." The soldiers then opened ranks and the ambulance going through the ranks of soldiers and on to Wounded Knee creek, carrying white flags.

Now we came to Wounded Knee creek, and camped west of the creek in a half circle with soldiers all around us. The tents were set up and we had supper. We got into camp about 4 o'clock or about sundown and they gave us hardtack, bacon, sugar and coffee.

After supper I went to the soldiers' camp and saw a priest, Father Craft, talking with some Indians and telling them there was no danger, and not to be afraid, that Colonel Whiteside was a good man [and] that we would go to Pine Ridge next day. There were about two or three tepees of Sitting Bull's people with us. Now about 11 o'clock Colonel Forsythe [Forsyth] came with his troops and also some Indian scouts, who went into camp southwest [*sic*—northeast] of us. I could not sleep at all that night, because of the noise of the arrival of the cavalry and for fear of the soldiers all around. Not many of us slept that night. In the morning about seven o'clock a council was called by order of Colonel Forsyth. Big Foot in his bed was dragged out into the council circle. His voice was very low from weakness. He could hardly be heard. When he spoke he rose up from his pillows and then sank back. My father, Horn Cloud, and a brother of Big Foot named Goggle Eyes had sat up with him all night and the army surgeon attended him.

Colonel Forsyth said, "Big Foot, do you want war or peace?" Big Foot said, "I do not want war, I want peace." Then Colonel Forsyth demanded twenty-five guns. Big Foot ordered the guns to be delivered. This was done. Then Colonel Forsyth demanded fifteen more because he said, "I heard every man had a gun." So the fifteen were given up. Then he called for ten more and before the ten had been brought he said, "I will have the soldiers search for more guns." Big Foot said, "You may do as you please." Then the colonel sent soldiers who seized everything, guns, axes, crowbars, knives and even awls. At the time of making the demands and giving the order of search and seizure, Colonel Forsyth went on to say to the men in council through the interpreter that he would have them stood in line facing the line of soldiers. Each with his gun aimed at the forehead of the Indian opposite him, in order to punish them for leaving Cheyenne River.

There were eight men who had not yet been searched and another man[,] making nine altogether, was struggling with two soldiers who were trying to disarm him. This man was hard of hearing. Someone cried, "Look out! Look out!" and just then the gun went off itself in the air toward the east. Then there was a volley and it was just like a hail-storm with shots in all directions. The Indians who were not killed at the first fire seized again whatever arms they could and tried to defend themselves and protect the retreat of the women.

When Colonel Forsyth was making these demands a captain, Captain Wallace, beckoned to me and told me to go and tell the women to hitch up and get out of the camp because, he said, "I see we are going to have trouble. The Colonel is half shot [i.e., drunk]." I started, but was stopped by the soldiers, but Captain Wallace motioned with his hand to the soldiers to let me pass, [and] I went and warned the women, but the trouble had started before I got back. The women ran to get into the ravines and hid[e] themselves and save their babies, dragging themselves all wounded and bloody. The cavalry pursued them, shooting the women and children wherever they found them. Little Bear says that he saw three soldiers throw a baby into the air and shoot it. He also heard of a woman and two children kneeling and praying when soldiers came upon them and killed them all.

This day, the 29th of December, 1899 [sic—1890] was a mild, clear day, but that night a terrific snow storm and great cold fell. The snow covered the bodies of the dead and wounded. Then after the storm the snow partly melted from over the bodies. Babies were found crawling about their dead mothers and dying in the snow. The bodies looked like chickens on the snow. All this had been done while the Indians were under a flag of truce.

There were about 400 people in Big Foot's band. There were 126 men counting boys. Of the victims there were 164 [sic—146] bodies buried at Wounded Knee. There were about 100 survivors. The rest are not accounted for. They must have died in the prairie. Some bodies were found in Bad River, considerably more than 100 miles away. Some wounded girls got back to the Cheyenne river still further away, but they afterwards died of their wounds and exposure.

32. **Mrs. Mousseau's account, as told to Melvin R. Gilmore, 29 October 1913**

Mrs. Mousseau's account, as dictated to Melvin R. Gilmore and interpreted through Otto Chief Eagle at Pine Ridge Agency on 29 October 1913, is printed here as it appeared in American Indian Magazine *5 (Oct.–Dec. 1917): 251–52.*

They made us camp at Wounded Knee creek about four o'clock in the afternoon with soldiers all around us. The soldiers brought Big Foot in an ambulance because he was sick. When we came to camp the soldiers brought him from the ambulance and put him into an army tent. After we made camp they gave us coffee, sugar, hardtack and a small piece of breakfast bacon.

About midnight we wanted to get some water but the soldiers refused to let us get it. After refusing to let us get water the soldiers called all the women together and let them go by twos, a soldier with a gun going behind each two women. At this time Joe Horncloud was interpreter, but at daylight Philip Wells was interpreter. At this time (daylight) a herald cried out that the soldiers would take us to the agency and take good care of us. The soldiers marched round in single file round the hill and told us to break up the camp. (The morning of December 29, 1890.) Then the bugle sounded and the dismounted cavalry marched and surrounded the place where the talk was to be. Then another bugle sounded and the mounted cavalry took position in a second line behind the first.

The women started to run toward the west, but the soldiers from both sides shot them. There was so much smoke I could not see the way. I was wounded at the first fire, but I was so scared I did not feel it. My husband was killed there and my little girl, and a little boy baby on my back was killed by a bullet which also broke my elbow, so that I dropped the body. Many of my relatives were killed. Chief Spotted [was shot] in three places. I had two shots in three places. I had two shots through the muscles of my back from one side to the other. The third bullet killed my baby which I was carrying in my shawl on my back and then broke my right elbow. I fell, but I did not feel the bullets, [I] was so excited.

I don't know what happened next, I was unconscious, but when I became conscious it was about noon, I think, and I found myself in the ravine and my mother was there. She had several flesh wounds from bullets. We were awfully thirsty and went down to the creek and got a drink. Then went into a place of many trees a little way off.

In this place of many pines, west of Wounded Knee creek, we stayed that night. I had one blanket and I was wearing several dresses. I had to tear up part of them to make bandages for my wounds. At least I had three dresses on and it was very cold when the storm came on. Next day we walked through the storm to a place on Porcupine creek, where we stayed in a lonely place till the thirteenth of January. We had nothing to eat, but we drank water. Then some Indian scouts found us. Their horses were gentle, so they put us upon the horses and brought us to Wounded Knee. When they found us they offered us a canteen of coffee, but we could not drink it because we had been so long without food. We were very thin and weak.

They took us to a house on Wounded Knee creek and prepared some food for us, but we could not eat. They found an old wagon and made a harness of ropes and put some gray blankets in and brought us to Pine Ridge agency. I was coughing all the time. Blood was caked on my wounds and on my broken arm. They took us across the creek (White Clay creek) to the camp of the soldiers and scouts, where they gave us some food and attended to our wounds.

33. Account of Dewey Beard, as told to Melvin R. Gilmore, 27 November 1913

This account from Dewey Beard (Iron Hail), as told to Melvin R. Gilmore at Pine Ridge Agency on 27 November 1913, appeared in American Indian Magazine *5 (Oct.–Dec. 1917): 248–51.*

Some time near evening [on 28 December] we arrived at Wounded Knee [with the soldiers under Major Whitside's command]. When we arrived they gave us rations of sugar, coffee, crackers and bacon. I, myself, distributed these rations to the people. We had supper. While [we] were doing this the soldiers guarded around our camp. Then they put Hotchkiss guns where [the] cemetery is now. ([Note in original:] He refers to the place where the victims of the slaughter were buried, now inclosed by a fence. The site is under the care of the Holy Rosary Catholic mission.)

There were so many guns all around us I could hardly sleep at all that night. I was rather afraid and worried in my mind about those guns. Early in the morning, about 6 o'clock, the guards were changed, new guards were put on. On the south side, across the ravine, the Indian scouts were standing in a line. Now Big Foot was lying in a wall tent, an army tent. Someone called, "All the men are wanted at Big Foot's tent in the soldiers' camp." The men went to that place and while they were sitting in a circle there they put two ranks of soldiers all around where they sat. But I was not there, [as] I was staying in my tent. If I was not called I had a notion to stay in my tent.

While I was sitting inside there was some noise, the women seemed to be excited and in fear. I looked out and saw some confusion among the women. I saw, when I looked out, that a gang of soldiers was searching the women and taking away all axes, crowbars and old guns that had been left; and they opened the women's shawls and took their awls and knives. Now when I saw this I did not want to give up my gun, so I took my knife and dug a hole by the fireplace and hid my gun. After I had hid my gun a sergeant opened my tent and saw me sitting there. He pointed toward the place where the men were sitting and told me to go there.

While I was going to that place I saw my brother Joe [Joseph Horn Cloud] coming towards our camp. When I went into that place I saw the faces of all the men changed, showing fear and excitement. While I was standing there the heralds said to the people, "The officer wanted twenty-five guns yesterday, but you have not given them." Then the interpreter, Philip Wells, said, "Now all you men that have a gun or a knife, put it down in this place (indicated). Now you men, after you have given up your arms, go towards the ravine to the south and stand in line facing the officers toward the north. A line of soldiers will stand facing you and each soldier will aim his gun at the forehead of the one of you in front of him and pull the trigger and snap the hammer. The gun will not be loaded. Now on account of this, saying that the guns would be aimed at our foreheads, there was fear and confusion among us. At that time my legs were trembling and my heart was thumping and I was afraid. [This menacing assertion appears in other Beard statements; it is perhaps most cogently explained in Beard's interview with James R. Walker, No. 19 below.]

Then I knew that we should get into trouble, so I remembered my knife. I had my knife in my belt. And while this thing was going on there was a man who was hard of hearing who came into the midst between the soldiers and I thought he was coming to give up his gun. When this man held up his gun in the middle, two sergeants sprang out and struggled with him and the gun went off in the air. Nobody was hit, the gun went off in the air towards the northeast, and then all the soldiers standing round fired at once, just like one gun. All those Indians sitting there were shot down. They did not hit me at first. I ran toward the north and met a soldier and he fired his gun at me, but the bullet went close to my ear and I took his gun away from him and took out my knife and killed him right there. Just as I was astraddle of the soldier, stabbing him, another soldier behind me shot at me, the bullet going through the muscles of my back, breaking my shoulder-blade and coming out at the top of my shoulder, it struck the first soldier in the head. I rose and went southwest towards the ravine. Now when I got to the edge of the ravine another bullet hit me in the front of the leg above the knee and I fell down. This was a flesh wound. But I rose up and ran into the ravine and followed a little way up the ravine. Now when I came into that pocket I saw my brothers there, except Joe [brother Joseph Horn Cloud]. All the soldiers, dismounted cavalry, came toward us there and the artillery brought a

Hotchkiss gun and set it up at the edge of the ravine pointed toward that pocket. We heard the guns cocked and right after that it was just like a storm of thunder and hail as the bullets came into that pocket. As soon as the storm of bullets was past we rose up and I shot off from his horse a soldier with shoulder straps. My shoulder was very painful, but I had to defend myself the best I could. Now I shot that soldier off his horse and I killed five other soldiers around the edge of the ravine[.] I fired among the gunners of the Hotchkiss gun[s] many times and about noon the Hotchkiss was not fired so frequently. I may have killed some of those gunners, but I do not know. The ravine was full of smoke from the Hotchkiss and from the cavalry carbines, and from the guns of the scouts. The firing into this pocket continued and I had no chance to think of the passage of time, but after a long time the firing stopped and I came up out of the ravine and the shadows of the hills lay far extended along the ground. The sun was very low. Some soldiers saw me, but they did not fire at me anymore.

When I came upon the hill I heard the Hotchkiss gun[s] far behind me where the cemetery is now. They shot at me but they did not hit me. When I came up on the divide I saw some Indians on horseback west of me, so I went towards them. Now these four men told me that a number of us had escaped, men, women and children wounded, and all had been taken by the Pine Ridge people (Indians) to a place on White Clay Creek about five miles below the mission. Now just a little way from there on a hill a mounted man came at full speed. I met him. He said[,] "Go along with these men to White Clay Creek." So we left these four men and they went down south of Pine Ridge to where White Clay post office is now to the Cutoff Band (Kiaksa). And we went down five miles below the mission where the Pine Ridge, Rosebud, Cheyenne [River] and other people were, at the bluff. There we found thousands of people wailing for the dead, singing death son[g]s, some Messiah people dancing the [Ghost] dance. Now when we arrived there I first realized that I was alive again. When I got there the people saw my wounds and blood. Relations cried, some fainted, they were excited and frightened at my wounds.

34. Supplemental information about Wounded Knee from Philip F. Wells, 1914

Philip F. Wells detailed his recollection of the broad placement of troops around the Indians at Wounded Knee in this account, which appeared in the Black Hills Weekly Journal, *10 January 1914. A portion of Wells's report, transcribed from the journal by Thomas E. Odell, can be found in Folder 41, Drawer 6, Odell Collection, Case Library.*

Now let us see what that "hollow square" was, and the "unusual battle formation of soldiers." Just before the fight began, the Indians were camped on the north side of the canyon [ravine] along the brow of [the] bank and the soldiers were drawn up in line about twenty or thirty yards to the east. Captain [George D.] Wallace's troop was drawn up in line within a few feet on the north side of the line of Indian teepes [*sic*], forming an angle with a line of soldiers on [the] east and the north line of the "hollow square," . . . was Sickle's troops [First Lieutenant Horatio G. Sickel's Troop E], a little over a quarter of a mile to the northwest and partly behind a hill. And what formed the west line was [Captain Henry] Jackson's troop [C] about a mile and a quarter away [across the large deep ravine] and behind the hills out of sight of the camp; and the south line consisted of [Captain Edward S.] Godfrey's troop [D, also across and below the deep ravine and] about half a mile to the southwest, and all the Indians, except women and children, were within the above described angle[s] and the Hotchkiss guns were stationed over a hill about one hundred yards to the north. The Indians were called up and placed in a group for the purpose of surrendering their arms, but only a few of the old men surrendered their guns, and it was the disinclination of all the younger Indians to surrender their arms. . . . The fight was started by an Indian firing the first shot, and . . . the fight at that place did not last over two minutes and including a battery of mountain howitzers. There never was a cannon shot fired into the so-called hollow square. [It was] not until the Indians had gained the canyon [ravine] and began to open fire on the soldiers that the cannon [Hotchkiss guns] were used to dislodge them. It is all true that the fight lasted several hours, but most of that fighting was against the main body of Indians that came from the main camp, which was a few miles northeast of the agency.[3]

3. Here, Wells properly differentiated between the mass killings at Wounded Knee and the later efforts of the Lakotas from Pine Ridge and Rosebud who came out to aid the victims.

35. Statement about Wounded Knee by members of the Big Foot Survivors' Association, September 1915

Members of the Big Foot Survivors' Association offered this statement about Wounded Knee in September 1915, translated and transcribed by Violet Catches of the Pierre Indian Learning Center, Pierre, S.Dak, in 2012. It reposes in Envelope 5, pp. 233–43, Folder 4, Box 4, Camp Manuscripts, Lilly Library.

The within is a statement of the battle of Wounded Knee by the survivors who have signed it Sept 1915. Around 8 a.m. this morning [29 December 1890] all the men were called to council. The soldier leader who met Big Foot yesterday said to do this. ["]These soldiers want all the guns in your possession.["] The soldier leader said ["]I want all of your guns,["] so Big Foot told his men to bring all of their guns. The men returned to their tepees by tens to get their guns[,] returning with however many guns they each had and put them down. Those who had more guns at camp went to get them and turned them in. While they were doing this, they (soldiers) blew a whistle and all together the soldiers loaded their guns. While they were doing this, a soldier leader on a bay horse gave a command for them to shoot and now they were shooting their guns. Some white men stood here and there watching and listening as this happened.

    [Signed]
Peter One Skunk
Jessie Shunkaluzahan (Swift Dog)
Alex High Hawk
Chas Blue Arm
Solomon Afraid of Enemy
Daniel Blue Hair
Send Typewritten copy of English translation to Swift Dog
    at Cherry Creek
Big Foot Survivor's Association.
The within is a statement of the battle of Wounded Knee,
    by the survivors who have signed it[,] Sept. 1915.

36. Notarized statement by Dewey Beard, given in Washington, D.C., on 12 March 1917

Dewey Beard (Iron Hail), translated by Henry Standing Bear, gave this notarized statement in Washington, D.C., on 12 March 1917, during an early unsuccessful effort to gain compensation for the Lakotas at Wounded Knee. Copy provided by Michael Her Many Horses, Wounded Knee, S.Dak.

In the latter part of December, 1890, Big Foot started from Cheyenne River Reservation with all his bands and stock belonging to them in reply to the request contained in the communication from Chief Red Cloud in reference to making peace. They reached a point on the Pine Ridge Reservation, known as Red Water Creek, where they left part of their stock to graze until they returned on the way home when the weather was warm. At this time Chief Big Foot was very sick. On their way, after they had eaten their dinner and started towards Pine Ridge Agency, between Wounded Knee and Porcupine Creeks the soldiers were coming to meet them. Big Foot being sick was lying in a wagon which another Indian was driving for him. In front of the wagon containing Chief Big Foot rode an Indian on horseback carrying a flag of truce to meet the troops.

The commanding officer came and asked if this man in the wagon was Chief Big Foot. He was told yes. The officer then removed the blanket which was over the face of the Chief and seeing his face covered with blood asked if he, Big Foot, could talk. The chief replied "yes." Then the officer asked the Chief where he was going to and what for. The Chief answered to visit his friends and tribesmen at Pine Ridge and to assist them in bringing peace amongst his people. The army officer told the Chief that he wanted twenty[-]five guns from the Chief. The Chief replied that he was for peace and if that meant a peaceful act then he was willing to give over the guns but not at a place like the one they were then at for fear of the unfaithfulness of his (the officer's) soldiers at that place. The chief was willing to deliver the guns but did not feel that the troops could be trusted out in the open where they then were but desired to have the officer wait until they had reached a suitable camping site so that the transfer could be made in a proper and orderly manner. Chief Big Foot said that the Pine Ridge Agency was where they were going, and that upon reaching there they would formally surrender their arms to the officer in charge of the United States troops. The army officer replied that he was looking for him (meaning Chief Big Foot) because he had heard that he had left the Cheyenne River Reservation and had come in that direction; that he had been looking for him all this while and had now met him and that the army officer was pleased that their meeting was in a most friendly way and he shook hands with Chief Big Foot for the second time. The army officer invited the Chief to ride in a better wagon to the place where the troops were camping. They took Chief Big Foot and his band to the Wounded Knee Creek where the troops were camping, and the Indians camped there along side of the troops of the United States. Big Foot was carried to a tent provided by the army officers near the scouts. The soldiers surrounded the band and gave them fuel to make fire and also rations for the Indians.

Next morning one of the Indians was calling to the Indians that they were going to have a council of their men with the army officers and when that is over they are all to start to the Pine Ridge Agency. A cavalry line was thrown clear around the Indians. All the men had gathered in a crowd to hold this council. Then an infantry [i.e., dismounted] line was thrown about the camp but within the circle made by the cavalry [i.e., mounted troops]. At this time through an interpreter [Wells] it was announced that the army officers had demanded on the previous day twenty[-]five guns which were not handed over but the delivery was postponed until they all reached Pine Ridge Agency. It was then announced that the officers were going to collect all the guns and weapons which they, the Indians, had. In obedience to this demand the Indians placed all their guns and weapons in a pile at a distance removed and at a place where the army officer could take the same. This was willingly done by the Indians when Chief Big Foot told his men to obey the order of the army officer. After all the weapons had been given up there was one Indian standing off still holding his gun in his hand, who raised the gun in the air to show that he was going to give his gun up also, although it had been agreed that they were to give up their arms and weapons when they reached Pine Ridge Agency. This Indian started towards the pile of arms, and at this moment an officer went up to him and grabbed the but[t] end of the gun. Another officer came towards him from behind and also grabbed the gun. The officer did this to take the gun away from him forcibly. The Indian was holding the gun by the barrel, and before he could place it in the pile these two officers attempted to grab the gun from out of his hands. In the scuffle caused by these two officers trying to take the gun away from the Indian it was accidently discharged.

Immediately after the discharge of the gun the voice of a soldier was heard in the direction of the south and instantly fire was turned on the Indians by the two lines of soldiers that encircled the camp and the soldiers continued firing upon them, shooting down and killing the disarmed Indians, [besides] women and children who were scattered throughout the camp on the prairie. Many soldiers, who were standing amongst the Indians and holding friendly conversations, fell under the fire of the troops. There was no firing by the Indians as they had been previously relieved of their arms and weapons. All the time during the continuance of the council and also while the shooting was in progress the flag of truce, which had been carried by the Indians, was still standing and waving in the smoke. After the firing was over, men, women, and little children were lying dead on the field; and some of the little children whose mothers had been shot were running about the place crying and calling for their mother. Three women who were just about to give birth to child were also killed. Some little children, whose mothers were killed, were found feeding upon the breasts of their dead mothers.

While this firing was continuing, I, Dewey Beard, ran against a soldier who aimed a gun at men but I succeeded in taking the gun from him. This soldier was shot down by another soldier who aimed at me but missed me and killed the soldier from whom I had succeeded in taking the gun. I followed a crowd of women and children who were running to a place of safety and having ammunition, I kept the soldiers from advancing upon the helpless women and children who were running to safety. The women and children found a deep place to hide from the flying bullets; I took a position near them and defended the women and children all the way through and saved them. After the firing had ceased the soldiers went about and shot to death those who lay wounded on the field. After all the firing had ceased the survivors escaped over the hill; and when they had reached the hill, I, Dewey Beard, looked back and saw the camp and also saw the dead men, women and children scattered about the place where the flag of truce was still standing and flying, and which had been planted by the Indians.

I, Dewey Beard, came here to place this matter and the facts in connection therewith before the good white people, in order that those who are now living, being survivors of that massacre, might be given some relief or redress by the good Government of the United States. I feel that every time that I recall this history, the matter is so vivid in my mind that it seems to me as though it had happened just yesterday, but I hope that we, the survivors be given by the Government of the United States relief of some nature or other or some re-imbursement. In view of the fact that Chief Big Foot while on his way to perform his good mission, namely to bring about peaceful conditions among the tribes of Chief Red Cloud, met with this misfortune never to return to his own Agency and draw his right for annuities in rations and clothing to which he and his band were entitled to under the treaty stipulations for that year, therefore, their survivors should not be re-imbursed in money to that extent, besides what other monetary considerations the Government might hereafter donate for the relied [*sic*—relief] of the surviving members of this band of Chief Big Foot.

37. Notarized statement by Joseph Horn Cloud, given in Washington, D.C., on 12 March 1917

Joseph Horn Cloud, translated by Henry Standing Bear, offered the following notarized statement in Washington, D.C., on 12 March 1917, while seeking compensation for the Lakotas at Wounded Knee. Copy provided by Michael Her Many Horses, Wounded Knee, S.Dak.

I am a Sioux Indian, now about 44 years of age and was present at the Wounded Knee Massacre mentioned below.

Colonel Whitside is the name of the officer of the troops which we met between Wounded Knee and Porcupine Creeks. I heard Colonel Whitside say that he was pleased to meet these Indians and would return to his camp with the Indians. At this point where they met they put Chief Big Foot, he being very sick, in an ambulance which was more comfortable than the rough wagon and carried him to the soldiers['] camp. After they camped [at Wounded Knee] the soldiers issued ration[s] to the Indians. The following night [of 28 December], just about eleven o'clock, there were some more soldiers came to this place from the Agency. This body of last arrived troops was under Colonel Forsyth. In the morning about eight o'clock there was an old Indian calling the men to a council. It was then announced at this council that these Indians be taken to the Agency where the troops will kill twenty heads of beef for them. Colonel Forsyth demanded over twenty guns from these Indians and Long Bull, one of the Indians, replied by being the first one to give up his gun. After the Indians had given up their weapons and arms, General [*sic*] Forsyth ordered a search through the Indian camp for any weapons that they may had [*sic*] left under cover. Big Foot, who was lying sick advised that this be done and that the order be obeyed. After they had gathered all weapons, the interpreter for the General [*sic*] announced that all the men be lined up and an equal number of soldiers be lined up, face to face, and the soldiers were to cock their guns, barrels being empty, pointing to the forehead of each Indian and pull the trigger in order to impress upon the Indians what could happen to them if the guns were loaded. When this was explained, Chief Big Foot told the Indians to be firm in mind and in courage, and to be patient and behave rightly as he was in fear of dying. Just at this moment, Captain Wallace came to me and whispered in my ear asking which one was my father and where he was. I pointed to my father. Captain Wallace told me that the commanding officer was half-shot, meaning thereby that the commanding officer was drunk, and that he (Captain Wallace) feared that something wrong might happen on account of the fact that the officer was half-shot and Captain Wallace told me to tell the women to have their ponies ready and try to save themselves if something wrong is started. I started towards my camp but was stopped by the soldiers. Captain Wallace then motioned to the soldiers to allow me to pass and I was then permitted to go to the camp.

When I reached the camp I saw soldiers amongst the women, uncovering their blankets and raising their dresses in search of weapons, and pushing the women about; all during these proceedings the soldiers were laughing. I started back towards the council and at this moment I heard somebody cry out "Look out, Look out" and I looked around and saw one Indian holding a gun in the air showing that he intended to lay that down when he got to the Agency but now he is going to lay it down like the rest of the Indians, and he started towards the pile with the gun. Instantly there were upon him two soldiers, who wore stripes, and they grabbed the gun and tried to snatch it from him but the Indian held on to the barrel of the gun. The gun went off in the air in a northerly direction. Immediately after this fire was turned on us from all directions, and I heard too, at the same time that a command to fire came from the soldiers from the southerly direction. After the firing had started, I ran and got ahold of two horses. As I was trying to get one of my sisters on one of the horses right close to me stood a soldier who told me to hurry up and get on the horses immediately. After this short conversation[,] beyond me but right close by me stood a white[-]haired soldier. This white[-]haired soldier cried out two times "remember Custer, remember Custer." Just about this time there was an old Indian woman running past him with some children following her and on her back was an Indian child. This white[-]haired soldier after saying "remember Custer" shot the old Indian woman down. On the second shot he shot one of the little children and then this other soldier, who stood nearby turned around and shot down the white[-]haired soldier who was shooting the Indian children. After I got up on the hill I looked back to the camp and saw the flag of truce still standing and flying.

At this point I met my brother, Dewey Beard, and we both went on and away from the firing. . . .

We two brothers, Dewey Beard and myself, have succeeded in building up a little fund by our own efforts so that we might be able to come here at our own expense to bring this matter before the authorities of the Government and the good white people looking to some relief and redress from the Government.

38. James McLaughlin's interrogations of Wounded Knee survivors, 1920

Indian Inspector James McLaughlin provided this report of his interrogation of Lakota survivors of Wounded Knee regarding their human and material losses and potential government compensation. McLaughlin to Commissioner of Indian Affairs Cato Sells, 12 Jan. 1921, Wounded Knee Compensation Papers, 476.24, Folder 14, Box 3564A, SDSHS. McLaughlin's notes for this report appear in the James McLaughlin Papers, Roll 17, SDSHS. McLaughlin had a long career with the Bureau of Indian Affairs and had served as Indian agent at Standing Rock, where he experienced a tempestuous relationship with Sitting Bull during the months preceding the medicine man's death two weeks before Wounded Knee. The following reports generally mention the various reservation administrative districts in which the persons interviewed resided.

Washington, D.C.,
January 12, 1921
Hon. Cato Sells,
Commissioner of Indian Affairs,
Washington, D.C.
My dear Mr. Commissioner:
As directed by instructions of May 5, 1920, relative to the conflict between certain Sioux Indians and U.S. troops at Wounded Knee Creek, Pine Ridge reservation, South Dakota, on December 29, 1890, I have the honor to report that in a recent tour of the Sioux reservations in North Dakota and South Dakota, I met nearly all of the Indian survivors of that affair now living, and interrogated them with reference thereto, having met them in the order herein listed.

The Indians involved in that affair, numbering about 420 persons, were under the leadership of Chief Big Foot of the Cheyenne River Agency, South Dakota, all of whom—except about 35 belonging to Standing Rock Agency—were of the Cherry Creek district, Cheyenne River reservation, of which Indian settlement the said Big Foot was the recognized leader, and the headquarters of which about 90 miles southwest of the Cheyenne River agency, with most of the Indians of that district being at that time among the least advanced in civilization of any of the Sioux bands, nearly all of whom having returned from Alberta, Canada, in 1881, where they had fled with Sitting Bull after the Battle of the Little Big Horn[,] June 25, 1876.

I was U.S. Indian Agent in charge of the Standing Rock reservation during the Messiah Craze of 1890-91 and [was] personally acquainted with all of the Indians of said reservation at that time, including the Ghost Dancing fanatics who fled from Standing Rock reservation on December 15, 1890, upon the death of their leader Sitting Bull, and joined Big Foot and his disaffected followers of the Cheyenne River Agency in their stampede from Cherry Creek to Pine Ridge reservation and were therefore of the Big Foot party in the disastrous affair at Wounded Knee, South Dakota, on December 29, 1890, and I still retain a distinct recollection of the dazed condition of the fanatical Ghost Dancing Indians involved in that affair.

The larger number of the Standing Rock contingent of the Big Foot party were killed in the Wounded Knee conflict and the survivors having subsequently returned to their former homes, it was to meet and interrogate them regarding the matter that I visited the Standing Rock Agency first when entering upon this investigation under my instructions, and on May 18, 1920[,] I met one of the said survivors of the Wounded Knee Affair, named Bear Gone, 60 years of age, who is now the wife of an Indian named High Cat and living with her husband about seven miles west of Standing Rock Agency, North Dakota. She is quite well informed and stated to me that at the time of the Wounded Knee affair she was the wife of an Indian of Standing Rock Agency named Charota (Ashes) and was with him in the Wounded Knee conflict with U.S. troops; that her said husband was killed outright in the melee and that she was wounded in the neck near base of the brain, the lacerated scar still showing very plainly. She also stated that they had with them at Wounded Knee 5 horses, [a] Winchester rifle, 8 antelope pelts, a woman's dress decorated with Elks teeth, 2 riding saddles, bedding[,] clothing and camping outfit, all of which property was lost to them there and none of it ever recovered. She further stated that a Standing Rock Indian of their party, named Hawk Bear, together with his son and a daughter were all three killed in the conflict, and that his wife was shot through the body from which wound she died some years later and that only one member of said Hawk Bear's family, named Hakektawin, escaped uninjured. She further stated that Swift Bird, Flying Hawk, Mrs. Fat Bear and Mrs. Fat Bear's mother who were of their party of stampeders were all four killed outright and that each of these persons had one or more horses and other property with them at the time, all of which was lost there and never recovered by their families, and on May 24, 1920, I met the following named Standing Rock survivors of that disaster at the Bullhead substation, viz:

John Spotted Bear, of Little Eagle district[,] Standing Rock Agency, aged 52 years, stated that he was in the Wounded Knee affair and escaped uninjured, but that his grandmother, named Scarlet Smoke, was killed and that his saddle horse was killed and saddle and briddle [*sic*] lost to him there.

James Red Fish, also of Little Eagle district, South Dakota, now 59 years of age, stated that he was 9 years old at the time and was in the Wounded Knee affair, in company with his grandfather, named *Singing Bull*, his grandmother named *Un-pan-ska-win*, his uncle named *Ha-shi-ta*, then 35 years of age, and his sister named *Scarlet Coat*, 7 years of age, all four of whom were killed outright in the melee, and he himself was wounded in the right thigh, but recovered from the wound. He also stated that he had 3 horses killed in action which with saddle and bridle were lost to him, and he further stated that his grandfather, *Singing Bull*, had 10 head of horses, 1 wagon, set [of] harness, Winchester rifle, tepee, bedding and cooking utensils with him at Wounded Knee all of which disappeared there and never recovered.

Hakiktawin, 47 years of age, now the wife of William Knocks Them Down of Bullhead district[,] stated that she was in the Wounded Knee conflict with U.S. troops, that she was then 18 years of age and was wounded in the right foot; that her father *Hawk Bear*, her sister Yusonpawin, 12 years old, her brother Zuyachigela, 6 years of age, and grandmother Oipagelutawin, were all four killed outright, and her mother *Cetan-Wanbliwin*, shot through the body, left side, from which she subsequently died, and she further stated that her father, Hawk Bear, had with him at Wounded Knee 9 horses, 1 tepee, Winchester rifle, family bedding[,] cooking utensils, 2 riding saddles, 3 pack saddles and several bridles all of which property was lost to the family there and never recovered.

Mrs[.] Bad Horse, 48 years of age of Little Eagle district, stated that during the Ghost Dancing Craze of 1890, she was the wife of Bear-Skin Vest and was with him in the Wounded Knee affair of December 29, 1890, where her said husband was killed and their child which she was carrying on her back was wounded and died from its effect. She further stated that they had with them at Wounded Knee, 2 horses, set harness, wagon, tepee, rifle, bedding and cooking utensils, all of which were lost to them and never recovered.

Crazy Bear, 59 years of age, of Bullhead district, formerly known as *Used-as-a-Shield*, stated that his brother Flying Hawk, was killed in the Wounded Knee affair, also his saddle horse was killed and saddle and bridle lost there and never recovered.

Mrs[.] Takes the Hat of Bullhead district, 45 years of age, daughter of Naki-hi-hi-la who died 5 years ago, at Standing Rock Agency, stated that her mother Naki-ki-hi-la was in the Wounded Knee fight but hid in a ravine and was uninjured, but lost 3 horses, harness and wagon, which were never recovered and she further stated that her brother, Wolf Necklace and his daughter named Scarlet Woman, were killed in the conflict.

Mrs. Holy Medicine of Little Eagle district, stated that she was not in the Wounded Knee affair, but that her uncle Little Owl, was wounded in that conflict and died of his wounds; that when he left Grand River with the stampeders he took with him 4 horses, set of harness and wagon which were lost to him there and never recovered.

Mrs[.] David Seventeen of Bullhead Station, stated that her brother-in-law, Patrick Seventeen of Bullhead Station, recently deceased, was in the Wounded Knee Affair, had his horse killed in the Melee and saddle and bridle lost to him.

Mrs. Walter Iron of Bullhead district, 43 years of age stated that her younger brother then 8 years of age was killed at Wounded Knee.

The foregoing list of survivors of the Wounded Knee affair reside on the Standing Rock reservation, and the following list of survivors residing on the Cheyenne River reservation, South Dakota, were met and interrogated by me with reference thereto between June 5th and June 12th, 1920, viz.:

John Black Hawk of Cherry Creek district, age 58 years, stated that he was not in the Wounded Knee melee, but that his father, mother, sister and a 4 year old daughter of his who was with his parents were all four killed there; that he was an Indian Policeman of Cheyenne [River] reservation at the time and did not accomp[a]ny his father's family in the stampede [toward Pine Ridge]. He further stated that his father lost 7 horses, set of harness, wagon, bedding, etc. in that affair, none of which property was ever recovered.

Mrs. John Black Hawk, also known as Marion Slowly, of Cherry Creek, 48 years of age, was not in the Wounded Knee affair, but her 2 brothers, Good Hawk and Eagle Wing were both killed in that conflict, and Good Hawk's wife was also killed there. Good Hawk had [a] team of horses, harness and wagon with him which were lost to the family there and never recovered.

John Shell Necklace, 60 years of age, Thunder Butte district, was not in the Wounded Knee affair, but his father, Industrious Bear, his mother, Smoke Woman, and two brothers were killed there and a sister, now Mrs. Wasica Mato of White Clay district, Pine Ridge reservation, was wounded but recovered from her wounds. He stated that his father had [a] team of horses with him at Wounded Knee, also wagon, tepee, bedding, etc.[,] all of which was lost there and never recovered, and further stated that his wife was not in the Wounded Knee affair, but that her father and step-mother were and both of them were killed outright.

Hard to Kill, also known as Brown Eagle, age 54 years, of Cherry Creek, South Dakota, stated that he was unmarried at the time of the Wounded Knee affair; that he escaped injury, but that his mother was killed, his sister, Chief Woman, received three gunshot wounds and died from her wounds and that his brother Edmond Owl King was wounded but recovered and is now residing in Cherry Creek district. He further stated that the family had 6 mares, 2 yearlings and 2 colts with them all of which were killed, which together with set of harness, wagon, tepee and clothing were all lost to them and none of the property ever recovered.

Frank Corn, age 43 years, of Thunder Butte district, stated that he had 3 horses killed in the Wounded Knee affair, also lost saddle and bridle.

Philip Black Moon, of Cherry Creek, 40 years of age, was with his mother, Mrs. Black Moon, in the Wounded Knee affair, his mother still living near [the] town of Faith, South Dakota, his older brother, White Dog, was killed in the conflict, sister, Brown Ear, was wounded and died of her wounds, and his brother High Back, now at Poplar, Montana, was wounded in the ankle and both arms broken, but recovered from his wounds. They had 6 head of horses with them[,] all of which were killed or otherwise lost to them there.

Afraid of Enemy of Cherry Creek, aged 66 years, stated that he received 6 slight wounds and one serious gunshot wound from a rifle bullet which entered his breast at the right nipple, and passed out under the right shoulder, from which he bled profusely from his mouth and nose as well as from the wound. He showed me the scars of his wounds[.] He also stated that his wife was wounded in the left thigh from which wound she recovered and died on White Clay Creek [on the] Pine Ridge reservation about 12 years ago; that his son named Scares the Hawk, 19 years of age, was also wounded but lived about 5 years after receiving that wound. He further stated that he had 10 horses and 2 colts with him all of which were either killed or appropriated by others as he never saw any of them afterwards; that he also had set of harness, farm wagon, 2 saddles, tepee, full camping outfit and 2 rifles which he turned over to the military, all of which property was lost to him and never recovered. He remained at Pine Ridge for about 10 years after the Wounded Knee affair and then returned to Cherry Creek where he received an allotment of land and now reside[s].

Brings Plenty of Cherry Creek, aged 56 years, now the wife of Charles Industrious, stated that she was in the Wounded Knee party, being there with her aunt, named Runs after Her, who was accompanied by her married daughter, named *Never Misses It*, and husband, named Owankauka, also known as *White Man*. This woman, Brings Plenty, stated to me that she was wounded in the right hip, that her said aunt received 2 wounds and the daughter, Never Misses It, was wounded in the left elbow, and all three recovered from their wounds, but that Owankauka was killed in the conflict; that she lost 2 horses and [one?] saddle there, also 2 haversacks together with her clothing and bedding.

Brown Sinew, also known as Axe, of Cherry Creek, aged 53 years, states that he was in the Wounded Knee affair, was unmarried and accompanied his sister and her husband, named Black Hair, that his sister was killed and her husband wounded but recovered therefrom; that he, Brown Sinew, was wounded in [the] left hand, the unsightly scar showing that his wound was serious. He further stated that he delivered his rifle to the military there and lost his horse and saddle which he never recovered.

Charles Blue Arm, of Cherry Creek, aged 46 years, now a citizen Indian, stated that he was in the Wounded Knee affair, was unmarried at the time and there with his two older brothers and their families, that both of his brothers and the wife of his eldest brother were killed in the conflict; that his eldest brother had 4 horses, set of harness and wagon with him and that his second brother had 3 horses, set of harness and wagon, also that he (Charles Blue Arm) had 2 horses and saddle, all of which horses and other property was lost to them there and none of it ever recovered. He further stated that the wife of his second b[r]other was uninjured, her name is *Brings Her* and now resides in White Clay Creek district of Pine Ridge reservation.

Swift Dog of Cherry Creek, aged 57 years, stated that he was in the Wounded Knee affair and was wounded in the right side and left elbow; that he was unmarried at that time and had accompanied his two older brothers, named *Runs After* and *Strong Fox* respectively; that both of his brothers were killed and the wife and son of his brother Strong Fox were also killed; that Strong Fox had team, harness, wagon, tepee, bedding, etc. with him and his brother Runs After had horse and saddle and that he, Swift Dog, had had horse and saddle, all of which property was lost there and never recovered. He further stated that his brother Strong Fox was the only member of their family who possessed a rifle and that he had delivered it to the Military before the fight occurred.

Edward Owlking [also Owl King], also known as Fast Boat, of Cherry Creek, 39 years of age, stated that he was in the Wounded Knee affair and was wounded in right hip; that his mother, two brothers, and one sister were killed in the conflict and another sister wounded who died from the effects of her wound one year later at Cherry Creek. He further stated that his father, Owl King, was not in the Wounded Knee affair; that the family did not possess any firearms, but had 3 horses killed in the melee [and] also lost 3 saddles, tepee, bedding, etc.[,] none of which was ever recovered.

Her Black Horses, also known as Her Gall, of Cherry Creek, 78 years of age, stated that her husband, Red Eagle, was killed in [the] Wounded Knee conflict and that she had 2 horses killed, also lost her tepee, bedding and clothing there.

James High Hawk, of Cherry Creek, 35 years of age, stated that he was in the Wounded Knee affair with his parents; that his father, mother and grandmother were killed in the conflict and he [was] wounded in the right thigh and right ankle, and his younger brother was wounded[,] from which he died 2 years later. He also stated that his father had with him there 4 horses, set harness, wagon, tepee, bedding and cooking utensils[,] all of which property was lost there and none of it ever recovered, and he further stated that his father had delivered his Winchester rifle to the military before the fighting commenced.

Alex High Hawk of Cherry Creek, 42 years of age, is an older brother of James High Hawk, and stated that he was wounded in the left ankle; that his father, mother and grandmother were killed in the Wounded Knee affair, as stated by his brother James High Hawk [immediately above]. . . . I also met *Jonah High Hawk* of Cherry Creek, 33 years of age, brother of the two preceding survivors of the Wounded Knee affair, who was only 4 years of age at that time and had escaped injury and had very little recollection of what transpired there.

Her Good Shawl, of Cherry Creek, 60 years of age, stated that she was in the Wounded Knee affair; that her husband, Horses Ghost, and her son named White Horse, were both killed in that conflict; that they had 4 horses with them there, also 4 Indian saddles, tepee, bedding, bucksking [*sic*] clothing and cooking utensils, all of which property was lost there and none of it ever recovered by her.

White Owl Woman, of Cherry Creek, aged 58 years, stated that she was not in the Wounded Knee affair, but that her mother, Walks Red, and brother[,] named Chief Boy, were both killed in that conflict and their horses and other property lost and never recovered by any of her family.

Leon Kills the First, of Cherry Creek, aged 33 years, was absent from home, working on the C. & N.W.R.R. [Chicago & North Western Rail Road] near the town of Washte, South Dakota, and his father-in-law, Daniel Blue Hair, of Cherry Creek, South Dakota, 45 years of Age, stated that Leon Kills the First was only about 4 years of age at the time of the Wounded Knee affair and was there with his father, named Kills First[,] and mother, named Holy Woman; that his father was killed outright and his mother received 4 wounds but lived until about 3 years ago when she died near Eagle Butte; that Killed [*sic*] First had with him at Wounded Knee 2 horses, set harness, wagon, tepee and full camping outfit, all of which property was lost to the family and never recovered by them.

Iron Horse Woman, now known as Mrs. Charles Knife of Thunder Butte district, aged 48 years, stated that she was then the wife of an Indian named Chase near the Lodge, who was killed in the Wounded Knee affair; that she and her husband each owned a horse and saddle which with 2 haversacks containing their best clothes were all lost to them there and none of their property thus lost was ever recovered by her.

Daniel Blue Hair of Cherry Creek, aged 45 years, stated that he was at Wounded Knee with his father, mother, sister, a married brother with wife and child, all of whom were killed in that conflict except himself; that he was wounded in the left thigh; he stated that his father's name was "His Wounded Hand," and that the family had 26 horses with them when they reached Wounded Knee creek, 24 of which horses were killed in the fight and the other 2 found by him before returning to Cherry Creek about 3 months later; that the family had [a] set of harness, wagon tepee, bedding and cooking utensils, all of which were lost there and nothing ever recovered except the 2 horses subsequently found. This survivor, Daniel Blue Hair[,] is a patentee Indian and receives a pension of $6.00 per month from having served in the U.S. Army at Fort Meade, South Dakota, in 1891–1892.

Her Good Voiced Horse, of Thunder Butte district, 60 years of age, now the wife of an Indian named . . . *Brave*, 68 years of age. She stated that she was in the Wounded Knee affair, that she was then the wife of an Indian named Wicaka-badeca, who was killed there, also 2 brothers named *Tokola Washaka* and his wife, named Yellow Leaf Woman and their little son were killed, also her unmarried brother named Runs After was killed; that her sister, named Snawin[,] and her little daughter were also killed, and further stated that the family had 2 horses, set harness, wagon, tepee and fully camping outfit, all of which were lost and never recovered.

As stated on first page of this report[,] nearly all of the Indians involved in the Wounded Knee conflict belonged to the Cherry Creek district of Cheyenne River Agency, South Dakota, the survivors above listed having subsequently returned to their former homes, but many of the Big Foot party elected to remain on the Pine Ridge reservation where they were subsequently allotted and now reside, of whom the following named survivors of that affair were met and interrogated by me in my tour of the Pine Ridge reservation between July 12 and July 31, 1920, viz.:

I met *James Pipe on Head* of White Clay district, Pine Ridge reservation, at Oglala, South Dakota, July 12, 1920, who stated that he was 40 years of age and a grandson of Big Foot, the leader of the Messiah[-]Crazed Indians involved in the conflict with U.S. troops at Wounded Knee Creek, South Dakota, December 29, 1890; that he was then about 10 years of age and was of the Big Foot party in that disastrous affair, but escaped uninjured; he further stated that his grandfather Big Foot and his wife were both killed in the fight; that they had quite a number of horses with them at Wounded Knee, also some cattle, together with wagon, buggy, harness, tepee, etc.[,] all of which property was lost there and never recovered by any of their relatives. This James Pipe on Head has wife and 3 children, is nice appearing and progressive.

John Little Finger, of White Clay district, aged 46 years, stated that Chief Big Foot was his grandfather and that he was of the party of Cheyenne River Indians who fled from Cherry Creek district under the leadership of his grandfather Big Foot and became involved in the Wounded Knee disaster, of December 29, 1890; that he had accompanied two of his uncles on the trip whose names were Long Bull and Short Haired Bear, respectively; that he himself was wounded in [the] right thigh, also in [the] right foot; that his uncle Short Haired Bear and 3 of his children were killed in the conflict and his wife died about one year later from shock, fright and exposure at Wounded Knee, and that his uncle Long Bull was also killed outright in the melee. He further stated that said Short Haired Bear had 13 horses with him and Long Bull 4 horses, all of which were killed or lost to them, and that each of his said uncles had a set of harness, wagon, tepee, and full camping outfit with them at Wounded Knee all of which property was lost there and never recovered by any of their relatives.

Mrs. Pipe on Head of White Clay district, a widow, 69 years of age, stated that her mother was Big Foot[']s sister and that she was reared in Big Foot[']s family; that she was not in the Wounded Knee conflict but was following the Big Foot party and did not reach Wounded Knee Creek until after the disaster had occurred. She stated that Big Foot was 65 years of age when he was killed at Wounded Knee and that his wife[,] Sinte-Chi-ola, who was also killed, was then 63 years of age. This woman further stated that Big Foot had about 25 head of horses with him at Wounded Knee, also about 30 head of cattle, together with harness, wagons, tepee, and full camping outfit, and that 9 head of her horses were in Big Foot[']s herd, all of which horses, cattle and other property disappeared there and [were] never recovered by any members of the family.

Jackson No Crow, of White Clay district, 38 years of age, stated that he was at Wounded Knee with his father, He Crow, and his mother, Louisa Weasel Bear; that his father was killed in the conflict and mother wounded in right thigh, but survived her wound and is now living with him in White Clay district. He further stated that his said parents had with them at Wounded Knee 6 horses, 2 riding saddles, tepee, 6 blankets, 4 quilts and 2 deer skins, all of which property was lost to them there and none of it recovered by the family.

Max Bald Eagle, aged 46 years, of White Clay district, stated that he is a Pine Ridge Indian and was not in the Wounded Knee Affair with U.S. troops; that he had at that time 24 head of cattle ranging on Corn Creek, Pine Ridge reservation, which were appropriated and killed by the Big Foot Stampeders for food on their route to Wounded Knee; that the reason he did not report this loss at the time it occurred was owing to matters being in great turmoil on the reservation at the time and that by soon after this occurrance he enlisted in a company of U.S. cavalry then stationed at Fort Meade, South Dakota, and therefore neglected to report the matter to Special Indian Agent James A. Cooper who paid off claimants for losses sustained of this character.

Little Bull No. 2, of White Clay district, 76 years of age, stated that he was in the Wounded Knee affair, and was wounded in the left leg which broke the bone and has left an ugly scar between the knee and ankle. He further stated that his present wife, name Ora Little Bull, was at that time the wife of an Indian, Wolf Ear[,] who was killed in the conflict; that two of her sons and one daughter were also killed outright and she shot through the left thigh, but recovered from the wound and is now his wife and living with him in White Clay district; that she had 2 horses killed and lost set of harness, wagon, tepee and camp equipage, all of which was lost to her and never recovered.

Lucy Morrisette, aged 51 years, wife of Oliver Morrisette of Wakpamini district, stated that she was not in the Wounded Knee affair, but that her father named High Hawk, who was of the Big Foot party from Cherry Creek district, was killed there; that her father had 3 wives, 2 or whom were also killed there, together with their children. She further stated that her mother was one of High Hawk[']s 3 wives, who had been residing on the Pine Ridge reservation that time and for some time previous[,] and she is living with her mother, therefore she and her mother were not with her father High Hawk at Wounded Knee where he and his two other wives were killed. She further stated that her father had team, harness, wagon, tepee and camping outfit with him at Wounded Knee, all of which was lost there and none of it recovered by any of the family.

Viola Running Hawk, 34 years of age, White Clay district, a divorce[é] with one child, stated that her father's brother, named Shoots Straight, and one of his children were killed in the Wounded Knee affair; that his wife and one child were wounded but recovered from their wounds and both of them have since died. She also stated that her said uncle had some horses [but] don't know the number, and other property with him at Wounded Knee, that his horses were killed there and all other property lost and never recovered, except one farm wagon.

Her War Bonnet, also known as *Julia Spider Backbone*, 41 years of age, wife of Luke Spider Backbone of White Clay district, stated that she was in the Wounded Knee affair with her father, mother and two brothers; that her father and mother were uninjured but her 2 brothers were killed; that her father and mother died recently; that her father's name was Hair Pipe who died at Cherry Creek in 1917. She further stated that her father had with him at Wounded Knee 5 horses, set harness, wagon, tepee and camping outfit, all of which property was lost to them there and none of it ever recovered.

Dora High White Man, age 39 years, wife of Grant High White Man of White Clay district, stated that she was in the Wounded Knee affair with her grandmother, name Snow Over Her, who died at White Clay in 1904; that she and her grandmother were uninjured there, but that the team, harness and wagon belonging to her grand-mother in which they were traveling, and driven by an uncle named Black White Man, was lost to them there and never recovered, and that her said uncle was seriously wounded and subsequently died from effect of his wound.

Mary Frog, widow, 87 years of age, living in White Clay district with her son, Alfred Frog, 45 years of age, stated that she was at Wounded Knee with her family; that her husband, now deceased, was wounded in the melee and that her son Alfred Frog[,] with whom she now lives, was wounded in both legs but recovered from his wounds; that they had with them 6 horses, set of harness, farm wagon, tepee and full camping outfit, all of which property was lost to them there and no portion of it ever recovered.

Susie Bear Horse, aged 37 years, wife of Philip Little Killer of White Clay district, stated that she was not in the Wounded Knee affair, but that her grandmother and uncle, named Shooting with Hawk Feather[,] were both killed there, and that they had 3 horses, set of harness and wagon with them which were lost to the family and none of the property ever recovered.

Black Hair, aged 64 years, of White Clay district, stated that he was in the Wounded Knee affair and received 7 wounds in the conflict (he showed me the scars in both legs, left arm and back of his neck); that the wife he had at that time was killed outright, also his 5 year old son was killed and 7 year old son wounded, from the effects of which he died 2 years later; that he had with him at Wounded Knee 4 horses, set of harness, wagon, tepee and campint [camping] outfit, all of which was lost to him there and none of the property ever recovered.

Red Hair, 85 years of age, of White Clay district, stated that he was not in the Wounded Knee affair, but that his widowed cousin named Bad Ear Woman,. . . was wounded in that conflict and her son killed outright and that she died from the effects of her wound some years later. He further stated that he is the nearest living relative of the woman, and does not know what property she had with her there, but knows that while she was traveling in company with the Big Foot stampeders that she had her own means of conveyance, all of which was lost to her there.

Leon White Bird, aged 50 years, of White Clay district, stated that he was at Wounded Knee during the conflict of Dec. 29, 1890, as a scout with the U.S. troops; that a woman, named Stands With, daughter of Wahpataukaska of Standing Rock reservation, was with the Big Foot party [and] was wounded and her saddle horse killed; that she had formerly been his wife and was the mother of his son, James White Bird, but had been living with a relative named . . .

Hakiktawin of Standing Rock Agency for some time previous to this affair and died in 1907.

Simon Helper, age 45 years, of White Clay district, stated that he was not in the Wounded Knee affair, but that a woman named Thunder Hawk Woman, then unmarried, and [who] subsequently became his wife, was in the Wounded Knee conflict, accompanied by her grandfather and an uncle named Akipa (Trouble)[,] both of whom were killed[,] but that she escaped uninjured and is now the wife of this Simon Helper and living with him on White River, White Clay district. He further stated that her grandfather and uncle, had each a team of horses, set of harness, wagon, etc.[,] including tepees, bedding and cooking utensils all of which was lost there and none of the property ever recovered by her or any other member of those families; that they had also fire arms and knives which were lost to them there.

Lydia Looking Elk, age 61 years, of White Clay district, stated that she was with her husband, Looking Elk, in the Wounded Knee affair and that her husband received 2 wounds in that conflict, one in the right leg and the other in the body, the bullet of the latter wound remaining in his body until his death in 1918. She further stated that they had 4 horses with them there, one of which was killed outright and the other 3 lost to them; that they were traveling with travois and lost 2 riding saddles, 2 Indian pack saddles, tepee, 7 blankets[,] one of which was a Navajo [blanket], 1 Winchester rifle and 1 shot gun, all of which property was lost to them and never recovered.

Dog Chief, age 59 years, of Wounded Knee district, stated that he and his family were with Big Foot[']s following in the Wounded Knee affair, in which he received 3 flesh wounds, one in right cheek, one in left shoulder and one in left thigh[—]he showed me the scars of his wounds. He stated that he had 2 horses killed there, also lost 2 saddles, tepee and camping outfit, none of which were ever recovered by the family; that his wife and one child with them were uninjured in the affair, and that his said wife died about 18 years ago. He further stated that he was known at Cherry Creek, Cheyenne River reservation, by the name of Wicasta Tamaheca.

Thomas Blindman, age 34 years, of Wounded Knee district, stated that he was a small boy at the time of the Wounded Knee affair, and was with his parents in that conflict; that his father, named Spotted

Thunder[,] was killed outright there, and his mother, named Blue Whirlwind[,] was wounded, shot through the body on right side but recovered from the wound, and died on White Clay Creek in 1918, at the home of her son Charles Blindman with whom she made her home. He stated further he was too young at the time to remember particulars as to what property his parents had with them and lost there, but that his Brother Charles of White Clay who was several years his senior would know the facts, but that he has always understood that his parents lost all property they had with them there.

Alice Kills Right, age 50 years, wife of Straight Forehead, of Wounded Knee district, stated that she was not in the Wounded Knee affair, but that her father named Scares the Bear, and mother named Yellow Bird Woman, with two of their grand children whom they had reared were all four killed in that conflict. She further stated that her parents had with them at Wounded Knee 5 horses, 2 riding saddles, and 2 Indian saddles for conveying their travois, tepee, and camping outfit, all of which property was lost there and none of it ever recovered by any members of the family.

Frank Iron Hawk, age 23 years, of Wounded Knee district, who is living with his wife and 1 child on Grass Creek, Washington County, South Dakota, stated that his mother, named Slohamani, was wounded in that conflict, shot in her left arm which shattered the bone above her elbow; that his mother lost 2 horses and other property she had with her there. He further stated that his mother died near Manderson issue station about 17 years ago, and that he and his brother Louis Iron Hawk, now 20 years of age, are the legal heirs of their deceased mother.

Yellow Woman, age 70 years, now the wife of Good Crow, of Wounded Knee district, stated that at the time of the Wounded Knee affair she was the wife of an Indian named Ijihazee; that they belonged to the Big Foot party who had fled from Cherry Creek, and were therefore with him in the Wounded Knee disaster; that her said husband and her son, aged 30 years [and] named Bear Lays Down, was killed in the conflict; that she escaped uninjured, but that her daughter-in-law, Mrs. Bear Lays Down[,] was wounded and died from the effects of her wounds. She further stated that the family had with them at Wounded Knee 7 horses, set harness, wagon, tepee, bedding and cooking utensils, all of which property was lost to them and none of it ever recovered.

Helen Long Bull, age 47 years, now the wife of Baptist Ladeaux of Wounded Knee district, stated that she was in the Wounded Knee affair with her father and mother; that she and her father, named Long Bull, now of White Clay district, escaped injury, but that her mother and grandmother, also a younger sister were all three killed outright; that they had with them at Wounded Knee 6 horses and saddles; that they were traveling on horseback and carried no tepee poles with them, but had tepee cover which they used for shelter when camping;, that they also had bedding and cooking utensils, all of which property was lost to them and none of it ever recovered.

Richard Afraid of Hawk, age 47 years, of Wounded Knee district, stated that he belonged to the Pine Ridge Agency and had been on a visit to Cheyenne River Agency and when returning home fell in with the Big Foot Stampeders, and was with them when they reached Wounded Knee Creek and thus became involved in that unfortunate affair; that he escaped injury in the conflict but his horse was killed and riding saddle lost to him and never recovered; that he was carrying a [.]44 Winchester rifle which he turned over to the U.S. troops which was also thus lost to him.

Little Cloud, age 57 years, of Porcupine district, stated that he and his family were with the Big Foot Stampeders in Wounded Knee affair, and that his father, mother and three of his brothers (8-10 and 12 years of age, respectively) were killed in that conflict; that his father's name was Spotted Elk, which was also Chief Big Foot's proper name. This witness stated that he and his wife escaped injury, but that he lost 3 horses, set of harness, farm wagon, bedding and cooking utensils, and that his father had 4 horses killed and lost set [of] harness, wagon, tepee, bedding and cooking utensils and had also delivered [.]44 Winchester rifle to the U.S. troops, none of which property was ever recovered by any of the family. [This man was Big Foot's son. His itemization apparently includes Big Foot's property lost at Wounded Knee.]

Henry Kills White Man, age 34 years of Porcupine district, stated that he was about 5 years of age at the time of the Wounded Knee affair and was with his father, named Kills White Man, accompanied by his mother, one sister and a 10 year old brother; that they belonged to the Big Foot following who fled from Cherry Creek and that his father received two wounds in the breast in that conflict with U.S. troops, and although he lived several years afterwards he never fully recovered from said wounds. He further stated that he and his older brother were uninjured but that his mother and sister were killed in the melee; that his father had 3 horses killed there, also lost set of harness, farm wagon, tepee, bedding and camping outfit, and that his father had delivered his [.]44 Winchester rifle to the troops before the conflict occurred, all of which property was lost and none of it ever recovered by any of the family.

Mrs. Young Bear, formerly known as Mrs. Beings White Horses, age 50 years, of Porcupine district, stated that she is a niece of Chief Big Foot[,] the leader of the Cherry Creek Ghost Dance Stampeders, that she was living with the Big Foot family at the time and was with them in the Wounded Knee affair; that her 3 year old daughter was killed, but that she was uninjured; that her uncle Big Foot who was ill at the time was killed outright during the conflict and his wife was wounded and died of her wounds at Pine Ridge Agency soon afterwards. She further stated that her uncle Big Foot had 14 horses with him at Wounded Knee, also [a] spring wagon and harness, tepee, bedding and cooking utensils, all of which property[,] including a Winchester rifle which he had delivered to the troops[,] was entirely lost to the family; that she and Mrs. Pipe on the Head, of White Clay district, are nieces of Big Foot and his nearest living relatives. [This itemization apparently includes more of Big Foot's property present (and lost) at Wounded Knee.]

Mary Runs on the Edge, age 50 years, of Porcupine district, stated that she was not in the Wounded Knee affair, but that her father named Kills First, step[-]mother named Wakan, a brother, named Waniyatu Opi, and two of her sisters were in that conflict; that all of them were killed except her step-mother who was wounded, but recovered from her wounds and returned to Cherry Creek district where she died about 2 years ago. She further stated that the family had with them at Wounded Knee 7 horses, set of harness, wagon, tepee and full camping outfit, all of which was lost there, and was informed by her step-mother that her father had delivered his Winchester rifle and her brother a Colts revolver to the U.S. troops before the conflict occurred, and further stated that she is the only member of her father's family now living.

Young Bear, age 65 years, of Porcupine district, stated that he was not in the Wounded Knee affair, but that his sister, named Roan Horse

Woman, and her husband, named Hale [Hail?] Eagle, and their two children were in that affair and all four of them killed in the melee. He further stated that his sister and her husband had with them at Wounded Knee 5 horses, set of harness, wagon, tepee and full camping outfit all of which property was lost to the family and none of it ever recovered by any of their relatives; that Harry Wounded Knee of Wounded Knee district is a grand son of said Roan Horse Woman and her husband Male Eagle.

George Randall, age 43 years, of Medicine Root district, stated that he was in the Wounded Knee affair, with his father and mother; that his father whose name was Good Hawk, was killed outright there, but that he and his mother escaped injury, and declined to make further statement as to property lost or anything connected with the affair.

Pain in the Hip, age 60 years, of Medicine Root district, stated that he was in the Wounded Knee affair, as one of the Big Foot party, talked a lot of nonsense, but would not give me any information as to what property, if any, he lost there, and I was subsequently informed by several Indians present, including Dewey Beard, that this man Pain in the Hip was not in the Wounded Knee affair, as frequently claimed by him in talking with persons who did not know him, upon which occasions he was usually very boastful of his participation in the conflict and the great lost [*sic*] of property sustained by him there, which bombastic talks, as stated to me by the Indians present who know him, as [*sic*–are?] nonsensical and without foundation.

Dewey Beard, age 56 years, of Medicine Root district, stated that he was in the Wounded Knee affair; that he and his family were of the Cherry Creek Stampeders who accompanied Chief Big Foot the leader of their party. This man, Dewey Beard, bears a good reputation and impressed me very favorably, and being unable to speak English intelligently, he desired to await the presence of his brother Joseph Horned Cloud, who has taken an active interest in this Wounded Knee matter and who had heretofore submitted written statements thereon, and upon Joseph Horn Cloud's arrival, Dewey Beard submitted a paper to me dated October 21, 1913, signed by General Nelson A. Miles, U.S.A.[,] retired, in which it was stated that said Dewey Beard had received two serious wounds in the Wounded Knee conflict, and that his father, mother, two brothers and one sister, together with his wife and one child were killed in that affair, and that all the property the family had with them at Wounded Knee was lost to them there except 8 horses which he and his brother Joseph subsequently recovered.

Joseph Horn Cloud, age 47 years, of Medicine Root district, stated that he was in the Wounded Knee affair with his father and mother, also his brothers Sherman and William and cousin (by Indian custom sister) named Pretty Enemy, were killed outright, and his brothers Dewey and Daniel both seriously wounded and his brother Dewey's wife and son named Tom, 10 days of age at the time[,] were killed; that he (Joseph Horn Cloud) escaped uninjured; that they were a large family and had a lot of property with them at Wounded Knee all of which was lost to them except 8 horses which he and his brother Dewey subsequently recovered.

At my request Joseph Horn Cloud, on July 23, 1920, furnished me a list of the property which as claimed by him was entirely lost to their family at Wounded Knee, which list I attach hereto.

Before leaving the Sioux country the early part of last November, I learned that the above referred[-]to Joseph Horn Cloud, died at his home in Medicine Root district, Pine Ridge Reservation, South Dakota, about the middle of September, 1920.

(SEE ATTACHED LIST OF JOSEPH HORN CLOUD)
COPY
Pine Ridge Indian Reservation, S. Dak.
December 29, 1890.

July 23, 1890.
Dear Major McLaughlin,
Washington, D.C.
I had put it down here what we lost at Wounded Knee massacre: 1 mare; 1 yearling; 1 2-years old mare; 2 gelding; 2 work horse[s]. Total horses 7 head horses.

1 wagon, set of harness, 4 saddles, 1 tepee, 9 quilts, 6 pillows, 1 blue cloth blanket, 2 heavy beaver shawls, 3 overcoats, 1 kettle, 1 water pail, 1 coffee pot, 24 dishes and cups.

We are a large family, 2 guns, 1 shot gun, 4 briddles, 2 good lariot ropes, 1 wagon cover, 2 beaded bags, 2 raw haversacks, to keep dried meat in it, 1 ax. This is all nothing from home Cheyenne River.

I do this according to your advise.

That is all (ate), Your friends,

Joe Horn Cloud,

Per Daniel White Lance or Horn Cloud.

Some valuable government papers, some from Generals Harney and Sherman, papers all gone too. Belong to my father he used to served the Government in early days under [Brevet Brigadier] Gen. S. W. [W. S.] Harney and son born also. We are innocent of this Big Foot Camps.

Kyle, S.D. July 23, 1920.

Miss Pretty Enemy our sister or first cousin during the Wounded Knee massacre, South Dakota.

2 Big mares, 1 yearling, 2 2-years old, some mare, 1 Buckskin gelding, beddings whole outfit, 1 little tepee, 2 beaded bags, 1 beaded dresses [*sic*], 1 heavy bearer shawl, that is all she is got valuable property with her [*sic*]. We know the things with her because she stay with us. That is all (ate)

Joe Horn Cloud

Daniel White Lance or Horn Cloud

Daniel Horn Cloud, also known as Daniel White Lance, age 52 years, of Medicine Root district and one of the prominent Horn Cloud family of that district, stated that he was in the Wounded Knee affair with his father, mother, brothers and sister (cousin [Pretty Enemy]); that he received three wounds in that conflict, one of which was in the right leg above the knee, another in the right ankle and another in the head, the bullet passing through his scalp; that he has never fully recovered from the wound in his ankle which still suppurates occasionally and from which he is still a sufferer, and walks with a decided limp. He further stated that his brother Joseph Horn Cloud was going to furnish me with a list of the property lost by their family which he subsequently did and which is attached to Joseph Horn Cloud's oral statement, immediately preceding this entry.

Elmore Red Eyes, age 43 years, of Medicine Root district stated that his grandmother (his father's mother) named Red Jumper was killed in that conflict; that his said grandmother belonged on Pine Ridge reservation and was on a visit to relatives at Cherry Creek, Cheyenne River Agency, and was returning home with the Big Foot Stampeders and was killed in the Wounded Knee disaster. He further stated that when she left Pine Ridge on her visit to Cherry Creek she took 8 horses with her, which she is supposed to have had with her upon her return, but that whatever property she may have had with her at Wounded Knee was entirely lost to her family.

George Little Dog, age 56 years, of Medicine Root district, stated that he was not in the Wounded Knee affair, but that an adopted sister of his, named Plenty Horses, and her husband named Iron Eyes, together with their 6 children were in that conflict; that the father, mother and 5 of their children were killed there and the 6th child, named Guy Buffalo, who with James Buffalo, both now residing at Cherry Creek[,] are the only direct heirs now living of said Iron Eyes and his wife Plenty Horses; that as to what property this family had with them at Wounded Knee he was unable to state but that Dewey Beard would doubtless know as he was of the Big Foot followers and knew this family well, and upon meeting Dewey Beard on July 22nd 1920, I interrogated him with reference thereto, whereupon he stated that this family were very well provided with camping outfit including tepee and bedding, that said Iron Eyes also possessed a Winchester rifle which he probably delivered to the troops.

Samuel Two Tails [Few Tails], an old time scout of Medicine Root district, stated that his father, named Two Tails [Few Tails] who was well known on the Pine Ridge Reservation was killed by cow boys in the fall of 1890 when returning home from a hunt on a pass from the Indian agent; that he having been absent some time did not know of the unsettled condition of matters then existing on the reservation and was shot down by cow boys without any provocation.

George Blue Leg, age 37 years, of Eagle Butte district, stated that he was with his father and mother of the Big Foot party in the Wounded Knee affair; that his father, named Takes the Bow, was killed there, but that he and his mother escaped uninjured; that he was too young at the time to know what property his parents had with them at Wounded Knee but that his sister, Mrs. Nancy Little White Man of Medicine Root district, who is older than he, would probably know.

Spotted Eagle, age 53 years, of Eagle Butte district, stated that he was not in the Wounded Knee affair, but that his father and mother were of the Big Foot Stampeders from Cherry Creek and both of them were killed in that conflict; that they were traveling with travois conveyance and had 2 horses with them, also bedding and clothing and 45 calibre rifle which his father turned over to the troops, all of which property was lost to the family.

Mary Mousseaux, 64 years of age, wife of Alex Mousseaux, of Porcupine district, she was also formerly known as *Medicine Woman*. She stated that her husband at the time of the Wounded Knee affair, was named *White Man* who was killed at Wounded Knee and that she was wounded in the right arm in that conflict, also a son 5 years old and another son 1 year old, [were] both killed there; that they belonged to the Big Foot band of Cherry Creek and fled therefrom with the Big Foot following; that they had 6 horses with them, 5 of which were killed in the conflict and that they lost set of harness, wagon, tepee, bedding cooking utensils, 1 buffalo robe, 1 Navajo blanket and that her husband had turned over to the troops his Winchester rifle before the conflict occurred. She further stated that she had 3 full grown brothers killed there, whose names were Shaving Bear, Long Bull and He Crow, whose property was all lost there; that Shaving Bear's 4 children were also killed there, that his wife Tiwashtewin yet living; that 2 children of Long Bull was killed in the fight, also 1 child of He Crow was killed, his wife yet living].

Peter Stands, age 50 years, of White Clay district, stated that he was in the Wounded Knee affair as one of Big Foot's party from Cherry Creek district; that he was wounded in the left arm above the elbow, also in the left hand; that he was unmarried at the time and was at Wounded Knee with his father, mother and older brother; that his father, whose name was *Pte-he* was killed outright and his brother named Joseph Black Hair, who is still living, was wounded above and below the knee in the left leg. He further stated that his father's family were traveling by travois conveyance and had only 3 horses with them at Wounded Knee; that their 3 horses were killed, 2 Winchester rifles turned over to the troops, and the following property lost to them there, viz.: 5 deer skins, a buckskin coat, pants and leggings, 2 quilts, 2 blankets, 1 riding saddle which cost $30.00 and 2 Indian saddles used in hauling their travois, none of which property was ever recovered by the family.

Black Elk No. 2, age 56 years, of Wounded Knee district stated that he was not in the Wounded Knee affair but took care of one of the Big Foot party of survivors named Bad Woman for 10 years after the Wounded Knee affair, in which conflict she had received nine wounds and whose son about 27 years of age at the time was killed in that conflict; that this old woman lived about 10 years after being thus wounded and died about 20 years ago, and that he did not know what property, if any, she and her son had with them at Wounded Knee.

Alice Soldier Hawk, age 44 years, of White Clay district, stated that she was not in the Wounded Knee affair; that her father named Flying Horse, was on [*sic*—an] Oglala Sioux belonging to and residing on the Pine Ridge reservation at the time of the Wounded Knee conflict and hearing the report of the fire arms went out on horseback to ascertain what the gun shot reports meant and before reaching Wounded Knee Creek he met a detachment of cavalry who fired upon him killing him and his horse and his rifle was taken by the troops of the detachment, and that this Alice Soldier Hawk and her brothers Joseph Fast Horse of White Clay district, and Howard Fast Horse of Pass Creek are the only living children of said Flying Horse.

Chasing Bear, age 75 years, of Wounded Knee district, stated that he was not in the Wounded Knee affair; that he was living on Pine Ridge reservation at that time, and that a son of his, named Bird Shaking Himself, was then living in Cherry Creek district, Cheyenne River Agency, S.D. and was one of the Big Foot following at Wounded Knee and was killed in that conflict. This Chasing Bear's wife, named Good Cloud Woman, aged 70 years, was present with her husband during our interview and she stated that her father named Yellow Bull and his wife, named Humming, were both killed in the Wounded Knee conflict; that two of her sisters were also killed there, one of whom had 3 children and the other 2 children with them, and that the said 5 children were also killed there. This old couple further stated that said Yellow Bull and family had with them at Wounded Knee 10 horses, set of harness, farm wagon, tepee and full camping outfit, all of which property was lost there and never recovered.

Mary Rough Feather, age 56 years, of Wounded Knee district, stated that she was one of the Big Foot Stampeders from Cherry Creek district, and was in the Wounded Knee affair, with her father and mother and their entire family; that she was a widow at that time and had a son 5 years of age with her who received 2 wounds there, one in the chin and the other in his neck, from which wounds he recovered; that his name was Charley Rough Feather who died at the Haskell Indian School some years later. She also stated that her family had with them at Wounded Knee, 5 horses, riding saddle, pack saddle, and good tepee, which latter they packed on saddle horses, all of which property was lost to them there and never recovered. And she further stated that her father, mother, grandmother, 2 sisters, and 3 small brothers were all killed outright in that conflict and that she is the only member of said family now living.

The foregoing list of seventy-five persons met and interrogated by me, are all survivors of the Wounded Knee affair of December 29, 1890, except a few who represented deceased relatives, and their respective statements, as above set forth, were made in a straight forward manner in the presence of quite a number of Indians, and impressed me as reasonably probable as remembered by the relators.

It will be observed that nearly all of those interrogated claimed to have had a specific number of horses with them at Wounded Knee, and asserted that all of them were either killed in the conflict or otherwise lost to them, and further claimed by those thus interrogated, that about 40 sets of harness, 40 wagons, quite a number of tepees, together with bedding, clothing and other property was also lost to them there.

In this connection I desire to submit that the horses then owned by the Big Foot Indians were chiefly Indian ponies of a market value not exceeding $50.00 per head, while the harness and wagons they claim to have thus lost, had in all probability been issued to them by the government at various times subsequent to their return from Alberta, Canada, in 1881.

The Indians of Big Foot's following in the Wounded Knee affair, had for several weeks prior thereto been engaged in the wild revelry of the so[-]called Ghost Dance Craze . . . unrest among nearly all of the Indian tribes during the summer and autumn of 1890. . . . The Big Foot following on the Cheyenne River reservation and Sitting Bull faction on the Standing Rock reservation [were] the more firm believers in that absurd doctrine from which, through long periods of fasting and exhaustive dancing, they became emaciated and dazed in appearance and heedless to the advice of persons interested in their welfare.

That the attitude of Big Foot and his following for some weeks prior to the Wounded Knee affair may be the better understood, I enclose herewith, marked exhibit A, copies of six certain reports of U.S.

Indian Agent Per[r]ain P. Palmer of Cheyenne River Agency, South Dakota to the Commissioner of Indian Affairs, dated, respectively, October 11, 1890, October 25, 1890, October 29, 1890, November 10, 1890, December 17, 1890, and December 22, 1890 [not included], which show the disaffection of Big Foot and his band then residing in the Cherry Creek district of the Cheyenne River reservation, also that on December 22, 1890, Big Foot surrendered to Lieutenant Colonel Sumner of the 8th U.S. Cavalry.

Upon Big Foot's surrender to Lieutenant Colonel Sumner, he requested permission to return to his camp which was only a few miles distance from where he surrendered, which request was granted by Colonel Sumner, with the understanding that he (Big Foot) and his band would rejoin the command the following morning, which promise Big Foot failed to keep but [instead] escaped during the night accompanied by his entire following, and his whereabouts was unknown from the evening of December 22, 1890 until the afternoon of December 28, 1890, when he and his stampeders were intercepted near Porcupine Creek on the afternoon of December 28, 1890, by a detachment of the 7th U.S. Cavalry, under command of Lieutenant Colonel Whiteside [*sic*—Major Whitside] of that regiment, and taken by said command south to Wounded Knee Creek where they encamped the night of December 28, 1890, and where the conflict between the U.S. troops and the Big Foot Indians occurred the following morning.

Being personally acquainted with Philip Wells, an intelligent Sioux mixed-blood, of the Pine Ridge reservation, residing near the town of Kadoka, South Dakota, and knowing that he had taken an active part in the Wounded Knee affair, he having been then attached to Lieutenant Taylor's troop of Indian scouts as Interpreter, and that on the morning of the conflict he had also interpreted for Colonel Forsyth, who was in command of the U.S. troops in that affair, and desiring to interrogate Interpreter Wells with reference thereto, I sent for him to meet me at Pine Ridge Agency for that purpose, and as requested he came from his home on Pass Creek to the Agency, a distance of about one hundred miles, arriving at Pine Ridge the evening of August 21, 1920, whereupon he related to me his observations and official connection with the affair in the presence of General H[ugh] L. Scott, member of the Board of Indian Commissioners, who was then at the Pine Ridge Agency.

There was no stenographer present to take notes of Mr. Wells['s] statement and he being anxious to leave for his home early the following morning, he promised that upon returning home he would prepare a written statement of his personal knowledge of the affair and mail it to me at Pine Ridge, with which he would also forward copies of statements of certain Indian survivors of that affair which he possessed, that I might submit with my report as pertinent to the matter, and his written statement with reference thereto, dated September 3, 1920, was duly received by me which I transmit herewith marked Exhibit B [not included here], and with which he forwarded me the promised copies of statements of three of the Indian survivors of that conflict which I also enclose herewith, that of an Indian named *Frog*, Exhibit C; of an Indian named *Help them*, Exhibit D; and of an Indian named *Hehakawanyakapi*, Exhibit E [all previously presented herein], and I also enclose herewith as Exhibit F, letter of Colonel James W. Forsyth, Colonel of the 7th U.S. Cavalry, dated at Fort Riley, Kansas, March 5, 1891, to the Adjutant General, U.S.A. which is a complementary indorsement of Interpreter Wells, and he having mailed the same to me for my information, I concluded to forward it with this report for consideration in connection with his statement of September 3, 1920, transmitted herewith, Exhibit B [not included herein].

I desire to add that I was unable to find any record at either Cheyenne River or Pine Ridge Agencies as to the number of Indians killed in the Wounded Knee affair, but found in the files of the Indian Office, copy of a telegram from Special Indian Agent James A. Cooper, dated at Pine Ridge Agency, South Dakota, December 30, 1890, reporting that about 150 Indians were killed and 30 wounded, and that 25 soldiers were killed and 35 wounded in that conflict, but from the best information obtainable there were doubtless many more Indians killed in the fight than as given in this telegram of Special Agent Cooper [not included here].

In conclusion I would respectfully submit that in considering all phases of this matter, including the fact that the crazed condition and heedlessness of the Indians involved in the Wounded Knee affair was largely responsible for the unfortunate occurrance; together with the further fact that thirty years have elapsed since that occurrance and that the Indians now seldom refer to it, I am therefore strongly of the opinion that the peace of mind of the Sioux and interests of the government would best be subserved by not agitating the matter further at this late date, but should it be determined, as a matter of justice, to reimburse the Indians for the horses and other property lost to them in that unfortunate affair, an appropriation approximating $20,000 would, in my judgment, be necessary to reasonably compensate them for the losses there sustained. . . .

Very respectfully
Your obedient servant,
[signed] James McLaughlin
Inspector.

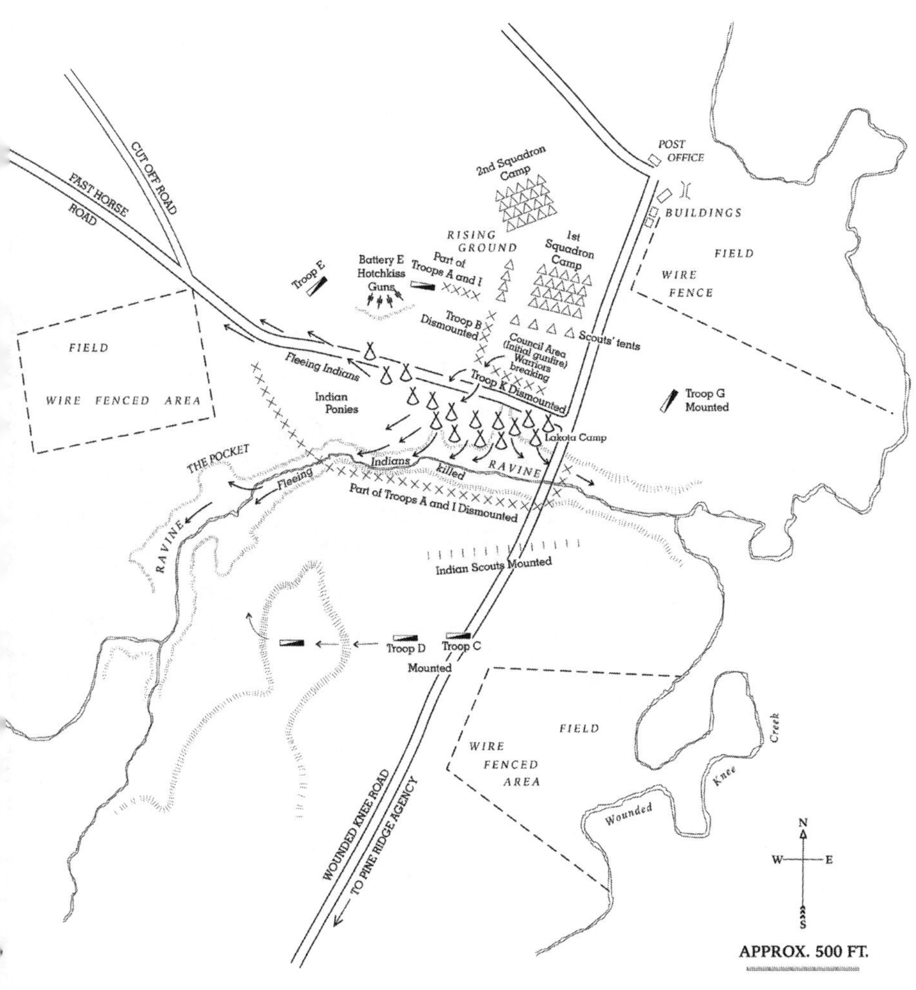

This map of Wounded Knee shows the positions of troops and the paths that many in Big Foot's camp took in the aftermath of the massacre. Robert G. Pilk

Soldiers of Battery E, First United States Artillery, are pictured here with several Lakota scouts and a Hotchkiss mountain gun. Library of Congress

A destroyed wagon sits above bodies in the ravine in this image taken following the massacre. South Dakota State Historical Society

Several figures stand on the frozen field amid bodies awaiting burial. South Dakota State Historical Society

In 1903, survivors erected this monument to memorialize those who died at Wounded Knee. South Dakota State Historical Society

Charles A. Eastman tended to many of the casualties of the massacre and wrote several accounts of the scene. South Dakota State Historical Society

Luther Standing Bear, pictured here in 1891, later recounted what he had seen at the massacre site. Library of Congress

Brothers Daniel Horn Cloud, Joseph Horn Cloud, and Dewey Beard (Iron Hail), (from left) were all present at Wounded Knee, and the latter two offered lengthy reminiscences of their experiences. History Nebraska

Eli S. Ricker conducted an extensive series of interviews with survivors of Wounded Knee beginning in the early twentieth century. History Nebraska

39. Description of the field at Wounded Knee within days of the massacre, recalled by Luther Standing Bear, ca. 1925

Luther Standing Bear recalled the field at Wounded Knee within days following the massacre in this description, circa 1925, in My People the Sioux, *ed. Brininstool, pp. 225–26. Surprisingly, Standing Bear did not mention the presence of the recently established mass grave atop the hill where just days earlier at least 146 of the Lakota victims had been buried.*

[In early January] I started over [from Rosebud Agency to Pine Ridge Agency] to find out how bad the reports were which we had heard about the fight. My father and mother and their family were at Pine Ridge at this time and I had heard nothing from them. It had snowed in the meantime, and the weather was very cold. It meant a ride of thirty miles on horseback, but I had a good horse, plenty of warm clothing, and I did not mind the jaunt.

When I arrived at the place where the fight had occurred between the Indians and the soldiers, all the bodies had been removed. Here and there lay the body of a horse. The tipi poles were broken and lay scattered about in heaps. Cooking utensils were strewed around in confusion; old wagons were overturned, with the tongues broken off. Everything was confusion. It was early in the morning when I reached this place, and the silence was oppressive and terrible.

There were many little pools of water here and there, some with clear water and others red with the blood of my people. I was enraged enough at this sight to shoot any one, but nobody was to be seen. The place of death was forsaken and forbidding. I stood there in silence for several minutes, in reverence for the dead, and then turned and rode toward the agency.

40. Account of Alice Ghost Horse, 1920–1940s

Alice Ghost Horse related this account to her son, John War Bonnet, sometime between 1920 and the 1940s. She was thirteen years old when the events occurred. Alice Ghost Horse, "A True Story of What Happened at Wounded Knee in December 1890," trans. Sidney Keith, as published in Twin Light Trail *2 (1992): 11–14. This notable account provides an extensively detailed recollection of the Big Foot people's journey south from Cherry Creek to Wounded Knee. Another account by this woman (later named Mrs. Alice Dog Arm or Kills Plenty) and also included herein appeared in James H. McGregor,* The Wounded Knee Massacre from the Viewpoint of the Sioux *(Baltimore: Wirth Brothers, 1940), pp. 122–23.*

We were camped at the mouth of Cherry Creek in the latter part of December 1890. I was 15 years old at the time. There was my father, Ghost Horse, [mother] Alice Her Shawl, her maiden name, we both have the same first names, Alice[,] and my two brothers, [and] our "Wicasa Itancan" [leader] was Chief Big Foot (know[n] to his friends as Spotted Elk). Up and down Cherry Creek Chief Hump and his people were camped. The Hohowjus or Minnekojus [also known as Miniconjous and Minneconjous] were also camped in this area towards Takini (now known as Bridger). The Minneconjou lived in the East. These people . . . were already assimilated [and living on the Cheyenne River Reservation], they were under military rule, they were trained to be farmers, and were given land.

At this time people were Ghost Dancing, across the river from Cherry Creek up on the plateau where one crosses the Plum Creek. We went up there where they had dances, but children were not allowed in, so my brothers and I played around the wagon until they finished dancing which was well after dark.

The Ghost Dances are held one a year, like a Sun Dance. They form a big circle with all the participants, [and] they hold hands and some sing. They close their eyes as they dance on the spot, not like the Sun Dance where they move in circles. The ceremony starts at almost sun down, and it's over when it gets real dark. They dance till someone falls down into a trance. While in that condition, their spirit winds up in heaven, where the dead relatives are[.] They claim they see them but they can't talk to them. The Great Mystery doesn't permit them to talk to anyone who is not permanently dead. After one is dead and goes up there, then they can talk to their relatives. It is a sacred dance, some can do it and some can't. After it's over we usually go back to Cherry Creek but some camp close to the dance area because the ceremony can last up to four days.

One day some people came from Standing Rock and told Chief Big Foot that Chief Sitting Bull had been shot and killed for letting his people Ghost Dance. The killing was provoked by the agent there. His name was Major [James] McLaughlin.

Chief Big Foot decided that they should flee to Pine Ridge for safety, [and] everyone agreed with him. On a short notice, it was decided to move out the very next day, so they staked out their horses and all went to bed early.

Early next morning we all packed our wagons ready to move out. I was on my horse as I planned to ride all the way to Pine Ridge, and my two brothers rode in the wagon. The youngest one sat with my mother in the back, and my older brother rode up front with my father. An extra horse was tied to the team, which can also be ridden. We crossed Cherry Creek right at the mouth where it empties into the Cheyenne River, and we followed the wagon trails that went west along the north side. The old wagon trails led us to Takini, a settlement of Minneconjou, who live the furthest away from us.

We ran towards the river and stopped half way before the river bank to have lunch of pemmican (dried meat and berries) that my mother had served. The men watered their horses nearby and we then continued at a trot. I followed the wagon behind, real close.

Before we left Cherry Creek the military agent would send Lakota scouts to the Ghost Dance, asking questions and spying. I am sure they knew we left Cherry Creek in a hurry. That's the reason we were running, making our way towards Takini (Bridger) community.

Late afternoon, we finally arrived at our destination, amid clusters of tents, tipis and lean-tos. The people here were getting the colder weather which was evident by the huge piles of wood at every tent. After we put up our tent my brothers and I went down to the river to look for wood and sticks so my mother could start supper. Not too long afterwards she had us a good meal ready. Hot coffee, gabooboo bread and wahanpi (dried meat soup). After a hearty meal my father went to a meeting at Chief Big Foot's tipi, so we played around for a while and then went to bed. My father said they planned to leave bright and early next day.

When I woke up my father was already hitching up his team, so I got up and saddled up Old Paint, [and] right after breakfast I got on my horse, ready to ride. I still planned to ride all the way to Pine Ridge. First wagon to leave was Chief Big Foot's, with all his relatives following behind, some on horseback, some were walking alongside, for the time being. We crossed the river and headed up the hill towards the southeast direction. I looked back and saw more wagons joining in and so the caravan moved at a faster pace as the horses broke into a trot. It was exciting for me, [as] we were running from the military. We ran like this all morning without stopping. Late afternoon, we stopped in a draw (a land basin that water drains into) to eat what little we had, but we were not to start a fire, lest we would be seen from a distance. When we are on the move usually some riders will fall back to check everyone at the request of the chief.

After a brief rest we were on our way again, keeping to the draw, and sometimes the going was hard on the wagons, because we were running along the creek beds. Going in a southerly direction, again we trotted most of the time, keeping to the low land, valleys and washouts. Finally we went below Porcupine Butte. The going was tough because there was no trail and the ground was frozen.

Sometime later the head wagons stopped on top of a hill and people were looking down at something. My father went to investigate, my mother got down from our wagon and came to me and started to tighten my saddle girth and said, "Stay close by, we may have to run for it." She said there were cavalry people camped down below along the Wounded Knee Creek. Just then, my father returned and said that Big Foot was sick and he was laying in the back of his wagon all bundled up. He said they're going to send some men down there with a white flag to talk to the cavalry officers.

I saw four riders going down the hill with a white cloth tied to a long stick. As soon as the riders crossed the creek all the soldiers laid down and aimed their rifles at them, but they kept on going towards the centre of their camp, [and] finally they arrived. There were some big guns positioned there, soldiers and officers were standing around. The party dismounted and they had a short talk. After a while a lone rider galloped up to where Chief Big Foot's wagon was and told him to go down to the centre of their camp, but the relatives objected. They told the rider that he [Big Foot] was very sick. So the rider went back to tell the cavalry.

Sometime later a doctor was sent up in a hospital wagon. The doctor examined Chief Big Foot and told them that he had pneumonia and gave him some pills. They loaded him into the hospital wagon and took him down to their camp. They talked a long time and finally one of our riders came back to tell the people to camp along the Wounded Knee Creek on the west side across the creek. So everyone pitched their tents there, as ordered. Pretty soon the army was coming around issuing crackers, coffee, flour, bacon and army beans.

By sundown we were completely surrounded by guards and foot soldiers with rifles. My mother and I went down the creek to go to the bathroom and pick up some sticks for the fire, but two soldiers were following us around and they appeared to be drunk. They were saying bad words to us. Everyone went to bed hungry and early, as it was a long hard journey and everyone was very tired. Some of the young men were detailed to watch the soldier guards all night.

Early next morning a bugle woke me up so I went outside and I noticed a lot of activity going on at the soldier camp. We ate hastily because most of the Lakotas were loading their wagons already and my father already had his team harnessed, so I saddled up my horse and I was ready to go.

At this time a crier was making his way around the Lakota camp telling the menfolk to go to their [the soldiers'] camp for more talks. The men left so the women continued to pack their wagons. I was on my horse just standing there and I could hear what seems to be an argument and it turned into a shouting match. Then pretty soon some cavalrymen rode in from their camp at a fast gallop and they started to search the wagons for guns, knives, axes, awls and bows and arrows, anything that the Lakotas might use against the soldiers. They were really rude about it, [and] they scattered our belongings all over the ground. The soldiers picked up everything they could find and took it to their camp and dumped it in front of the officers and continued to argue with the Lakotas, but they wouldn't give in.

During the heated argument a medicine man appeared out from no where, by the name of Yellow Bird. He stood facing east right by the firepit, which was not covered up with dirt. He was praying and crying. He was calling on the eagles and the buffalo spirits. He sent his voice to Wakan Tanka[:] "Let me die first but save my people." He picked up some dirt and threw it in the air, saying, "This is the way I want to go, back to dust." He must have sensed something was going to happen to the Lakota.

At this time there were cavalrymen, all on bay horses[,] lined up on top of the hill on the north side. One officer rode down the hill at full gallop towards the confrontation. He made a fast halt and shouted something to his commanding officers and retreated back to his company. Right away they all drew their rifles and their long knifes [*sic*—the troops at Wounded Knee carried neither swords nor bayonets] and you could hear them load their rifles with live bullets.

In the meantime, more cavalry soldiers were lined up on the south [*sic*—north] hill. They set up a big gun on wheels aiming at the centre of our camp. I heard the first shot coming from the confrontation followed by rifles cracking in the cold air. Occasionally a big gun would "boom" from the hill to the south [*sic*—north]. The Lakotas scattered in all directions. Since the soldiers confiscated all the axes, awls and guns, a hand[-]to[-]hand fight was pursued at times. The two cavalry troops swooped down shooting at every Lakota who was running and it didn't matter if you were a child or woman. They shot you anyway.

My father made it to the wagon and my horse was trying to bolt so my father told me to jump off, so I did and the poor horse ran like a scared rabbit into the woods. In the meantime we fled into the ravines where the plum bushes were the thickest and dived in like frightened rabbits. The gunfire was pretty heavy and people were hollering for their children and children were crying everywhere. My father said he was going out to help the others and my mother objected, but he left anyway. Pretty soon my father came crawling back in. He was wounded below the left knee and was bleeding. He took my youngest brother and left again, saying he was taking him further down the creek and would come back after us.

Soon afterwards my father came crawling back in again and said, "they killed my son," and started to cry, so we cried a little bit, lest we be heard. There was no time to think. My father said we should move to a better hiding place but my mother objected again, saying we should all die here together. She told me to stand up so I did, but my father pulled me down.

With a little effort, we crawled to a deeper hiding place. Bullets were whistling around us but my father went out again to help the others. Some people crawled in and I recognized Black Moon and his mother. They were okay. More women and children came in. The young ones were whimpering. Groups at intervals came crawling in, and four of them died right there, but there was nothing anybody could do. A man named Breast Plate (Wawoslal Wanapin) came in and told us that my father was killed instantly. We all cried for a little bit because the soldiers were still firing their rifles at anything that moved. Charge in Kill and Back Hip (Nistute) came in later but left again. They were brave. It seemed like eternity but actually it didn't last that long. It was getting late in the afternoon and [at] about dark the shooting ceased all of a sudden, and soon after a long wagon was going around picking up their dead for these were the soldiers that were killed in the cross-fire.

At a given moment a signal was made for us to stand up and make our way in a northeasterly direction, tip-toeing our way through creek beds and ravines, occasionally we would stumble over dark objects which turned out to be dead horses or even dead Lakotas. We heard a child crying in the distance asking for water, and many more crying for their mothers. It was a cold night.

We walked in the creek bed, heading now in a northerly direction. It must have been Wounded Knee Creek where we met up with more people. There was little talk, and it was decided to split up while each group moved off in a different direction so as not to be caught all together. So we escaped with our lives.

Our group reached a hill by morning [30 December] and we rested there. We could see a long ways off, [and] there was flat country to the east of us and hilly country towards the north and west. We were heading north. The sky showed polka-dot white puffs with blue background. The wind watered our eyes. The wind was changing patterns in the fast flowing clouds. It looked like a storm was coming.

We had some boys staying on the hill watching back towards the south for any movement or sign of horses when suddenly the boys hollered down to us, "a rider is following our tracks." We all scampered into the draws like rabbits. We continued deeper into the bushes and waited. But it was a man wearing a lady's scarf riding towards the hill where we were. It was Back Hip (Nistute) whom we met at Wounded Knee. He was not hurt.

After we shook hands with him we all cried. He told us that after the shooting he escaped to Pine Ridge, but most of the Oglalas all evacuated to the hills. He walked back to Wounded Knee and found his horse. Luckily he caught him. He then started to track north, thinking some of them might have escaped and hoping to meet up with them. He was persuading us to go with him towards Pine Ridge. Before anybody could decide, some more riders appeared, heading in our direction, so we took off for the ravines. Back Hip stayed on to meet the riders who galloped in, hollering "Don't run, we are Lakotas." They dismounted at the sight of four Lakotas who emerged from their hiding places. Finally we all came out to shake hands and we all cried with them. There was one woman with them and she had some pemmican, so we ate with them. We hadn't eaten since we left Wounded Knee, a day and a half earlier. One of the men said he saw cattle way back there foraging down a draw. They said they were going after some meat, and they left.

So we started out again, covering some miles before dark. It started to cloud up, rolling in from the northwest, cloud waves seeming to roll over the hills and valleys like water. Misty fine drops of rain were falling, more of a drizzle. Then the wind came sometime later and it turned into snow. It started to blizzard, but one of the men steered us towards a cabin, which he spotted from a hill. This blessed haven we reached along a creek, so we stayed warm sitting there waiting out the storm. We had meat from the last butchering to keep us fed. Later in the night their voices woke me up, loud voices, high pitched women's voices arguing whether to scatter or stay. The calmer voices of the males I listened to, most of the talk was in a whisper as we listened. I sat up in a hurry when a new meaning came to my senses. I got scared for the first time. My heart was beating faster, my breathing became shorter and harder. Quickly I moved closer to my mother's body which was to me as natural as a cottontail jumping into its lair. The noise the women heard was maybe the rumbling of horses running or buffalo stampeding. Maybe even cavalrymen, but it turned out that they may have heard something, then [began] imagining their fears into loud noises.

For some time we just sat there staring at the darkness, only the occasional flickering of the embers to see by. During the night some riders went out to scout around. Later they came back and said in a low voice that it was time to go. No one complained. All acted on instinct to survive. It was still cloudy and cold when we left the cabin.

Luckily the cabin had a wooden floor and a stove. Some of the men loaned us their horses again, so my brother and I rode double, as well as the others. Sometimes the snow would blow, but we kept to the low lands, [and] it wasn't that windy down in the draws. There were about 13 of us in the party. Despite the hardships, we kept moving in a northwesterly direction. The hills were getting denser all the time and we were glad that we were out of danger.

Finally we stumbled onto a camp of Oglalas. They were camped in a nice place among the pine trees. Towards the end of the camp we came across Short Bull's tent. All of the Oglalas came to welcome us, [and] they fed us. Each were given a family to stay with. We stayed at this camp for three months, and the sun kept coming on higher every day. Soon all the snow started to melt, and everyone knew it was spring. There was a lot of rejoicing in the camp.

One day a lone rider came to the camp and said there was a meeting at Pine Ridge. Next day, early as usual, we all headed for the home of the Oglalas. It must have been quite a ways because we camped some place in the hills. The caravan was long with travois, buggies, horseback and people on foot. The chiefs were walking ahead with the warriors following behind. Over the last hill we could see many tents and cavalry all over the place. Dust was flying. Horses were tied to the hitching posts, face to face. After we made camp near the fort [*sic*—army camp], Can Hahaka (Vertebrae) and Wakinyan Maza (Iron Thunder) came to our camp to talk to us. They said they came after all the Minneconjou (Cheyenne River Sioux) survivors, deceased or wounded. They said we all belong to the Minneconjou band.

In Pine Ridge my mother reluctantly signed the papers that say we are survivors. The families of these survivors usually tell of the "Wikisleyapi" (Rape) of the young maidens. The soldiers started a bonfire and all the young that were captured, they literally raped them— some escaped to tell of the ordeal. Later, some had babies that were not full-blood Lakotas. The cavalry pitched up three big tipis in the middle of the post [camp] where they told us to go. I remember there was Black Moon and his mother and brothers, Iron Horn and Wood Pile were there. There were many Minneconjous that showed up at the tipi, even some we thought had been killed.

One day we left for Cherry Creek towards the Cheyenne River

Reservation. We left in five wagons, one loaded with oats and hay, another one of rations and one wagon full of soldiers, who escorted us, taking us around Wounded Knee so we won't see the place again.

Some nights I cried, because they killed my brother and father for nothing.

41. Reminiscence of John Ghost Bear, November 1928

John Ghost Bear shared this reminiscence, as interpreted by former Indian scout Ben Janis, at Pine Ridge Agency on 1 November 1928. NA Identifier: 285586, File 053, Historical Data 1927-32, Box 172, Main Decimal Files, 1900–1965, RG 75, NA, Kansas City, Mo. (Courtesy of Lori A. Cox-Paul and R. Eli Paul, Kansas City, Mo.).

The Indians who took part in the Wounded Knee battle were what was known as the Big Foot Band, who lived on the Cheyenne River, about twenty-five miles above the mouth of Cherry Creek and six miles below the mouth of the Belle Fourche River.

Big Foot had something like 350 Indians with him, including men, women and children; and they left home about the middle of December, 1890, presumably to join the hostile Indians who were on the Pine Ridge Reservation.

General Miles [actually Major General John R. Brooke] was in command of all the soldiers and Indian scouts on the Pine Ridge Reservation; and he heard that the Big Foot Band of Indians were coming, and sent out a troop of cavalry, under Major Adams [actually Major Whitside], and several Indian scouts, to head them off before they came to White River; but, before the soldiers got to what is now called the Big Foot Pass, the Indians had gone down, so Major Adams [Whitside] and his soldiers and scouts came down the pass after the Indians, but there were too many of the Indians; so he just followed them towards Pine Ridge, and did not attempt to head them off or stop them.

General Miles [Brooke] heard that Major Adams [Whitside] had not succeeded in heading the Indians off, so he sent five [four] troops of the 7th Cavalry to meet them and bring them to Pine Ridge, so they could not join the hostile Indians. The soldiers met the Indians at Porcupine Butte, and brought them down to Wounded Knee Creek, where they camped for the night.

It was decided to disarm the Indians at Wounded Knee before they brought them to Pine Ridge; so the Indians were lined up, and the soldiers started to take the guns away from them. Most of the soldiers were placed on small hills around where the Indians were lined up, and the artillery was on the small hill where the Indians that were killed in the fight are now buried. There were five [four] field guns and a Gattling [*sic*] gun placed on this hill. The soldiers were ordered to fire on the Indians if they did not give up their arms peaceably.

After most of the Indians were disarmed, Lieutenant [*sic*—Captain George D.] Wallace stepped over to an Indian named Slippery Skin, who was not in the line, and Slippery Skin shot and killed Lieutenant Wallace. That started the fight, and the Indians started to run, most of them up the large draw, just south of where the Indians were being disarmed.

The fight lasted about two hours. There were about 170 Indians killed, including women and children; and there were more women and children killed than there were men. There were about 35 soldiers killed, presumably most of them having been shot by each other, as nearly, if not quite all, of the Indians had been disarmed. A few of the Indian men picked up the guns of the soldiers that had been killed, and used them to fight the soldiers; but most of them had nothing to fight with. Colonel Forsythe [Forsyth] was in immediate command of the soldiers who were in the fight. The fight took place December 29, 1890.

As told by John Ghost Bear, who was an Indian police [policeman—i.e., scout] on duty, and actually took part in the battle.

Interpreted by Ben Janis, who was an Indian scout during the Indian war of 1890-91.

42. Statement of Afraid of the Enemy, May 1932

Superintendent James H. McGregor obtained the statement of Afraid of the Enemy, interpreted by Ben American Horse, on 25 May 1932. The published and edited version appeared in McGregor, Wounded Knee Massacre from the Viewpoint of the Sioux, *pp. 126–27.*

I am 78 years old, so you can judge that I know quite a lot of things which occurred. I am not going to talk about these creeks and rivers. I know that I was with Big Foot's band that was called over here. We came over here to see some of the Oglala Chiefs and just unconcerned about anything else. When we saw the soldiers coming we tied a white flag to a pole and held it so the soldiers could see it. We went into camp with them and I never thought that anything would happen. I saw some of the soldiers and Indians and some of my relations and was not afraid of anything that evening. I went over to see Big Foot in a soldier's tent where he was sick.

The next morning the officer told Big Foot that they wanted all his guns. He was our chief and we looked to him to say something but he was coughing all the time. Finally he said you men better give him your guns, we are not on this trip to do any fighting but we came over here to see our relatives and to be at Red Cloud's council.

[The following part of Afraid of The Enemy's statement comprises part of the original unedited portion provided by Michael Her Many Horses. Readers might further consult the edited version in McGregor's book, as cited above.]

Shortly after Big Foot said that, there was an officer said, now yesterday I seen quite a few of your fellows with guns and I want you to give them to me and I will have some of my men collect them. Shortly after that a soldier started out among the Indians [and] searched them and also where the women were packing up. Some of the soldiers came from where the Indians were [camped?] had axes and even these hide tanners and kept a[-]yelling "No more, No More" and took those weapons to where the guns were piled. As I noticed now in looking back that I had heard them unloading and instead of unloading they were drawing in another fill[?]. The gun was quite long. They place[d] the gun in position and aim[ed it] right at us. We neve[r] thought anything was going to occur. We were a band of people that respected God and we didn't think there was going to be any harm done and any intentions of that happening. As I looked over towards the soldiers they were surround[ing] us [and] I noticed an officer on a sorrel horse that came around the left end. As he came around I heard him give one comman[d] and right after the command it sounded like a lightning crash. That is about all I know. When I became conscious I was lying down. As I arose and started to go I began to get unconscious again. Again when I became conscious again I found myself on the ground again. For that reason I do not know a great deal of things because I was unconscious most of the time. I have got my old cloak and it has nine bullet holes in it, but I didn't bring it. I am shot all through my body. I am ready to die any time from the effects of those wounds. I was bleeding from my nose and mouth and that is all I am going to tell. I just wanted to tell about the firing.

[The following closing elements of Afraid of The Enemy's statement are from McGregor's book:]

We were a band of people that respected God and we did not think there was going to be any harm done. . . . I want my good friends to tell the good white people what they did to us here at Wounded Knee. We know he [McGregor] is our friend and we know that some white people are good friends of the Indians, but most of them do not like us and [do] not have sympathy for us poor Indians. The missionaries have been good friends to the Indians and love them. We don't have hate in our hearts for the white people, but the soldiers tried to murder us and we want the Government to find out the truth, not like the picture show [production] that came here [with William F. Cody in 1913] and had the Indians to act just like they wanted but not the truth.

43. Account of Dewey Beard,
recorded by James H. McGregor, 1933

James H. McGregor obtained this account from Dewey Beard (Iron Hail), interpreted by William Bergen in 1933, which was published seven years later in his volume Wounded Knee Massacre from the Viewpoint of the Sioux, *pp. 103–9.*

I was a member of the band that was killed here. Just a little beyond Porcupine Butte we were coming this way when we were met by the soldiers. Big Foot, who was sick and had been sick then for four days, had a hemorrhage, came up with a flag of truce tied to a stick. We were traveling in a peaceful manner, no intention of any trouble. I was told that this was an officer that came around to where Big Foot was laying, so I followed him up possibly a yard right behind him. I wanted to know what his intentions were. This officer asked Big Foot—"Are you the man that is named Big Foot and can you talk?" He asked him where he was going. ["]I am going to my people who are camped down here.["] The officer then stated that he had heard that they had left Cheyenne River and the Army was on the lookout for him. "I have seen you and I am very glad to have met you. I want you to turn over your guns." Big Foot answered. "Yes, I am a man of that kind." The officer wanted to know what he meant by that, so the interpreter told him that he was a peaceful man. He says, "you have requested that I give you my guns, but I am going to a certain place and when I get there I will lay down my arms."

"Now, you meet us out here on the prairie and expect me to give you my guns out here. I am a little bit afraid that there might be something crooked about it, something that may occur that wouldn't be fair. There are a lot of children here." The officer then said they are bringing a wagon and I want you to get in that and they will take you down to where we are camped. Shortly a wagon drew up and they wrapped a blanket around him and placed him in the wagon and started to camp, so we followed. This side of the [modern trading] store, where you see these houses [in 1933], is where we were camped and right this way is where the soldiers were camped. In the evening they unloaded some bacon, sugar and hardtack in the

"

center and stated that someone should issue this out, so the women all came into the center and I am the one that issued it out to them. We heard a mule braying over this way and also heard the soldiers making a complete circle from the south to the north direction. I forgot something too that I wanted to repeat. That evening I noticed that they were erecting cannons up here, also hauling up quite a lot of ammunition for it [*sic*]. I could see them doing it. Shortly after we erected our camp, guards were stationed around. They were walking their beat. I also noticed that night besides the store there was some fires built there and we knew that they were the Indian Scouts. The following morning there was a bugle call shortly after that another bugle call, then I saw the soldiers mounting the horses and surrounding us. Even though they had surrounded us and we noticed all these peculiar actions, I never thought there was anything wrong. I thought it wouldn't be no time until we could be starting towards the Agency. It was announced that all men should come to the center for a talk and that after the talk that they were to move on to Pine Ridge Agency. So they all came to the center. Shortly after that I also followed and came to the center where they all were gathered. After I got there and looked around and the men were just sitting around unconcerned. Big Foot was brought out of his tepee and sat in front of his tent and the older men were gathered around him and sitting right near him in the center. The interpreter said that the officer said that yesterday we promised some guns and that he was going to collect them now. I don't remember how many soldiers there were, but these soldiers were climbing on top of wagons, unpacking things, taking axes and other things, and they were taking them to where the guns were already laid down. Some of the Indians were further east that had guns in their arms but were not seen for some time. They were out over where the soldiers were so finally they called to them to bring their arms to the center and put them down. One of them started towards the center with his gun. This fellow that started said: "Now it was understood yesterday that we were to put down our guns after we reached the Agency, but here you are calling for our guns so he took the gun and showed it to them." He started towards the guns where they were laid down and one soldiers [*sic*] started from the east side towards him and another from the west side towards this Indian. Even so, he was still unconcerned. He was not scared about it. If they had left him alone he was going to put his gun down where he should. They grabbed him and spinned him in the east direction. He was still unconcerned even then. He hadn't his gun pointed at anyone. His intention was to put that gun down. They came on and grabbed the gun that he was going to put down. Right after they spun him around there was the report of a gun, was quite loud. I couldn't say that anybody was shot but following that was a crash. The flag of truce that we had was stuck in the ground right there where we were sitting. They fired on us anyhow. Right after that crash, that is when all the people were falling over. I remained standing there for some little time and a man came up to me and I recognized him as a man known as High Hawk. He said, come on they have started this way, so let's go. So we started up this little hill; coming up this way, the soldiers started to shoot at us and as they did High Hawk was shot and fell down. I wasn't[,] so started back and then they knocked me down. I was alone so I was trying to look out for myself. They had killed my wife and baby. I saw men lying around, shot down. I went around them the best I could, got down in the ravine, then I fell down again. I was shot and wounded at the first time I told you that I fell. I went up this ravine and could see that they were traveling in that direction. I saw women and children lying all over there. They got up to a cut bank up the ravine and there I found a great many that were in there hiding. We were going to try and go on through the ravine but it was surrounded by the soldiers, so we just had to stay in that cut bank. Right near there was a butte with a ridge on it. They placed a cannon on it pointing in our direction and fired on us right along. I saw one man that was shot with one of these cannons. That man's name was Hawk Feather Shooter.

44. Account of James Pipe on Head, recorded by James H. McGregor, 1933

James H. McGregor obtained this account by James Pipe on Head, interpreted by Henry Standing Bear, in 1933, and included it in Wounded Knee Massacre from the Viewpoint of the Sioux, *pp. 107–9.*

These people coming from the other reservation [at Cheyenne River] reached the foot of the Porcupine Butte. At that point they realized that the soldiers were going that direction to meet them, or take them by surprise, or whatever it may be, so Big Foot, who was my grandfather, was sick and his wife was driving the wagon. Big Foot told these people to raise the white flag; that means peace. So on a stick they fixed a white flag and they carry it. The old man advised these people that if the soldiers meet them they must not be disturbed, the Indians must not start anything; that was the old man's advice at this place. An armed officer, with an Indian interpreter, told them that the soldiers were camped down on Wounded Knee and took Big Foot and his band down there. Big Foot was camped at some point on Medicine Root [Creek] the night before they reached the Butte. That day they came down here [to Wounded Knee Creek] and the soldiers took Big Foot off to one of the soldier's tents for care. The night I first visited my grandfather and some of the [other] Indians visited him. The next morning the Indians were issued a little hard bread for rations and then following that there was a request or call that all the Indian men should get together in some spot or some point, which they did. I was a boy, my grandfather asked me to take some tobacco over to Big Foot where he was lying, so I took it. Of course, at that time the Indians were completely surrounded by both cavalry and infantry [*sic*—by "cavalry and infantry," Pipe on Head apparently meant both mounted and dismounted cavalrymen]. I delivered the tobacco to the old man, and he was lying there in the center of all these Indians who were called together. That is where I delivered the tobacco to him. At this time, all of the Indians were unarmed, all their weapons taken from them and Big Foot told me that I had better go back to grandmother, so I started to leave to go back to my grandmother and to where the women folks were. Just at this moment there was a big noise; I couldn't see just what it was but it was sounding like quite a number of gun shots together. This [Then?] I knew it was guns fired on us. When these soldiers started shooting, I started to run towards the hillside over there at a distance [and] I came across a little boy. I took the little boy by the hand and all at once someone came on the side of me and took hold of my hand. This woman was my mother [Nest?]. She had a baby on her back, my sister, but this girl that she was carrying on her back was shot. While we were running we saw on the ground dust flying, some of the bullets struck near us. We managed to get around through the line and escape through this direction.

45. Account of Richard Afraid of Hawk, recorded by James H. McGregor, 1933

James H. McGregor included this account by Richard Afraid of Hawk, interpreted by William Bergen in 1933, in Wounded Knee Massacre from the Viewpoint of the Sioux, *pp. 129–31.*

Those people who were in the Massacre that were killed were all camped below the foot-hill here and I was among them. In the morning I heard some man, taking the part of a harangue, announcing that all men should come to the center to hold a meeting to talk over matters and after that they were to all go into the Agency. Those were the very words I heard. So we men all come to the meeting that is where they wanted us to meet, and some of the men that didn't come at once, they still were among the camps or tepees. The soldiers went down there and told them to come in, they have rushed or forced them into the meeting. Just as soon as all the men were gathered in the center, in fact, just as the last man came in, just as sudden, the infantry [dismounted cavalry] surrounded us.[4] When they surrounded us, some mix[ed]-blood or interpreter [Philip Wells] stated that all the Indians should take their arms to the center. So all those that listened to the man that announced this went and put their arms where they were told to. The soldiers saw that some of those were not placing their arms where they were told to so they went among the Indians, threw back their blankets, took their guns and even their knives, [and] axes away from the women. Shortly after all the weapons were gathered down where the infantry [dismounted cavalry] surrounded us and the cavalry surrounded the tepees right in between and we noticed some of the officers walk back and surround us. At the time one of the two [four] heavy guns or cannon were stationed up on this hill, and this officer was walking back and forth where we were surrounded. At the time one of these men that was riding back and forth after giving these commands, we couldn't understand what he said, but something was said in a loud command and then all at once all the guns were fired.

4. There were no enlisted infantry soldiers at Wounded Knee.

That is all that I can remember, that all the guns were fired and for quite awhile after I couldn't remember anything. As I said, for a time I didn't know what happened. When I came to my senses, people were all lying about where formerly they were all sitting or standing. It appeared that they were all dead. I started then for the creek intending to go down into the creek but as I got down to the creek I saw a company of soldiers so I went back and came to an empty wagon that was standing there and I sat down in that. While I was sitting there it seemed as though all these shots were aimed at this wagon box so I jumped up and started across the flat as fast as I could. I noticed that where the road goes up the hill I didn't see any soldiers so I started for that and got away through there.

46. Account of Dog Chief, recorded by James H. McGregor, 1933

Dog Chief offered this account, interpreted by William Bergen in 1933, which James H. McGregor published in Wounded Knee Massacre from the Viewpoint of the Sioux, *pp. 133–35.*

I was a member of that band and when we were near Porcupine Creek when we saw soldiers and this made us all take notice at once. Some of us on horseback were back at that time and we saw a gathering in front and then we went as fast as we could to the front as they might need our help. The soldiers just came on like they were going to run over us and then they spread out like they were going to fire on us but they did not. Our Chief told us not to make any attempt to fight but to hold up a white flag as he said that was the way the Palefaces had of saying that they were for peace. Well we had the white flag but the soldiers did not[,] but took the cannon off from the mules and was working at them like they was going to fight.

The Chief and the Army officer had some talks and then we all were told that we were going to where there were more soldiers on Wounded Knee Creek, and so the soldiers led us into the camp and gave us some little rations and we were told that we must camp and not get away from the Indian camp, so we stayed there all night. That night I heard a noise and I learned that they had sent for more soldiers and they arrived during the night.

The next morning the Indians and soldiers all got up and had some little eats and the women were getting ready to move as we were told that we were going into Pine Ridge, and that made us happy, as that was where we were going anyway as Big Foot wanted to be at a Council that Red Cloud had called. About that time all the men were told to go to Big Foot's camp and they would have a talk and then go to the Agency. Big Foot was sick and he had a comforter or blanket around him and he looked very sick, but he still was Chief and the Army officer told him that he must have the Indians bring their guns to the center and give them up. We did not like this but Big Foot told us to do what the soldiers say so the guns were piled in the center. I noticed that the soldiers were moving around and they were strung around the camp. Then I saw the sergeant take some soldiers and go to where the women were getting packed to go to Pine Ridge. They would go right into the tents and come out with bundles and tear them open. They kept this up for some time and returned to the center where we had piled the guns and they brought our axes, knives, and tent stakes and piled them near the guns. I heard one of the white men say something but as I don't understand white man's talk, I do not know what he said. Right after that there was an awful roar as it seemed all guns fired at one time. That is all I know as I was lying on the ground when I regained my mind. I raised up my head and the awful firing was going on. All the men lying around me were killed or wounded. I tried to get up and when I did, I ran toward this ravine down towards the [later] store and down into quite a coulee and there I saw women and children, some of them wounded and bleeding, even the small children were bleeding. Then some soldiers came and saw us and began to shoot us again so we ran up the ravine. We were being killed as we moved up toward the head of the valley [ravine]. We went as fast as we could. Two boys were with me, one is Little Finger and the other one Red Shell, but he is dead but Little Finger is living and is with us today. After a while some Indians on horseback came to the top of the hill, not very far from where we were hiding and these Indians had guns and were our friends that had come out to fight from Pine Ridge. When the soldiers saw them they quit killing us and went back to where there were more soldiers. The Indians that were on horseback took all of us that was able to ride on behind them and we got away from the soldiers.

47. Statement of Nellie Knife, recorded by James H. McGregor, 1933

Nellie Knife gave the following statement in 1933. James H. McGregor included it in Wounded Knee Massacre from the Viewpoint of the Sioux, *pp. 138–39.*

I will just tell about the Massacre. When we camped with the soldiers we did not think of war or fighting. The soldiers gave us some eats and we needed them very much.

When we got up the next morning [29 December] the soldiers were still guarding us. We were going to Pine Ridge to see our relations and Big Foot was to be in a Big Council. While I was packing, a soldier from headquarters told the men and the large boys to go to Big Foot's tent, and while they were away soldiers came to where the women were and took axes, knives and other things that the Indian women had. I kept on packing and all at once I heard an awful noise. As the shots were fired the women and children ran for a safe place to hide. I ran toward the flat and as I ran I saw many people were already killed. I was running with a young girl named Brown Ear Horse, but she got shot so I went on and left her. I saw a woman, she was the wife of One Skunk, she was shot and she screamed and cried, but I could not help her as the bullets were flying thick and I wanted to get to a safe place. I saw a woman named Red Stone and she was on a horse and a small boy was near her and I put the boy on the horse with her and we kept going to a place to hide, and after the firing stopped and the soldiers went away I returned to see if I could find any of my people. My mother-in-law, my sister-in-law and many brothers were dead and my father-in-law, Little Bull, was alive but his leg was broken.

48. Story of Charley Blue Arm, recorded by James H. McGregor, 1933

"Story of Charley Blue Arm (Cherry Creek, S.D.)," as obtained by James H. McGregor and interpreted by William A. Bergen in 1933, was published in Wounded Knee Massacre from the Viewpoint of the Sioux, *pp. 136–38. Here, it appears in an early unedited format as provided by Michael Her Many Horses of Wounded Knee, S.Dak.*

To start with, I wish to say that I was among those that were with Big Foot, [and] the band that was moving this way en route. We were over here at the Porcupine Butte when we saw two soldiers. There was no intention to carry on any warfare. We had no intention of that kind, so we so we [*sic*] stuck up a stick with a white flag tied to it. I didn't for once think that there would be a fight of any kind. From there we moved on to right below on this hill and camped where there was already soldiers. The Indians were camped along the creek there and the soldiers were camped right down below the hill here [east of the present cemetery]. The following morning it was announced that we men should all gather to the center to have a meeting or discussion to talk. So the men start[ed] for the center and I was also among them. Shortly after they gathered to the center and were seated around, the officer requested that they all give up their arms, or guns[,] so I saw all those that had guns give up their guns and those that left their guns in their camps went back after them and brought them to where they were piling them up. After that they [soldiers] went along among the men, threw their blankets back, looked at their belts to see if they had knives or other things that could be used as a weapon and took them away from them. As I saw it, the soldiers all wear their guns up in this position (stock under their arms) that is what I saw where we were, then looking over where the women were I saw some soldiers over there un-tieing [*sic*] their bundles, etc.[,] looking for weapons. I saw the soldiers were returning from over there with axes, knives and what guns they could find they brought over and placed where the other guns were piled. I do not understand English and it was stated here that one of th[e] officers gave a command. Of course, I didn't understand that or didn't hear it, rather. I did not hear the report of any gun prior to the time general firing was done by the soldiers. The truce flag, or white flag, that we had was stuck in the mud it seems and we were gathered around that and I noticed that all the Indians were lying about dead under that truce flag. After seeing that I started for the creek and on my way I saw a great number of men, women and children lying dead. I went past them on down into the creek. I ran up the creek a short distance and there I saw a number of men and women gathered so I went up to them and stopped there. At that time there were two cannons stationed up here [on the hill top] and that is what they were firing at us. I stayed where I last stated I got to and remained there all day until sundown and then went from there on home.

Q. About how far were you from where the soldiers were?

A. A fourth of a mile.

Q. Did the soldiers disturb them at that time?

A. Yes, the soldiers were shooting at us where we stopped there.

Q. Hit some?

A. Yes, they killed some there.

Q. Why didn't they run on?

A. The reason we did not was on account of the women. There was some women there and we didn't want to desert them. That is about as much as I know.

49. Account of Rough Feather,
recorded by James H. McGregor, 1933

*The account of Rough Feather, then sixty-nine years old, as
interpreted by Henry Standing Bear in 1933, was published in
McGregor,* Wounded Knee Massacre from the Viewpoint of the
Sioux, *pp. 109–11.*

I am going to just tell about the way that they surrounded us, right
below here, and I am going to tell only that which I saw, and the
things I heard will be the only things that I will tell about, also my
activities and how I came out alive. Right down here, all the Indians
were placed in a group and were surrounded by the soldiers. So I had
a blanket on, don't know where I got it from, someone gave it to me,
I covered my head up and stood there among them, and I understood
that the soldiers wanted the guns. I was facing that way and I could
see Big Foot, he was lying in a tent. Right near where Big Foot's tent
was I saw a soldier. He had his gun in his hand, and in a loud voice
made some remarks. So I looked over at him. It may be possible that
very soldier is still living. He was the one that again said something
in a very loud voice. About that time I heard some noise behind so
I looked back. I saw them aim the guns at us. It sounded much like
the sound of tearing canvas, that was the crash. As I heard the crash
I became unconscious. Something struck me. As I was standing there
I happened to look up and the smoke was awfully dense, but I could
now make out a face right in front of me. As I saw him he turned and
started the other way so I followed. As I started to follow him I saw
him get in front of the soldiers and [he] grabbed hold of one and they
both fell down together. I was right up on them and I had to jump
over them. The other soldier standing nearby struck me with his gun
in the chest. I missed something that I wanted to state. That soldier
that hit me with his gun from the effects of that my breast bone here
is smaller and thicker. I ran down along the flat down here towards
the cut bank. As I was nearing the bank it frightened me to hear
some Indian calling my name.

[The following portion of Rough Feather's account is taken directly from the partial transcription of his original unedited testimony as provided by Michael Her Many Horses, Wounded Knee, S.Dak.]

Come, he said, as fast as you can, it is terrible. The man that said that was Ghost Bear who is still living. I believe that that man is the cause of my living today. He said again, there are a lot of women and men laying down over here [and] you had better go over here and lay down, so I went down there where they were laying and stayed there with them. Shortly after that they ceased firing. Then again I heard some one say "all of you that are still alive get up and come on over you will not be molested or shot at any more." I heard them state that but I was still a little bit afraid so I just remained there. The second time he repeated that, well then I got up. They told us to come in a bunch to where they were so in going that way I ran into a man. His face was all covered with blood. The man had a gun and, of course, he looked horrible. So I just stopped and stood there. Then the man came up to me and asked where he was shot. This man said there was 7 men that were shot or wounded. ["]You fellows go and get him some of the survivors['] horses and bring them.["] He told me[,] ["]You go and get one of the wagons that belongs to those that were killed and bring it over.["] So I went up to a wagon that was pretty well loaded, but I took it. He told me again—["]these are some of your relatives laying here, they are not dead yet but you better load them on the wagon.["] I didn't know who they were but I started to lead [*sic*] them on the wagon. I recognized one, an old small lady who was the wife of Big Foot. This man that I told you had his face all bloody that was giving me these instructions I believe that man is still living and I believe his name is Philip Wells, who is called in Indian, the Fox. After loading all those wounded people up I was escorted by the soldiers right down below. Right on the other side of the [modern] store, I met some scouts and they told me that on the ridge on the other side of the store that [there] was a young fellow lying. They asked me to also load him on. He was a cousin of mine. He was shot seven different places. I had no more room so I laid him across my lap and drove the wagon that way to the quarters of the Agent at Pine Ridge. I believe that my living today is caused by Ghost Bear and Philip Wells.

50. Account of Mrs. Rough Feather, recorded by James H. McGregor, 1933

Mrs. Rough Feather gave this account, obtained by James H. McGregor and interpreted by Ben American Horse in 1933, and published in Wounded Knee Massacre from the Viewpoint of the Sioux, *pp. 127–29.*

I started from Cherry Creek with Big Foot's band. We were going to Pine Ridge to visit relatives. I am now [ca. 1934] 73 years old but I remember lots of things that happened. I was a widow and was with my parents. The soldiers met us near Porcupine Butte, and after they talked to Big Foot we went on to Wounded Knee Creek, where the soldiers were camped and we camped there too. The next morning we were getting ready to break camp when the Indian men were ordered by the soldiers to come to the center of the camp and bring all their guns. After they did this, the soldiers came to where the Indian women were and searched the tents and the wagons for arms. They made us give up axes, crowbars, knives, awls, etc. About this time an awful noise was heard and I was paralyzed for a time. Then my head cleared and I saw nearly all the people on the ground bleeding. I could move some now, so I ran to a cut bank and lay down there. I saw some of the other Indians running up the coulee so I ran with them, but the soldiers kept shooting at us and the bullets flew all around us, and a bullet went between my legs but I was not hit one time. My father, my mother, my grandmother, my older brother and my younger brother were all killed. My son who was two years old was shot in the mouth [and] that later caused his death.

We had ten horses, harness, wagon, tent, buffalo robes, and I had a good Navajo blanket. All this property was lost or taken by the Government or other people. I had a hard time in my life and you can see that I am having a hard time now. It is cold weather and this is an old house and I suffer from cold. It is hard to get wood as we have to go a long way to get it.

I was in Montana, where they had a big battle with Custer, and the Indians won and then lots of soldiers came and we escaped to

Canada. I was only about ten years old then and don't know much about that, but remember hearing lots of guns and hearing lots of war-[w]hoops. After a while we went to Standing Rock Reservation for four years, then I went to Rosebud for a short time and then to Cherry Creek, where Big Foot was camping.

51. Account of Edward Owl King, recorded by James H. McGregor, 1933

Edward Owl King gave the following account, interpreted by Henry Standing Bear in 1933, to James H. McGregor, who published it in Wounded Knee Massacre from the Viewpoint of the Sioux, *pp. 116–19.*

In the month of December, when the sun was well up, about eight o'clock in the morning, the Indians were just taking down their tents ready to travel. At that time we were surrounded by both cavalry and infantry. Over in this direction of the flat were white men's camps. The Indian men were called and asked to get together. They took along the grown boys too. At this time, there were soldiers going around among the teepees, picking up and taking up weapons. We were again surrounded by another line of infantry [dismounted cavalrymen], so that there was three lines of soldiers surrounding the men, not the women. How the firing started, I do not remember; all that I remember is that I was running up this ravine trying to get away. There were some ponies, women and children shot down and scattered and while running I stepped on them. This man [i.e., another Lakota member of the survivors convocation] was telling about a bunch of Indians running up the ravine and trying to find refuge in a deep place—I belonged to that crowd. It wasn't a very deep place, and that was where many of the Indians were shot and killed. I was shot too, but did not die. The soldiers came down, one of them, while we were there, so that soldier picked me up too and carried me up on the flat so when the soldiers saw these Indians coming up over the hill they shot and killed some of the Indians, just like this other Indian man was telling. There was an Indian that rescued me by taking me into a deep place. I was laying there all this while until darkness came. I was a boy, my sister and mother were killed. I was the only survivor of the family. I believe the white man broke the law by that act and think we are entitled to claim [compensation] for the killing of my people, as well as property that was destroyed. We made claim for allotment for my relatives that were killed because at that time we were entitled to allotment but we didn't get any.

These people are first time giving the straight story of it. Some years ago [1913] they had a moving picture taken of this Massacre [i.e., the Cody film]. The Indians without thinking went ahead and performed in the ways that were directed by some white people, not truthfully but just the way they wanted it presented in pictures. That tells the wrong story. There may be a book written on that but that would be an error if it was based on that picture. They all agree that the presentation of the Massacre by the picture was all wrong. These old men say that they are giving you the right truth now.

52. Account of Henry Jackson,
recorded by James H. McGregor, 1933

*Henry Jackson, also known as Harry Kills White Man, offered
this account, interpreted by William A. Bergen in 1933, to
James H. McGregor. Michael Her Many Horses of Wounded
Knee, S.Dak, provided this version of his account, which also
appears in* Wounded Knee Massacre from the Viewpoint of
the Sioux, *pp. 119–20.*

I am going to tell what I know from Porcupine [and coming] this way.
I was at the age of 6 then a little fellow when you get very curious and
wanted to see everything and know everything. When we stopped
over here at Porcupine, of course, we were behind and I didn't see
what was going on ahead. After we started to move again and we
came opposite to where they had the cannons and hitched mules to
them, I saw them taking those cannons right behind us. Right down
below here was where the soldiers were camped and the Indians
were strung along on this side and their camp was on the further-
est end. In the evening they didn't permit us to go after water and I
wanted water awful bad. The following morning I heard from where
the soldiers were camped an announcement made that they wanted
all the men to the center. The next I knew was the soldiers entered
our tepees. My sister was sitting down on some quilts and they raised
her up and searched in the quilts and elsewhere for weapons. My father was blind at that time so my brother-in-law, Wears Yellow Robe,
went over to where the men were called and I went along with him.
The next think [*sic*] I saw, after the men were told to sit down, and
after they sat down I noticed the Infantry [dismounted cavalry] were
coming around the other side of our camp and surrounded us. I noticed in looking at them that there was an officer that gave some sort
of a command and they drew their guns in position and I also saw
them load their guns. I was quite afraid of them so I started to go
around away from them. The soldier standing on the end motioned
me back with his hand. So I started back when another officer in
the center said something to this other one and then they told me to
go on so I went on. So from there I went on to my camp where my

mother was loading up the wagon. That is when I heard the volley or crash. My mother and I started to run out away from the camp and she was shot in the head and killed. My sister was on ahead of me and started back and got me and we ran to the head of the ravine that goes west. There was quite a number of them there and they were helping each other out of the embankment and when we got there they helped us out. I have never said anything about this. I didn't like to on account of my mother who was shot right with me and it appears that it just happened this morning; it makes a fellow feel bad.

53. Statement of George Running Hawk, recorded by James H. McGregor, 1933

Michael Her Many Horses of Wounded Knee, S.Dak., provided this early, unedited version of "Statement of George Running Hawk, Wanblee, S.D. 54 years of age," as obtained by James H. McGregor and interpreted by William A. Bergen in 1933. See also *McGregor,* Wounded Knee Massacre from the Viewpoint of the Sioux, *pp. 111–13.*

I am going to just speak with reference to this little place down here. The first thing that I heard, I heard a voice saying all men must come to the center to talk. These are just the very words that I heard. My father, I heard him say that the soldiers were asking for guns and he took his gun and said he was going to give it to him [them]. He took his gun and started for the center and told me to look after the horses. So I caught up the horses and tied them up. Quite a while afterwards, I also went over to where the gathering was. The first thing that I noticed after getting there was the guns that were piled up. What I noticed . . . in this way [was] that some gave up their arms. (Four that I noticed gave up their arms and my father was among them.) I was sitting near a man who told me that just as soon as the talk was over that we were going on to Pine Ridge Agency. Shortly my father came over and told me that I had better return to the camp and look after the horses so I went back to camp again. I went back and saw that the horses were tied alright, nothing wrong with them, so I came on back again. I came back to the same place where I was sitting by the man I spoke of before. Shortly after getting seated I noticed that the Infantry [dismounted cavalry] was circling all around us. This man that I was sitting with told me that he understood that just as soon as we were finished talking here that we are going on but I couldn't understand why these soldiers should come and surround us as they are doing now. Some one ought to mention this or say something about it. After telling me that, I looked around and could see where the women were picking up and getting ready to move. I saw soldiers there throwing out stuff from the wagons and getting all things that could be used as weapons and looking for things. While we were talking, I want to say here, that something similar, only worse [happened]. Yesterday we were out here to visit when it rained and there was a flash of lightning. We all got up and everybody ran for shelter—the flash or crash that we heard here [in 1890] was worse than that. The crash was on and they were fighting. I jumped and looked around—nothing could be distinguished, everything was smokey [*sic*]. I was going to start the other way and this man that I was sitting with was knocked over and shot and I had to jump over him. I became unconscious, lost my mind. First thing I became conscious like, I was down here at the creek. I went down to this ravine here [and] just as I was about to spring over the bank there were two soldiers there. They picked up their guns and instead of firing they snapped their guns at me. I continued on down east of the [later] store. . . . The sorrel horses were stationed there, so I ran on towards the river [Wounded Knee Creek?] then and they were shooting all around me and I saw some of the Indians gathered together there [in the pocket in the ravine?]. When I got up there I noticed a young boy that was wounded. He got up and he said, say partner I wish you would take my leggings off. So I sat down with him and took his leggings off the leg that he was shot. From there we started on the best we could down towards the forks of the river. We came along pretty near to the bank, and there was shooting all around us that . . . had a tendency to weaken our legs because we both fell over again. When we got down in the river he came up the river and I got up on the flat. While I was going through the flat there they shot at me again just as soon as they did the first time I spoke of. They didn't hurt me any where, [and] I had a blanket around me and must have been an awful good target because that was what they were hitting at the most. That is just as much as I remember. Beyond that I don't remember anything.

54. Account of Mrs. Mousseau, recorded by James H. McGregor, 1933

Mary Mousseau (Mousseaux) (Medicine Woman), who was a young girl in 1890, gave this account, as obtained by James H. McGregor and interpreted by William A. Bergen, ca. 1933. It was published in McGregor, Wounded Knee Massacre from the Viewpoint of the Sioux, *pp. 113–14. For more on Mousseau, see entry 38 herein.*

These [other Lakota] people have told the whole history of the event. The only thing I can add to that is that I was shot, and the white men were so thick here like a whole pile of maggots. One white man with a Roman nose seemed to have a whole lot to do with me. Every now and then he felt me around the waist to see if I had any knives. I threw my blanket back and showed them I didn't have anything. They took everything away from us that had a sharp point, any metal that had a sharp point, then fired on us. I had my brother with me. The smoke [from the guns] was awful thick. We were making our getaway. We had a child with us. The child was dead; my mother was packing it although it was dead. Right below here was where I was shot, right on this little bench here. All of those are my relatives, my nephews and I had an uncle here. All up and down here it looked as though something was sacked up and spread all over. There was some smoke and all of the women were headed down toward the store. My right arm was broken and I can just use my left hand now. I hardly remember anything. I was quite excited. The soldiers followed us up and kept firing. My mother and I kept going until we got to the spot these people had referred to, the end of the ravine; when we got there we were charged by the Army, they came in two squads.

After my mother and I passed that place, here these men were surrounded, [and] if we had remained there we probably would have been killed. I just went over these ridges. My arm was not cared for, I had nothing to eat, it was bleeding but I just kept on moving. We followed on down to Wounded Knee Creek. . . . There was quite a snow storm that night; we didn't have any bedding. There was a shack on the old mail route over here that time, that is where we went. We stayed there two days. We didn't have anything to eat or drink and we were found in that condition by the Indian Scouts and were taken to the Agency.

55. Statement of Bertha Kills Close to Lodge, recorded by James H. McGregor, 1933

Michael Her Many Horses of Wounded Knee, S.Dak., provided this early unedited version of "Statement of Bertha Kills Close to Lodge," as obtained by James H. McGregor and interpreted by William A. Bergen in 1933. See also *McGregor,* Wounded Knee Massacre from the Viewpoint of the Sioux, *pp. 114–16.*

I was 17 years old at the time of the Massacre and I was a member of the Big Foot band that was en route here. The object of coming over here was to visit relatives and to make a general visit and that is all I know anything about. I was not interested in anything else. I came over here for that purpose. Arriving here I saw the soldiers were camped on east and we were camped on the west side below from here. The following morning some men announced to break camp. In the meantime while they were calling they were issuing hardtack and we were packing up ready to travel. I was standing against the wagon looking this way when the men were called to the center. They had no arms with them. I noticed that all the men gathered together in the center. I also noticed that they [the soldiers] were all along this ridge . . . and right in here some were loading two guns. I also noticed some soldiers going from here down in that direction did have a few guns. Seems as though they were taking guns on down to the center. They also came over to where I was standing and my father had a gun and they took that, came along on the edge of camp over to where they were stacking the arms. Shortly after that there was some more soldiers came over to where I was and they searched our wagon, throwing down our dishes [and] what we had packaged in the wagon and took our knives, axes and awls and anything that could be used for a weapon. Shortly after that they left starting this way. The children dropped some of the hard-tack and I stooped over to pluck some up and just about that time, what appeared to me was a severe hail stone [hailstorm?] just rattled right under the wagon. Right after that I started in a Southeastern direction and as I went on I could see men that were shot down by the soldiers but the smoke got so severe I couldn't see anything so I went on a little way and started in a northern direction. We started and got to this ravine. There [were] my mother and I and three aunts and some of the children, who were small at that time. We got to the head of the ravine. While we are lying there, there was an Indian scout above us. I had a younger sister pretty seriously wounded, got to asking for water. Just about that time the scout went and got some water for my sister and my mother asked him [who] he was and he said he was Feather On Head. The scout then came over and of course we were having trouble with my wounded sister. I had another little sister that had gotten away from us in this affairs [*sic*] and she was wounded in the leg and crying. One of my aunts, this is the mother of James Big Hawk, cried and said that all her sons were killed and she didn't care to live. So we took one of the children and started back this way. There was some firing over there. One of my aunts ran back to where she was and found out they had shot and killed her. It was reported that there was some little girl her hands were all bloody. I went over there and it was my sister and her mother who was pregnant at that time. I found there [that] she was killed. I was wounded but able to go to where they were. My sister was near death and I stayed with her. When she died I straightened her out, laid her out the best way I could. We were all brought up here, loaded in the wagons in bad condition and were taken to the Agency. That is all I am going to say.

56. Account of John Little Finger, recorded by James H. McGregor, 1933

John Little Finger offered this account, obtained by James H. McGregor and interpreted by Henry Standing Bear, in 1933. It was published in McGregor, Wounded Knee Massacre from the Viewpoint of the Sioux, *pp. 120–22.*

The soldiers after surrounding us they lined the Indians up and took their weapons away from them and took them to a distance and lay them there, so they were without any arms. There was a soldier at the same time going around the camp outside where the women folks were and taking from them weapons, butcher knives, and anything that could be used as weapons, and put them in one place. Just about the taking knives and other things away from the women time the soldiers that were going around these camps folks [*sic*], I noticed that a line of infantry was standing nearby and had been commanded to load their guns and at that moment they gave us to believe that they were going to do some shooting, so at that time this infantry [dismounted cavalry] began loading their guns I saw that there seems to commence some trouble. I stepped out and then I struck through their lines to try to get away. Just as I was working from this line, that moment, I heard a white man's voice at the other end, sound just like somebody calling like, "hey." When that sound was made, it was about the same time that the report of the guns came in one sound. The soldiers commenced to shoot at that moment. When the soldiers started to shoot I ran to get away and before I could get to the deep place there was already some Indians shot and killed. A lot of them [were] shot down and I stepped on some of them already shot down, but I kept on going until I reached the cannon [canyon] this side of the [later] store. When I reached the ravine, of course, there was a lot of Indians following up the ravine and I was with them, and on each side of this ravine soldiers were shooting down on us until we got so far we couldn't go any further as a line of soldiers got in front of us so we took refuge in a big ravine. In this ravine where we took refuge, most of them were women and children and, of course, defenseless and helpless; above them the soldiers just got near them and shot these people down. This was kept up until I heard a voice, calling from some place in a very far distance, saying that these Indians were to come out of there because fighting is not to be continued, so some of these, not yet killed, left the big ravine of refuge and they went up on the flat, but I was not with them, because I was shot through in two places, one through my leg and my foot, so I crawled along until I got over where those that were ahead of me sat in a circle up there and the soldiers were surrounding them. I got up on the flat, a little distance from them and they started to shoot them again and killing them, [and] of course, those that were not shot down tried to get away. At the moment there was a number of old men, Indians, came up over the hill and they were on horseback and had guns, but was some distance from us but when the soldiers saw them they took on a run, so that it shows that when the soldiers that were killing us, saw that the Indians were our friends and that they might make a charge on them they lost their bravery and started to run. After the soldiers left that place, these Indians on horseback came down to the place where I was and they helped me on a pony and they took me over to the Agency, and this is my own experience. This is what I remember.

57. Account of Peter Stand, recorded by James H. McGregor, 1933

Peter Stand gave this account, interpreted by William A. Bergen, to James H. McGregor in 1933, who published it in Wounded Knee Massacre from the Viewpoint of the Sioux, *pp. 123–25.*

I was among Big Foot's band en route here at that time. If this was a nice summer day we could point out the various places. Right at the forks of the two creeks down here, we were made to camp and on this side of there and on the flat adjoining was where the soldiers were camping. That evening we were given rations such as crackers, coffee, sugar, etc. Soon after dusk, it was quite dark, nearly bedtime when we heard a sort of metallic sound as though soldiers were moving and came to where the men were camping and about that time we heard some Indians right across from us talking. The women went after water, came back and reported that the infantry [*sic*] and the cavalry had surrounded us. We didn't know what to think, after hearing all of that. We were kind of a little bit afraid and it bothered us a little through the night until morning. I want to state that there was a tent erected right near the soldiers for Big Foot, who was troubled with a hemorrhage at that time.

The next morning, from this tent, someone announced that all men should come to that spot to talk with the officer. This announcer was stating that the large boys were to come also so we all went. We boys were placed just back of the men, out towards the creek out here to one side right in a body. About that time there was about six soldiers that came to where the men were and commenced to search them, threw their blankets back and searched them, also searched them through the legs. When they were through with them they also went over to where the women were packing up to move. I saw the soldiers come to surround us, two lines of infantry [dismounted cavalry], two lines of cavalry [mounted soldiers] around us. As I stated there was some commotion, I raised my arm up and they fired the volley. As the volley was flying into us, we couldn't see anything—everything was smoking from then on; this valley was just covered with smoke so I didn't see anything. Right after the volley was fired,

I heard somebody bellow in Indian for them to throw themselves flat on the ground so I did as he announced.

Later I started for our camp but the smoke was so thick I couldn't see anything, [and] the first thing I knew someone hit me, on my right side, that is I ran into someone. I straightened up and started again, and ran into somebody's leg again but didn't fall that time. I kept running until I got where the camp was. I noticed there was one of the horses [that] was shot down and the other was still alive but all tangled up so I went on by the wagon box and on up the hill [and] laid flat on my back. From where I laid, I could see men, women and children coming. As I looked over that way I could see them shot down one after another. We were not harmed much in there because we dug a trench. There were women that dug in there, most of them with their hands. I got there too and just stayed there all day. There was lots of women and children and there was about sixty of us in this trench. Most of them were killed but four of us men [and] about seven women[,] and the rest were all killed. That evening after they had ceased firing we started up that creek on foot. We saw our relatives lying dead all around there. We looked them over as we went. We got up to these pines at the head of this ravine.

58. Partial Story of Peter Stand, recorded by James H. McGregor, 1933

*Michael Her Many Horses of Wounded Knee, S.Dak., provided
this early, unedited version of the partial "Story of Peter Stand
(Oglala, S.D.)," obtained by James H. McGregor and interpreted
by William A. Bergen in 1933.* See also *McGregor,* Wounded Knee
Massacre from the Viewpoint of the Sioux, *pp. 123–25.*

Q. Could anyone remember who it was that gave the command [to
throw themselves on the ground when the initial shooting erupted]?

A. No, I do not know who it was, just heard the voice. So then
I started for our camps but as I stated, the smoke was so thick I
couldn't see anything, the first think [thing] I knew some one hit
me, on my right side, that is I ran into some one. I straightened up
and started to run again, then we heard another crash. He fell and
I fell right near him, then I got up and started again, and ran into
somebody's leg again but I didn't fall at that time. I kept running
until I got to where the camps were. The smoke was so dense I didn't
know when I got to the pack so I felt all around down into the pack.
As Afraid of Hawk told you, there was a wagon box tipped over; I
went by that, [and] there was about six young men behind that and
I noticed there was one of the horses was shot down and the other
was still alive but all tangled up so I went on by the wagon box and
on up the hill and laid flat on my back. From where I laid,. . . I could
see men, women and children were coming. As I looked over that
way I could see them shot down one after another. You go up and
you will find that it is not very high[,] but down in that ravine the
men, women and children were coming, they were right behind them
surround[ing] them and firing. Right straight in this direction from
the [later-built trader's] store, along that valley, there was a wash-out
all along, about up to my waist, and as they reached that they all laid
in that wash-out all along [where] they were shot or killed right in
the wash-out. On the side of the store at that time there was kind of
a big bank and all those that got in there used what knives they had
in digging a sort of a trench and got behind that, so that the soldiers
were firing on all sides. We were not harmed much in there because

we dug a trench. There were women that dug in there, most of them with their hands. I got there to[o] and just stayed there all day. There was lots of women and children and, as this other man said [to] Blue Arm, there was about 60 of us in this trench. Most of them were killcd but [for] four of us men, [and] about seven women and the rest were all killed. That evening after they had ceased firing we started up that creek a foot [afoot]. We saw them lying dead all around there. Looked them over as we went. We got up to these pines at the head of this ravine. That is as much as I am going to tell.

59. Story by Donald Blue Hair,
recorded by James H. McGregor, 1933

*The "Story by Donald Blue Hair (Cheyenne [River] Agency),"
obtained by James H. McGregor and interpreted by William A.
Bergen in 1933, appears here in an unedited format provided
by Michael Her Many Horses, Wounded Knee, S.Dak.* See also
McGregor, Wounded Knee Massacre from the Viewpoint of the
Sioux, *p. 125.*

I am going to state here what I came for. Right down here, right below
where you see this land, is where we, the Indians, were camped. I was
with Big Foot's band. The morning after we made our camp there,
all the men were requested to come to the center, then they began to
search for arms, throwing our blankets back, and searching us. They
took everything, any kind of a knife, these beading awls. After taking
everything away from us that had a sharp point[,] all that could be
used as a weapon, we were all bunched up. They all stood around us
with their guns in this position (stock under their arms). Right on
top of this hill, the calvalry [*sic*] surrounded the entire camp. The infantry [dismounted cavalry] surrounded us after placing us together.
After these soldiers that were searching for arms returned, they shot
the volley into us. At that time they were using black powder and the
smoke was like a fog. I didn't know who I was running to or what assistance I would get. I notice some of the people get up and running
around all over. I didn't know where they were running to but they
were all running towards the store [i.e., the general spot where the
later modern trading store was located along the south edge of the
big ravine] or up the ravine. From the first volley that was shot into
us, they just continued to shoot. I took a run around this little ridge
over here then circled around and came back down into the ravine.
That is where I stayed or laid all day long. There were others with me.
That is all that I want to say.

60. Account of Frank Sits Poor, recorded by James H. McGregor, 1933

Frank Sits Poor offered this account, interpreted by Henry Standing Bear, to James H. McGregor in 1933. It was published in McGregor, Wounded Knee Massacre from the Viewpoint of the Sioux, *p. 129.*

I was just a child when our band was in the Massacre but I remember very little about it. I remember that I was with Big Foot's band en route here and that we camped here and the following day we had the Massacre. As I remember it, I was sitting in a teepee and all at once it sounded to me like a crash of lightning as though wire was falling over the teepee and I do not remember just how I came out of the teepee, but I had noticed that there was a soldier with a gun on his shoulder. I went close to him and he pointed the gun at me. I couldn't say whether he shot at me or didn't but I heard the report of a gun. As I started up this hill I overtook an old woman that was ahead of me. As I went past her she got hold of my hand but I jerked away from her and went right on past her.

---

61. Statement of White Lance,
recorded by James H. McGregor, 1933

*White Lance, a Horn Cloud family member and a brother of
Dewey Beard, provided this account, obtained by James H.
McGregor and interpreted by William A. Bergen, in 1933. At
the time, White Lance resided in Kyle, South Dakota and was
sixty-four years old. Michael Her Many Horses of Wounded
Knee, S.Dak., provided this early, unedited version.* See also
the published version in McGregor, Wounded Knee Massacre
from the Viewpoint of the Sioux, *pp. 118–19.*

In listening to all the statements made here in the past two days, I
find out that they were telling actual facts. I am not going to tell anything different from what they were telling. Practically on the same
line. I am going to tell such events as I saw. We met the soldiers on
the other side of Porcupine Butte near the home of a man. In coming
towards the soldiers we noticed they had two cannons erected and
their guns in position to fire. We were not on the war path, had no
intentions of it, but we came right up to where they stood. We had
along with us Chief Big Foot who was very sick. They placed him
in a buggy or wagon and came on with him [to the soldier camp at
Wounded Knee Creek]. Right down below here is where we camped
and to the left of us is where the soldiers were camped. The following
morning all the men were called and gathered so I came to where
they were gathered. They called for guns and arms so all of us gave
the guns and they were stacked up in the center. It was understood
that just as soon as all the guns were stacked in the center we were to
continue on to Pine Ridge Agency. Big Foot was placed right in the
doorway of the tent and I stood right to his left side. I could see that
there was commotion among the soldiers and I noticed on looking
back they had their guns in position ready to fire. There were two
officers in the center; the one that was standing to the left gave a
command in a loud voice then we couldn't see anything for smoke.
The smoke was so dense I couldn't see anything so I didn't make a
move [—] just stood there. When it cleared up a little I was going to
start to go away when I looked to my right side. I saw Big Foot lying

down with blood on his forehead and his head kinda to the right side. I never heard that they take advantage of a sick man. That is the first time I ever saw that happen. I went a little ways then. I was knocked down, [and] I was unconscious for a little while. I was shot then and wounded and I went to this little wide cut bank and there I found that we were surrounded by the Soldiers. We were surrounded by the soldiers and some [of us were] already wounded, some dead, but they continued to fire on us. There is no reason for shooting at us twice. They had already shot at us. I stayed there all day with these young fellows, boys then, and since then I have been unable to use my left [arm] but I struggle along. That is as much as I know to tell.

Q. Were the cannons stationed in the various places when you came, or were they placed there after you camped?

A. The cannons that I saw placed here were those that they un-packed and place[d] right up here on the edge. Do not recall of seeing any cannons placed in position when we arrived.

I want to say, I am not much of a story teller, but this I desire to say that prior to this time, there has never been an Agent that has taken the interest in us as the present Agent [James McGregor] has done and we appreciate what he has done for us and we all thank him for it. I also desire to say what he has done for us is the same as wiping away our tears. I want all the Survivors to always remember this man and what he has done for us. I want to thank him very sincerely for all of us. That is what I want to say about our appreciation.

We are in hopes that he will be able to assist us some way or another with a claim some time that we will make and for which we will be grateful for.

White Lance.

62. Statement of James High Hawk, recorded by James H. McGregor, 1933

Michael Her Many Horses of Wounded Knee, S.Dak., provided this unedited version of the "Statement of James High Hawk," obtained by James H. McGregor and interpreted by William A. Bergen in 1933. See also *McGregor,* Wounded Knee Massacre from the Viewpoint of the Sioux, *pp. 135–36.*

My cousin just narrated, or made a statement [of] what she knew and in that she stated that there were some small children and I probably was one of them that she spoke of. I had a little brother that was nursing then, an infant, and one brother a little bit large[r] and I was a little bit larger than he. He was about four years old at the time. The only thing that I want to narrate here, is that I personally was wounded twice, shot twice, had two wounds. My mother was wounded as she narrated but they again came and shot her and also my infant brother. My brother lived through his wounds but he was bothered a good deal from the effects of the wound and later died. I have an older brother also that was in the Massacre. He is not here but he took me towards this ravine where he claims some of the Indians were in hiding from the bloodthirsty soldiers . . . and we probably went to one of the places where it was narrated they were in hiding.

The white people say the Indians are treacherous, but we are not[.] We love our families and we do not bother the white people, but they came here, killed us—women and children, [and] we have the wounds to prove what they done. I just wish to say on account of that—Did not our forefathers and the U.S. lay that most sacred treaty on April 29, 1868 wherein both parties agreed to cease from all war-fare—to be accurate about it, it is the Article One of that Treaty [that] says—from this day forth in all wars between the parties to this agreement shall forever cease. This Massacre is absolutely a grave injustice and disgraceful act committed against Big Foot's band by the United States Army. It is the most shameful, cowardly and treacherous killing ever staged by [the] United States Government. In my opinion, it is no warfare but a coldblooded murder. The crime, evil and inexcusable action which the defendant cannot find just excuse to justify their action.

63. Account of Mrs. Alice Dog Arm (formerly Alice Ghost Horse), recorded by James H. McGregor, 1933

Mrs. Alice Dog Arm or Kills Plenty (formerly Alice Ghost Horse, who left another account, q.v., above) gave the following account to James H. McGregor in 1933. It was published in McGregor, Wounded Knee Massacre from the Viewpoint of the Sioux, *pp. 122–23.*

We were taken to the soldiers['] camp on Wounded Knee and we got there about the time the sun went down [over] the hill in the West. We got some food from the soldiers and after eating it we finished making our camp for the night. We were strictly guarded by the soldiers all through the night.

We arose early the next morning to make further movement. While we were doing this they took all the guns away from us and then took things from our tents and bed rolls.

I saw a soldier on a bay horse riding towards us and soon after that they began to shoot us. Bullets came from all directions already killing many women, children and men. I ran and hid in a ditch with my mother and two brothers. My father came and took my older brother to care for him. Soon he came back and said that they had killed my brother. Then my mother cried and as she wanted us all to be together and die together so my father took us to a safer hiding place and then he left us and soon a man named Air Pipe came and told us that my father had been killed.

We stayed there all morning till the afternoon and when it got dark we moved down the creek to an empty shack and stayed there all night. In that house was Philip Black Moon and his mother. Philip is living yet at Cherry Creek.

The next morning we left this cabin and went on down the creek and left some of the wounded people there. We didn't have any food since the day of the Massacre.

64. Account of Louise Weasel Bear, recorded by James H. McGregor, ca. 1933

Louise Weasel Bear's account, obtained by James H. McGregor circa 1933, was published in McGregor, Wounded Knee Massacre from the Viewpoint of the Sioux, *p. 111.*

You can see me, I am sick and I hurt every day. The soldiers nearly kill me. I never done them any harm or any other white man. That Massacre was very wrong to the Indians and Big Foot didn't want to fight the soldiers. He always had a white flag so that they would know he was for peace and for the treaty.

The soldiers did not fire in our camp till the guns were put down at Big Foot's tepee. Before they shot us some of them came to our tents where there were just women and they were not nice men. They searched our tents and wagons and the women. They took our knives and axes. After this they killed us and our children. We tried to run but they shot us like we were a buffalo. I know there are some good white people, but the soldiers must be mean to shoot children and women. Indian soldiers would not do that to white children.

65. Public document statement
of Annie Iron Lavatta, 1934

*Annie Iron Lavatta (Hakiktawin), a Wounded Knee survivor
who lived on the Standing Rock reservation, made the following
statement in a public document from 1934. It was published in
McGregor,* Wounded Knee Massacre from the Viewpoint of the
Sioux, *p. 140.*

AFFIDAVIT

STATE OF SOUTH DAKOTA,

CORSON COUNTY;

ss.

Before me, E.Y. Berry, a Notary Public, in and for the county and
State aforesaid, personally appeared Annie Iron Lavatta, or Hakiktawin, who, being first duly sworn (affirmed), deposes and says that
on or about the 27th day of December, 1890, after sun rise, the U.S.
Army came and called all the men folks to the front and after the
men came to the front some of the U.S. Soldiers went and searched
the tepees, and take [took] what weapons such as guns, ammunitions
[*sic*], even awls, needles, knives, and when they were through searching the tepees, all the weapons were taken to where the men folks
were and set it in the center of the circle and first thing I remember
the U.S. Army started to shoot into the men folks when they were all
disarmed of their weapons, and most of them were killed and those
[who] were not killed were wounded[,] even the women, and children, were killed and wounded.

I, Annie Iron Lavatta, or Hakiktawin, I was running away from the
place and followed those [who] were running away, with my grandfather, and grandmother, and brother, and [they] were killed as we
crossed the ravine or creek, going up the grade, and then I was shot
on the right hip clear through and on my right wrist where I did not
go any further as I was not able to walk, and after the soldier picked
me up where a little girl came to me and crawled into the blanket.

(Signed)

ANNIE IRON LAVATTA, HAKIKTAWIN.

Subscribed and sworn to before me this 20th day of
January, 1934.

E.Y. BERRY

Notary Public in and for the County of Corson; and State of
South Dakota.

My commission expires November 25, 1935.

66. Program, Wounded Knee Survivors Association, 1935

The following is a program from a meeting of the Wounded Knee Survivors Association in 1935. Wounded Knee Survivors Association Program, 1935 Pine Ridge File No. 160, Box 60, Central Classified Files, 1907–1939, Records of the Bureau of Indian Affairs, RG 75, NA, Washington, D.C.

PROGRAM
Survivors of the Wounded Knee Massacre
Wounded Knee, South Dakota
June 19[,] June 20[,] and June 21[,] 1935
June 19[,] 1935

Evening Prayer	Amos Fast Horse
Address of Welcome	Richard A.O. Hawk
Address of Response	Jack Bull Eagle
Address to Comrades	James High Hawk

June 20, 1935
Business Meeting
From 8 A.M. to 5 P.M.

James Pipe on Head	Presiding
Speech	Supt. James H. McGregor

June 21, 1935

9:00 A.M.	Decorate Graves
Prayer and Instructions	Clayton High Wolf
The Nature of Memorial	Leo C. Cunningham, S. J.
Graves of the Departed	Grant H.W. Man

Approved:	Committee:
James Pipe on Head, President	Richard A.O. Hawk
Leo Iron Hawk, Secretary	Charles Blind Man
Jackson He Crow, Treasurer	Henry Jackson
	White Lance
	George Running Hawk

Wounded Knee Survivors Association

67. "Claim of Survivors," as completed by Mrs. Nellie Knife (ca. January 1937)

Mrs. Nellie Knife, age sixty-seven years, completed the following "Claim of Survivors" (undated, ca. January 1937). Wounded Knee Files, Francis H. Case Papers, George and Eleanor McGovern Library, Dakota Wesleyan University, Mitchell, S.Dak.

Q. What claim do you have:

A. I claim that I am a survivor from the massacre.

Q. Were you wounded or injured?

A. No, I wasn't but the gun smoke got in my lungs, and [I] also swallowed dead person's blood and my health has not been good since.

Q. Did the soldiers intend to shoot or kill you?

A. Yes.

Q. How old were you at that time?

A. I was going on 20 yrs.

Q. Do you have any witnesses to prove that you are a survivor from the massacre?

A. Yes.

Q. Who are they?

A. John Did Not Go Home and Henry Grouse Running.

Plaintiff—Mrs. Nellie Knife   Mrs. Knife's mark. [thumbprint]
Address—Cherry Creek, So. Dak.

Name—John Did Not Go Home Age 78 yrs   John's mark. [thumbprint]
Address—Cherry Creek, So. Dak.

Name—Henry Grouse Running Age 72 yrs
Address—Cherry Creek, So. Dak.
[Signed] Henry Grouse Running

Witnesses to thumb mark:
Anna Hollow Horn
Lydia Hollow Horn

68. Two letters giving names of Lakota attendees who served in the hospital at Holy Cross Chapel, Pine Ridge Agency, 1937 and 1940

The following two letters to United States Representative Francis H. Case of South Dakota, in reference to his pending and ultimately unsuccessful legislation to compensate Lakota survivors for losses sustained at Wounded Knee, give the names of Lakota attendees who served in an improvised hospital in the Holy Cross Episcopal Church Chapel at Pine Ridge Agency. Wounded Knee Files, Case Papers, McGovern Library.

Red Shirt Table
Buffalo Gap, S. Dakota
Nov. 30, 1937
Hon. Mr. Case
Washington, D.C.
Friend:
I am sending in the list of names that [were] taking care of the wounded from the Wounded Knee massacre.

Henry Red Shirt	(Deceased)	
Silas Fills Pipe	(living)	Buffalo Gap, S. Dak.
Thom S[.] Tyon	Living	Oglala, S. Dak.
Paul Eagle Bull	"	Little Eagle, S. Dak.
John J. Bissonet	"	Pine Ridge, S. Dak.
Mrs. Red Rock	Deceased	
Mrs. Blunt Horn	Living	Wounded Knee, S. Dak.
Mrs. Eliza Last Horse	"	Kyle, S. Dak.
Mrs. Mary Fire Thunder	"	Hisle, S. Dak.

There are some work a day or two but this work steady day and
    nights taking turns in nights for about two months.
If you want to hear some more I'll be glad to tell you.
From Charles Red Shirt
Buffalo Gap, S. Dakota
Route R. S. T.
***

Busby, Mont.,
June 6, 1940
Mr. Francis Case
Member of Congress,
2nd Dist., So. Dak.
Hon. Mr. Case:

. . . I was appointed by the Supt. at Pine Ridge, after the battle to help care for the Wounded Indians. But I received no remuneration for this service.

My maiden name was Mary Bissonette, I worked for three months caring for the wounded Indians. About two years ago, Thomas White-Cow-Killer, enquired and found out the names of all of us women who served as nurse-helpers after the Massacre, and he made an effort to get remuneration for us, through Congress. No doubt you are familiar with this matter.

I would be pleased if you would write to me what has been done with regard to this matter. We had heard that favorable action was expected on it, and so I am anxious to learn the truth regarding the matter. . . .

Respectfully yours,
(Signed)
Mrs. Mary Fire Thunder

69. Testimony of James Pipe on Head, Dewey Beard, and James Grass, in extracts from hearings on H.R. 2535, House of Representatives, 1938

James Pipe On Head, Dewey Beard (Iron Hail), and James Grass gave the following testimony, as translated by Charles White Wolf, in extracts from U.S., To Liquidate the Liability of the United States for the Massacre of Sioux Indian Men, Women, and Children at Wounded Knee on December 29, 1890: Hearings on H.R. 2535, Before the Subcommittee on Indian Affairs, 75th Cong., 3d sess., 1938, pp. 16–24.

STATEMENT OF [SURVIVOR] JAMES PIPE-ON-HEAD (interpreted by Charles White Wolf)

Mr. PIPE-ON-HEAD. The reason why I come here, I figure you people are my friends, and I would like to prove to you that what I have seen with my own eyes I give you this morning.

I do not come here to condemn anybody, but I come here for the good of my people.

When Big Foot's band was conquered, and when they met the troops, they immediately stuck up the white flag, which meant peace.

The battle was on the 28th [*sic*] day of December. So we traveled with the soldiers and came to their encampment, and at that time Chief Big Foot was very sick. We came back to the point where the soldiers were camped.

On morning of the 29th day of December—it was in the morning—the Camp Crier announced to all men to come to the center of the camp. So all men in this camp went to the center and to the place where they asked them, and they all sat down. It was announced that this was to have a meeting, and after the meeting they were to move on to the agency, which I think would have been Pine Ridge Agency; and he said, "The Government says to turn in your firearms." So we did[.] They went out to the camps [—American Indian camp] and picked up all rifles. The soldiers went out to the camps and raided the wagons; they took axes, knives, and awls, and even the women's pins on their sides; they took them away from them. When it was all done, it was gathered up and piled up.

While they were piling up their guns, and the men were all sitting in the center, surrounded by soldiers, two rows of soldiers formed circle to the east, with their guns all ready. They were on a hill. Not far from there there was a bunch of soldiers, with two cannons. Away back over here . . . women and all helpless people and children of all sorts were standing, and behind them were troops with Indian scouts.

Mr. FRANCIS H. CASE. Mr. Chairman, I would like to interrupt to ask a few questions.

Mr. MURDOCK. Certainly.

Mr. FRANCIS H. CASE. Jim, what is this painting [exhibiting picture]?

Mr. PIPE-ON-HEAD. That is a reproduction of the massacre. That shows a reproduction of the massacre.

Mr. FRANCIS H. CASE. How was this made?

Mr. PIPE-ON-HEAD. This picture was made by me and a brother of mine. He was an old man at that time, and he knew [we] were coming for this, so we thought we would have some kind of proof to show just how and where that happened.

Mr. FRANCIS H. CASE. How long after the battle was this picture drawn?

Mr. PIPE-ON-HEAD. In 1933, when we formed what they call the Survivors' Association; that is when they started to plan on this picture.

Mr. FRANCIS H. CASE. And this was drawn from your memory of the battle at that time?

Mr. PIPE-ON-HEAD. Yes; this was drawn from the memories, as I saw it on that day.

Mr. FRANCIS H. CASE. Mr. Chairman, I would like to call the attention of the committee to the Fourteenth Annual Report of the Bureau of Ethnology of the Smithsonian Institution, made by J. W. Powell, Director, part II, published in 1893. This contains the report by James Mooney on the "Ghost Dance Religion of the Sioux," and tells the story of Wounded Knee. Between pages 868 and 869, is a map prepared by Lt. J. Q. Donaldson, of the Seventh United States Cavalry, which gives the position of the troops and the position of the Indians, the position of the camps, and the terrain, as made by Lieutenant Donaldson at the time. I would like to call the attention of the committee to the fact that the placing of the tents and the placing of the troops and of the Indians in the map corresponds very closely to that of the painting. I think that is important, not only because it supports Pipe-on-Head, but because, as the story develops you will see from the picture that the position of the troops was such that when the firing started by the troops, part of the troops themselves were in the line of fire.

Thus in firing on the disarmed Indians and the women and children, who were in the center, as they started to scatter and flee, the soldiers also fired on their own troops. The statement of General Miles which is incorporated in the report of the War Department calls attention to that fact—that the troops themselves were in the line of their own fire. His words are:

Thirdly, an examination of the accompanying map and testimony shows conclusively that at the beginning of the outbreak not a single company of the troops was so disposed as to deliver its fire upon the warriors without endangering the lives of some of their own comrades.

Mr. MURDOCK. May I ask what this represents here [indicating on painting]?

Mr. RALPH H. CASE. That is a battery of gattling [*sic*] guns.

Mr. MURDOCK. These troops were then placed on the brow of a hill, as the witness said a moment ago.

Mr. WHITE WOLF. He wants to prove to you gentlemen that this is how the condition looked after they wiped us out.

Mr. FRANCIS H. CASE. Were the tents set on fire?

Mr. PIPE-ON-HEAD. It was reported that after the massacre was all over with, and at evening, there was parties come through there and burned up the tents and all their belongings.

Mr. FRANCIS H. CASE. Was this a clear day?

Mr. PIPE-ON-HEAD. This picture was the day after this occurred.

Mr. FRANCIS H. CASE. Was it a clear day—the day of the massacre?

Mr. PIPE-ON-HEAD. Yes, sir; it was a clear day.

Mr. FRANCIS H. CASE. Did any storm develop the night following the massacre?

Mr. PIPE-ON-HEAD. After the massacre cleared over, they had a storm that night—a snowstorm.

Mr. FRANCIS H. CASE. That is all, Mr. Chairman. I wanted him to identify his pictures, because I thought it would be easier for the committee to follow him.

Mr. MURDOCK. The witness may continue with his statement, if he cares to proceed further.

Mr. PIPE-ON-HEAD. The soldiers surrounded us with their guns all ready, and I heard something just about that time, and somebody yelled out very loud. The minute that fellow hollered, it went like that [witness claps his hands]; the rifles all fired at the same time. Immediately after the firing the smoke got very thick, and right behind me I could see the muzzle of a gun, and at the same time I saw Big Foot, my grandfather, the first man to be shot.

Immediately after the firing I had some powder burns in my eyes, so I worked my way through the smoke, and right in front of me I saw an old woman who had already been killed; and as I passed that old woman I ran into a dead horse. I passed there and I ran across a woman who had a girl about 1 year old on her back. This little girl had her head blown off. The party I can identify as the daughter of a man by the name of Young Bear. She took the child off a little ways and laid it down on the prairie, and she went right on.

After they had stuck up a flag of truce, or peace, or what you call it, the people shed their blood. It was a case of slaughtering a bunch of defenseless mothers and some babies in the cradle; and one of the saddest parts was a little boy whose mother was killed and lying there, and the little boy didn't know that his mother was dead, and he was nursing on his mother's breast. That boy is now living, and his name is Black Fox. He is living in Rapid City at the present time.

That is not the only case, but there were many cases. There was one case of a mother carrying her child on her back, and they put a bullet right through the both of them. That was the son of a man by the name of High Hawk.

After they ceased firing, there were some that were lying on, probably, this canyon [indicating], and some were lying on the field wounded. The soldiers came up there and told them to get up, that it was all over. Some of them were so helpless, wounded awfully bad, that they could not get up, and the soldiers came up and shot them all over again.

So after that, up by the end of the canyon, there was a bunch of them taking refuge there, and the soldiers came up and told them it was all over and to get up, and when they came up they sat down on the hill and the soldiers surrounded them again. They thought it was all over with, and they sat on top of the hill, in good spirit, and the soldiers surrounded them and shot them down again.

Mr. MURDOCK. May I ask at that point: Were these warriors or men and women together?

Mr. WHITE WOLF. He asks what people are you referring to, Mr. Murdock.

Mr. MURDOCK. Those that came out of their hiding and were on the brow of the hill.

Mr. PIPE-ON-HEAD. A few men and one woman.

Mr. FRANCIS H. CASE. At that point, Mr. Chairman, may I call attention to the report of the Secretary of the Interior which quotes this from the narrative of General Miles:

Not only the warriors, but the sick chief, Big Foot, and a large number of women and children who tried to escape by running and scattering over the prairie, were hunted down and killed.

The official reports make the number killed 90 warriors and approximately 200 women and children.

Mr. BARTON. Major, you emphasized the fact that it was the Seventh Cavalry that was in the Custer Massacre?

Mr. RALPH H. CASE. I did.

Mr. BARTON. And that the Seventh Cavalry engaged in the Wounded Knee battle was the same Seventh Cavalry. Did you mean to intimate that there was a spirit of revenge that had been passed down in that outfit?

Mr. RALPH H. CASE. I did mean to intimate that; and I will show you, Congressman, that the commanding officer was Major Whitside. At the end of the late war I served under his son, who was then Lt. Col. Warren W. Whitside, and while this is not good evidence, nevertheless I will say for the record that Colonel Whitside told me that the Seventh Cavalry went to Pine Ridge with full intent of getting even for the loss of Custer at Little Big Horn 14 years before. That is not good evidence, but it is what a son of the man who was in command told me.

Mr. FRANCIS H. CASE. Of course, Mr. Chairman, a point I would like to keep clear is that the Seventh Cavalry under Custer at the Little Big Horn in 1876 was a military expedition invading Indian territory; while at Wounded Knee in 1890, Indians moving with their families under a flag of truce were in the process of surrendering to the military, and unarmed women and children were pursued and shot down without a chance to defend themselves. A desire to even scores may explain but does not justify what happened.

Mr. MURDOCK. I would like to ask the witness one more question. Your picture shows the Army camp—the camp with the soldiers around it, and to the one side women and children. When this firing began, did the soldiers fire on the women and children who were to one side?

Mr. PIPE-ON-HEAD. May I see the picture? [The picture was exhibited to the witness.]

Mr. MURDOCK. Here [indicating] I take it, are the men seated. Here [indicating] are women and children. In the first outbreak of firing, did the soldiers fire on these women and children, or were there women and children in the center?

Mr. PIPE-ON-HEAD. The troops, the white soldiers and Indians scouts were over here [indicating], but for the lack of space we did not put them in. When the firing started, this bunch [indicating] fired, and another bunch fired, and this [indicating] fired over here.

Mr. MURDOCK. Who were these Indian scouts; of what tribe?

Mr. PIPE-ON-HEAD. They were the members of what they call the Pine Ridge Scouts now.

Mr. MURDOCK. May I ask one more question: Was it the practice of the Army in those days to take Indian police and Indian scouts of the same tribe in that immediate neighborhood?

Mr. PIPE-ON-HEAD. It has been the practice. That is the reason that we write in here that some of the Indians scouts killed some members of their own tribe. And some members of the Big Foot Band were Indian scouts, but they did not know it. They shot them all down.

Mr. MURDOCK. In other words, the scouts in the Army itself were shot down in this battle?

Mr. PIPE-ON-HEAD. Yes; and some of the members of the Big Foot Band were Indian scouts.

Mr. MURDOCK. Do any members of the committee have any further questions? Mr. Dimond?

Mr. DIMOND. No, Mr. Chairman.

Mr. MURDOCK. Mr. Barton?

Mr. BARTON. How many were in the band, altogether?

Mr. PIPE-ON-HEAD. There were around in the neighborhood of 300 people.

Mr. BARTON. About 90 men were killed and 200 women and children; is that right?

Mr. PIPE-ON-HEAD. Yes.

Mr. MURDOCK. If that concludes this witness' statement, I would like to call the other witness for perhaps 10 minutes.

Mr. DIMOND. Before you call him, Mr. Chairman, I should like to ask a question: How many survived of the entire band of Indians who were present at that place and time mentioned?

Mr. PIPE-ON-HEAD. We have no exact record, but up to the time when they were taking evidence or statements from other Indians, there were only 55 alive at that time, and since then 11 of them have died, which would make forty-some odd.

There are 44 living survivors today.

STATEMENT OF DEWEY BEARD
(INTERPRETED BY CHARLES WHITE WOLF)

Mr. MURDOCK. We are pleased to hear you now, Mr. Beard.

Mr. BEARD. First, I wanted to come out with my friends, and I am glad to meet you all today.

I would like to tell you gentlemen today that there was no reason at all that the United States troops massacred the Big Foot band. I want to bring out the fact that the United States has done what we call one of the biggest murders, as we call them, and that the United States must be ashamed of it, or something, because they have never even offered to reimburse us or settle in any way.

At that time we stuck up our white flag, and they took our guns away from us. When we were bare handed they cut loose on us. The children did not know what was going on. We always had been told that when the white flag was stuck up there would be no trouble, and the people believed in that white flag. All at once they cut loose on us, and at that time I was shot in the leg, and up till today I never found out why they did that to me—shot me like that; and some time I would like to find out what was the reason why the American troops should do that; why they should ever injure anybody unless anyone was bothering the law. But still they shot me down.

The United States soldier murdered the bunch of us, and they have never made an offer of any kind of settlement.

In saying a few words on this massacre, I want to point out a very few of the things that I have seen with my own eyes at that time. At that time my wife and I had a baby of 22 days old, and right at the time when the firing started I missed my wife, and later I found out that she was shot through the breast. The little 22-day-old baby was nursing from the same side where the mother was wounded and the child was choked with blood. A few days afterwards the little boy died.

I saw on that field small children like that lying by the side of their mothers, and I saw about four or five of them lying there frozen to death.

After that—they knew I was wounded; I was shot in the leg, and I fell down; they knew I was wounded and helpless, and they came and shot me all over again, in the breast. I was laying off there to one side, right by the camp side, and the soldiers were going through the field, and the men and women were wounded and could not help themselves, and the soldiers came over there and put the bullets through them again.

Mr. MURDOCK. His statement was that he was wounded in the breast and in the leg?

Mr. WHITE WOLF. Yes, sir.

Mr. MURDOCK. Was he wounded in the leg first, and then afterward, while he was helpless, he was shot through the body?

Mr. BEARD. Yes, sir; I was helpless, lying there, and they came back and shot me in the breast again. If I was killed at that time, I would not be here testifying for my people.

The picture shows where the soldiers surrounded us. We did not have any guns—not a thing—and immediately when the firing started some of the soldiers and some of the scouts were on the line with us, and some of them were killed right along with us.

Mr. MURDOCK. About how many Indian scouts were with the troops?

Mr. BEARD. At that time, when they first met them, they had seven Indian scouts, and then there were some more came after that.

Mr. RALPH H. CASE. Mr. Chairman, may I ask the witness a question?

Mr. MURDOCK. Yes.

Mr. RALPH H. CASE. Did you ever see a gun like that [exhibiting a gun]?

Mr. BEARD. Yes, sir; a few years back I have seen quite a few guns like that.

Mr. RALPH H. CASE. I will state to the committee that this is one of the guns that was collected on the battlefield at Wounded Knee, transported to Pine Ridge Agency, and kept there in the warehouse for many years. I was permitted by the agent to take this gun from the warehouse.

There has always been some dispute as to whether or not these Indians did surrender their arms before the firing started. I picked this gun up at random from several hundred in the warehouse. I want to call the committee's attention to something that I did not find out myself until I returned to Washington. I wish you would notice as I drop the ramrod. I used to use a muzzle-loading gun myself.

Mr. MURDOCK. I was acquainted with one of those when I was a boy.

Mr. RALPH H. CASE. I wish you to note that the gun itself is still loaded; and this, I believe, tends to support the Indians' statement that their guns were surrendered in advance of the firing. This is a typical Plains Indian gun of the period—muzzle loading, smooth bore, Springfield make, which shoots either ball or shot.

Mr. MURDOCK. Have you made sure that that does not have a percussion cap on it?

Mr. RALPH H. CASE. I first made sure that it has no percussion cap. But at the same time, it still is a loaded gun, and things happen with loaded guns.

Mr. BARTON. Mr. Chairman, there were 24 soldiers killed, were there?

Mr. RALPH H. CASE. I think so.

Mr. BARTON. One officer and twenty-four soldiers.

Mr. RALPH H. CASE. One officer and twenty-four soldiers.

Mr. BARTON. And the claim of the Indians is that those were shot by their fellow soldiers?

Mr. RALPH H. CASE. By the cross-fire. As is indicated on this map, which is a Government publication, there were soldiers on four sides of the Indian group.

Mr. BARTON. The Army claims that there were at least 50 shots fired before the soldiers opened fire. That is mentioned in the letter from the War Department.

Mr. RALPH H. CASE. I know that is the statement made in the

War Department's records and reports. However, the story which others have told me is that one Indian walked up to that pile of guns, and in a gesture of defiance—can't you imagine that an Indian would throw that gun up in the air and fire it? That Indian was dead, they tell me, before the echo of the shot died away, and the firing became general.

Mr. MURDOCK. Have you other questions, gentlemen, to ask the witness?

Mr. RALPH H. CASE. I would like to add to the record that this is the first and only time that any witnesses have ever been heard on any pending legislation relative to the Wounded Knee Massacre.

Mr. MURDOCK. I have one or two questions that I would like to ask the witness.

Is it your impression that the Indians in this band were on their way to the Pine Ridge Agency to surrender?

Mr. BEARD. Yes, sir.

Mr. MURDOCK. Is it your best judgment that there was no warlike intention on the part of this band?

Mr. BEARD. They were on peaceful business.

Mr. DIMOND. How many soldiers were present on this occasion?

Mr. MURDOCK. It may be the records will show that.

Mr. DIMOND. I imagine so.

Mr. WHITE WOLF. He has no idea.

SUPPLEMENTARY WRITTEN STATEMENT OF DEWEY BEARD
To the Subcommittee on Indian Affairs:

Mr. CHAIRMAN, friends, first I want to thank the committee that heard us on H.R. 2535.

I wanted to remind the committee that in the last World War we sent our boys across. Some of them were killed over there; others were wounded and some luckily came back without wounds. Some of these boys are descendants of the Big Foot's band. They helped to defend our country, gave up their lives and fought for this Government which some 47 years ago shot down their helpless unarmed grandfathers and grandmothers at Wounded Knee Creek.

We were always friendly toward the whites and have been very loyal to the United States Government in every way, but someone told us that the War Department and the administration is opposed to H.R. 2535. I cannot understand why they want to do this. All that

I ask is that Congress pass this bill and pay those poor Indians back on the reservation the money which is provided in the bill and help us to forget the whole Wounded Knee affair.

I did not get to continue with my statement at the hearing, but I hope that the committee will be kind enough to read this additional statement and urge a favorable consideration of the bill H.R. 2535 in the Congress.

MARK DEWEY (his thumb print) BEARD.

A. T. H.

Mr. MURDOCK. We thank all three of you for your statements, and we will give them due consideration.

Congressman Case, have you further testimony that you would like to bring before us?

Mr. FRANCIS H. CASE. Mr. Chairman, I want to thank the committee for their consideration this morning, and with the permission of the committee I would like to make extracts from this Fourteenth Annual Report of the Bureau of Ethnology and insert them in the record to give the background and the details of the Wounded Knee tragedy as set forth in the record made at the time. It verifies the account that has been given us here this morning.

Mr. MURDOCK. Without objection, they will be placed in the record. [So done.]

[* * * * * *]

[Thursday, 12 May 1938]

STATEMENT OF JAMES GRASS

(INTERPRETED BY ADELBERT THUNDER HAWK)

Mr. GRASS. Mr. Chairman and members of the committee, the Wounded Knee massacre, before it occurred they were the people who were killed, who came from the northern Sioux country. They belonged to the northern band. They were part of the Big Sioux Band. They were coming—we heard they were coming to Pine Ridge and we waited for them. We were to meet them. I was a scout with the troops.

On the day they arrived on the Pine Ridge Reservation I was detailed to carry a message to the Indians so I was gone for 2 days and the day I left and the next day I left they were killed and when I came back we helped bury them. We buried old men and old women; women that were still with child and even infants. We saw those children, perfectly harmless who could not even harm anyone that were killed; even little infants. About 2 miles up the ravine along the creek there were people lying dead, some Indians were scattered all along right there dead. We picked them up and buried them and took them back and there were many women.

Mr. MURDOCK. I would like to ask a question at this point.

Among all those that you buried did you observe any Indian scouts who were connected with the Army who had been killed?

Mr. GRASS. There was only one scout [named High Back Bone] that was killed; he was not buried there but they took him back to the agency.

Mr. MURDOCK. You are positive that at least one Indian scout serving in the Army was killed in that affair?

Mr. GRASS. Yes; I did not get to see him and I was not there at the actual fighting. I was there later.

Mr. CASE. Did they bury them in individual graves or all in one ditch?

Mr. GRASS. They were buried in this one big trench.

Mr. BARTON. Do you mean they were buried like you would stack cordwood in one mass?

Mr. GRASS. Yes.

Mr. BARTON. How old were you at that time?

Mr. GRASS. I was about 27 years old.

Mr. BARTON. And then you are about 74 years old now?

Mr. GRASS. Yes, sir.

Mr. CASE. Thank you very much, Jim.

I wish to thank the committee for its kind consideration.

The CHAIRMAN. If there is nothing further for the committee to consider at this time, the committee adjourns.

The committee is now adjourned.

70. Account of Peter One Skunk, 1938

*Peter One Skunk, who lived at Cherry Creek on the Cheyenne River
reservation, recounted his experiences at Wounded Knee in the*
Mitchell *(S.Dak.)* Daily Republic, *29 December 1938.*

Peter One Skunk, a survivor, escaped in the thick of the fight after
being wounded. . . . One Skunk recounts how, after he had been
wounded in the head, he secreted himself in a nearby ravine and
managed to mount a stray horse and start away. The first horse was
shot from under him, but he caught a second one and escaped as bullets sang close to him. . . . "We didn't want to fight," One Skunk says
today. "It was Yellow Bird, a medicine man, who made us believe the
ghost shirts would keep the bullets of the white man from harming
us. We soon knew better."

It was Yellow Bird[, explained One Skunk,] who harangued the
Sioux while the soldiers were searching their blankets to determine
whether the Indians had guns concealed beneath them. It was Black
Fox who drew a rifle and fired a shot which precipitated a volley from
the soldiers—a volley which killed nearly half the warriors.

71. Account of Paul High Back, September 1940

Paul High Back gave the following account "on September 8th 1940 . . . in the Sioux language to John B. Williamson at Pine Ridge. . . . It took nearly 4 hours, from 8 P.M. until nearly midnight, in the telling" ("Paul High Back's Version of the Disaster of Dec[.] 29, 1890[,] at Wounded Knee," Wi-Iyohi, Monthly Bulletin of the South Dakota Historical Society *10 (1 June 1956): 1–3).*

My folks lived along Cherry Creek and were members of Big Foot's (Sitanka Os'Page [*sic*]) Band. The Ghost Dance (Wanage Wacipi) had been going on at Pine Ridge for some time. Messengers were sent from them to our reservation and also to the Standing Rock Reservation farther north to explain the dance and try to get others to join in the new religion.

Quite a few became interested and started dancing, among them being those at Sitting Bull's camp on the Grand River and those in the Cherry Creek band where I lived. After the fight in Sitting Bull's camp, during which he was killed, his followers became alarmed. They were afraid the soldiers would come and kill them all, so they scattered and most of them came south to our settlement on Cherry Creek. We did not know anything about the fight until they came. Their coming made us all afraid and we concluded we had better go to Pine Ridge Reservation where the rest of the Ghost Dancers were congregating.

We did not go with any idea of trying to fight the soldiers or to make any trouble. We went because we were afraid and did not want to be alone. We wanted to be together. So we left our homes and started for Pine Ridge. There was quite a big company of us. We went down over the prairie and then through the Bad Lands and across the White River.

I was one of the four young men who were scouts or outriders and who rode ahead or to one side of the caravan. One night we camped near Porcupine Creek and the next morning the three other young men and I were riding ahead. We had just climbed the hills to get out of the creek valley when we saw three men coming towards us on horseback. When they came up we saw that they were Indians. Two were regular Indians and one was a mixed blood. They had guns and we knew by their clothes that they were scouts for the white soldiers.

The mixed blood did the talking and told us many soldiers were ahead of us a few miles, but not to be afraid. He told us the soldiers would treat us well and take us to the agency where there were many other Indians and where we would have plenty to eat. He said everything would be alright if we would go with the soldiers. Pretty soon the soldiers came, and the officer talked with some of our leading men, with the scout as interpreter. Our leaders then decided to go to the agency, for there was nothing else that we could do since we could not fight them. So we came along with the soldiers.

Most of the soldiers went ahead of the wagon train but some rode along on each side of us. When we got to Wounded Knee Creek they said we could camp for the night. So we stopped and camp[ed] on the flat while the soldiers camped on the slope above us. That night we did not sleep well, everybody was afraid. All night long the soldiers had lights and were working at something. We could hear the noise and rattle of iron being moved around and it made us all very nervous and we could not sleep. All night long soldiers walked back and forth around our camp. In the morning we found that everything had been arranged differently. There was a row of big guns set up on the side of the hill and we found that they shot bullets very fast (Hotchkiss machine guns).

After a while we were all called out, men, women and children. So we came and stood up close to where the soldiers were. They told us we must give up all our guns, knives or whatever weapons we had. They said to come fo[r]ward ten at a time and lay down our guns and our knives. So ten of our men went up to them but they only had one gun to lay down. The soldiers did not like this very well, but we could not put our guns down because we did not have them with us. Those of us who had guns had left them back at our tents.

Then some soldiers went to our tents and began to look for our guns. They found quite a few and carried them out and threw them down on the ground. They did not lay them down carefully, but dumped them down in a pile, throwing them down hard. We were standing there, men, women and children, all of us very much afraid. We were defenseless as none of us had guns. The soldiers were standing all around us holding their guns in their hands ready to shoot.

But as it turned out, there were two men down at the lower end of our group who had their guns under their blankets. One of the soldiers who was walking back and forth in front of us saw the ends of those guns sticking out. He called out to the other soldiers that these men had guns.

I was standing at the upper end of the group where I could see it all and I can say that those two Indians never raised their guns or shot them, but as the soldiers started forward to take their guns from them, suddenly all the rest of the soldiers raised their guns and fired right into us. They shot right away into all of us men, women and children.

We had no chance to fight back as we had no weapons. All we thought about, those of us who were still alive, was to get away. The morning was cloudy and damp and the smoke from the guns did not rise but settled right on us. From then on nothing could be seen very plain. The soldiers were rushing around shooting all of us that they could see to shoot. I got shot thru the right hand, the bullet entering just as [at] the base of my thumb and coming out at the base of my middle finger. Somehow I finally got down into a washout or gully south of the fight, where a lot of Indians had taken refuge and where they had been shot down. I got down among them and kind of crawled down under the dead bodies, but the soldiers kept on shooting into us whenever they saw any of us move.

Twice more I was shot, one bullet going through the fleshy part of my left forearm and a third going through the fleshy part of the calf of my leg. Almost all of the day the shooting continued, the soldiers searching among the draws and brush for Indians still alive and shooting them down.

After dark I crawled out and though suffering greatly, I made my way to Wounded Knee Creek where I came across three women and four or five children, including two boys about 14 or 15 years old who had survived though some of them were wounded. We had made our way some distance down the stream when morning came. Soon afterwards we met some Indians coming down from the so[-]called hostile camp over near White River northwest of Pine Ridge Agency. They had heard of what had happened and were going over to see what was going on. They were very angry and in a very hostile mood. They took care of us and took us over to their camp. I was in pretty bad shape for a long time but my wounded [wounds] all healed up except that my right hand is a little withered. Outside of the fact that I can scarcely grip anything with that hand, there is nothing wrong with me. I am seventy years old and I am well and strong yet.

Now all I have told you is what I saw and experienced myself. It is all true and I have told it exactly as it happened. After the first shooting and the smoke settled, everything was in confusion. All the people thought about was to get away from the soldiers and many things may have happened that I did not see.

72. "After Wounded Knee—A Recollection," by Addison E. Sheldon, ca. 1941

Addison E. Sheldon visited the Pine Ridge Agency with several others two days after Wounded Knee and described the situation there respecting the Lakota survivors, offering a heartfelt non-Indian perspective. Sheldon later served as superintendent of the Nebraska State Historical Society from 1917 to 1943. Sheldon, "After Wounded Knee—A Recollection," Nebraska History 22 (Jan.-Feb. 1941): 45.

I still see them—the defeated, dejected Big Foot Sioux who were prisoners at Pine Ridge [on] December 31, 1890. It was near two o'clock in a gray, grimy morning as we drove—six of us—from Chadron in a stage coach with Winchester rifles in our hands, watching the shadows of the pine trees on the hills; drove on across White Clay Creek into the big yard in front of the Pine Ridge Agency. A band of men, women and children (mostly women and children) occupied the center of that yard. Some of them were prostrate on the ground. Some were sitting crow-legged, rocking to and fro in silent suffering. Some sat upon their ponies stiff and straight, but yet suffering.

In a circle around this band of Indians were other Indians in blue uniforms of the United States, with rifles. Even in the darkness the situation interpreted itself. One of us said to the others in the coach: "Those Indians are captured from the Big Foot band on the Wounded Knee Battlefield."

It was true. Their distress was so much deeper than the darkness that it told its own story. Their guards were the Pine Ridge police, famous, efficient, obedient Sioux warriors, transformed by the discipline and drill of a United States officer—and the force of necessity—into United States soldiers. They were standing guard over their own cousins, for the Big Foot band was closely related to the Pine Ridge Sioux. Not a word was spoken on either side. There was nothing but silence and dumb suffering.

Later we saw the mangled and dying brought in from the battlefield—about sixty of them. Women with legs broken by canister shot; little children torn and disfigured by rifle bullets. The Presbyterian

Church and Episcopal Chapel were quickly converted into hospital rooms, and with incredible speed doctors and extemporized nurses organized the last hospital service for the last Indian battlefield in America.

73. Additional commentary by Philip F. Wells, 1942

Philip F. Wells offered this commentary to Thomas E. Odell at the South Dakota State Soldiers' Home in Hot Springs on 27 December 1942. The document reposes in Folder 41, Drawer 6, Odell Collection, Case Library.

I forbad the whites to pick up the dead. Walking Bull, an Indian scout, approached three wounded Indians lying on the ground and said, "Don't be deceived because I wear soldiers' clothes. I want to save you." One of the wounded Indians shot Walking Bull in the leg, grazing his skin. Walking Bull then said, "I came to save you, but you have no ears." He then shot the wounded man.

The Indians were told that they were going to be taken to Pine Ridge Agency and must first give up their arms. Colonel Forsyth told them that through me, the interpreter.

That the medicine man threw up dirt as a signal is not true. The dirt thrower walked around and said "Ha! Ha!," an expression of regret that he would do something. He picked up the dust and threw it to illustrate that the bullets could not penetrate the ghost shirts. He showed that the bullets would pass as harmlessly as the wind carries dust away.

The soldiers did not shout, "Remember Custer!" That report was circulated two or three days after the fight. I was directed by Major Whitside and Lieutenants Robinson and Varnum about ten days after the fight to make inquiry about the rumor, but I found no evidence that the soldiers said that.

Women and children did not fight. They were busy getting away in order to save their lives.

74. Account of Black Elk, 1930–1940s

*The following account is from Black Elk, an Oglala Lakota who
rode over to Wounded Knee on hearing the distant Hotchkiss
guns firing while he was near Pine Ridge Agency on the morning
of 29 December 1890. Decades later Black Elk told his personal
reminiscence to poet, ethnologist, and historian John G. Neihardt
in a series of interviews. Neihardt transcribed much of the material
into manuscript form in the 1930s and 1940s. Anthropologist
Raymond J. DeMallie of Indiana University edited and annotated
the document for publication by the University of Nebraska Press
in 1984. These selections relate Black Elk's perspectives and detail
his personal activities in the area of Wounded Knee on 29 December
1890.* DeMallie, ed., The Sixth Grandfather: Black Elk's Teachings
Given to John G. Neihardt *(Lincoln: University of Nebraska Press,
1984), pp. 269–75. See also the published rendering by Black Elk
to John G. Neihardt, in Neihardt,* Black Elk Speaks: Being the
Life Story of a Holy Man of the Oglala Sioux, *ann. Raymond J.
DeMallie (Albany: State University of New York, 2008), pp. 208–12.*

We moved camp to the Cheyenne River north of Pine Ridge [Agency].
Most of the Oglalas were camping around Pine Ridge. . . . Two days
later I learned that the soldiers were marching toward Wounded
Knee. This was in the month of the Popping Trees—December. I
heard that Big Foot was coming from a young man who had come
there. Rough Feather I heard was going to get Big Foot, who was
coming from his camp near the mouth of Medicine Root Creek on
White River. At that time there were some soldiers camping somewhere around there on the other side of the river. Rough Feather
went over there in order to get Big Foot. He wanted them to come in a
southeasterly direction, but they did not do it. They wanted to follow
up Medicine Root. They followed it to the head and then scouts for
the soldiers saw them here at the head of Medicine Root. The scouts
represented this to the soldiers and from here it was represented to
Pine Ridge. On this same evening the soldiers went toward where
Big Foot was camped at the head of Medicine Root. Big Foot's camp

came to the creek of Porcupine Butte where the soldiers met them and they nearly had a fight here. The soldiers brought Big Foot back to Wounded Knee. That evening the soldiers gathered around where they had camped. The soldiers had them well guarded all night.

[The following description by Black Elk in the third person described events that he was not present to witness on 29 December, for he arrived in the broad vicinity of the Wounded Knee engagement after the principal action had occurred.]

It was December 29, 1890, the next morning. They carried Big Foot over to the officers, for he was sick. They told the rest of Big Foot's people to bring their guns over there. Everyone stacked their guns and even their knives. . . . The soldiers were searching all the tipis for weapons. There were two men near Big Foot's tipi who wore blankets made out of white sheets, with just their eyes showing. Some of them had probably hidden their knives. The officer who was taking the guns from them went up to these men and pulled their white blankets apart and one of them had his gun concealed inside the sheet. He proceeded to the other one and opened it and just as he was going to get his gun, this man shot him. This man's name was Yellow Bird. This fellow did not want to give up his gun, and did not intend to shoot the white man at all—the gun just went off. Of course the soldiers were all around there already with their guns . . . on the hill [to the] north, across the flat east, and across the creek [i.e., the deep ravine to the direct south]. Yellow Bird and the white officer were wrestling with this gun and they had rolled down together on the ground and were wrestling with it. Dog Chief was right there where they took the guns and was standing right by these men while wrestling. This man was a friend of mine and he saw the whole thing.

Big Foot was the first Indian that was killed by an officer before the . . . guns began [to shoot]. They had carried Big Foot over to where the guns were being given up and immediately after the shot of Yellow Bird the officer shot Big Foot. Yellow Bird went into a tipi nearby and killed lots of them [soldiers] probably before he died. The Indians all ran to the stacks of guns and got their guns during a lull while the soldiers were loading again. A soldier ran up to tear the tipi away to get at Yellow Bird, but the latter shot at them as they came up and killed them. They fired at the tipi and the soldiers' guns set it afire and he died in there.

[Black Elk personally participated in the following sequence of events at Wounded Knee:] The night before this I was over in the camp at Pine Ridge and I couldn't sleep. When I saw the soldiers going out it seemed that I knew there would be trouble. I was walking around all night until daylight. After my meal early that morning I got my horse and while I was out I heard shooting over to the east—I heard wagon guns [i.e., artillery] going off. This was a little distance from the camp and when I heard this gun I felt it right in my body, so I went out and drove the horses back to the camp for I knew there was trouble. Just as I got back with the horses there was a man who returned from Pine Ridge and had come back because he had heard this. He said, "Hey, hey son, the people that are coming [i.e., Big Foot's people] are fired upon. I know it."

I took my buckskin and saddled up. I had no gun. The only thing I had was the sacred red stick [i.e., his sacred bow]. I put on my sacred shirt. This was a shirt I had made to be worn by no one but myself, which had a spotted eagle outstretched on the back of it, a star on the left shoulder, the rainbow diagonally across the breast from the left shoulder downward toward the hip. I made another rainbow around the neck, like a necklace with a star at the bottom. At the shoulder, elbows, and wrists were eagle feathers. And over the whole shirt I had red streaks of lightning. This was a bullet-proof shirt. I painted my face red. I had another eagle feather thrust through my hair at the top of my head. Of course I was going out by myself, and I could see that there were some young men following me. The first two men who followed me were Loves War and Iron White Man. I asked them where they were going and they said they were just going over to see where the firing was. I told them that I was going there to fight for my people's rights and if they wanted to, they could come along. So they went with me and about this time some more older men came.

I just thought it over and I thought I should not fight. I doubted about this Messiah business and therefore it seemed that I should not fight for it, but anyway I was going because I had already decided to. If [I] turned back the people would think it funny, so I just decided to go anyway. There were now over twenty of us going. As we neared there was a horseback [rider] coming toward us. He said: "Hey, hey, they have murdered them!" Just then right before us I could see a troop of soldiers coming down a canyon. They [the men with Black Elk] stopped their horses and asked me what to do, so we decided we'd first see what we could do and then we'd do it. We started out and at the head of the gulch we went along the creek and got on top of the hill at the head of the gulch now called Battle Creek. . . .

In the morning when the battle started, I could hear the shooting from Pine Ridge. With about twenty other young men, I started out to defend my people. When we got on the hill at the head of the draw about two and one-half miles west of the monument, we could see some Indians being captured by two small troops of soldiers. This was at the head of the draw. I could hear the cannons and rifles going off down there and I could see soldiers all over the hills on each side of the draw. I then depended on my Messiah vision. As we faced them we sang a sacred song which went like this:

A Thunder-being nation I am I have said. (twice)

You shall live. (four times)

Then I said to the men whom I had led there: "Take courage, these are our relatives. We shall try to take the captives back. Furthermore, our women and children are lying dead. Think about this and take courage."

I had good eyes at this time and I could see cavalrymen scattered all over the hills. After I had said this to my young men I proceeded down on horseback and they followed me. Right by the yellow pine in the head of the gulch there was an Indian wounded through the legs by the name of Little Finger. Another man was following me, Iron White Man, and we put this wounded man behind [him on] his horse. At the very end of the gulch this wounded fellow fell off. Then another Indian came along and we asked him to take him over to a safe place. We took him across the hills northwest to safety. At the head of the gulch I saw a baby all alone. It was adopted by my wife's father. Its name was Blue Whirlwind. I was going to pick her up but I left her for she was in a safe place.

We started north toward where the horses are and we stopped right this side of the horses. We started out straight north under the first white clay spot a little ways up the hill. To the north was a troop of cavalry and about one hundred yards to the east was another troop of soldiers (by the pine trees). Two of my men went to where the captives were and there was another Indian riding a black horse standing right this side of the captives. Just as the two men got to where the soldiers were and got to where the black horse rider was standing, the farthest troop over there fired on us first and shot right across the draw as we retreated. Then after a little bit the main body of the men said: "Take courage, it is time to fight!" As the cavalrymen fired, the horses stampeded across the hills here.

Then the body of Indians charged down this draw toward the captives. I could feel the bullets hitting me but I was bullet proof. I had to hang on to my horse to keep the bullets from knocking me off. I had the sacred bow with me and all I had to do was to hold the bow toward the soldiers and you should have seen the soldiers run! They saw they couldn't hit me so they ran eastward toward the [present] monument. The other boys were not bullet-proof so they had to get behind the hill back there. I was alone. Every time I pointed the bow at the soldiers they couldn't run fast. If I had had a gun I could have killed a lot of them. When they got over the hill they peeped out ready to shoot. Just as I got up to them about twenty yards away, they shot at me and missed me. The soldiers on the other side came down the creek and lay down ready to shoot and they pumped away at me but they didn't hurt me. I proceeded back to where my men were. I had to hold my bow in front of me in the air to be bullet-proof but just as I had gotten over the hill after completing my charge, I let my bow down and I could feel some bullets passing through my ghost dance shirt near my hip. You could see the marks of the bullets on the shirt. I got shot but not much. I could feel a bullet graze my body, was all. Then I made another charge, as the soldiers had crept over by this time. (After I had made the charge the other young men came and got the captives while I had the soldiers chased away.) Then as I charged again you could hear the bullets whizzing by me.

In this draw there was another Indian. Then right in here I was surprised to see two boys about fifteen years old who had repeaters and who had evidently done quite a lot of damage. They killed lots of soldiers lying around. These two boys followed after the soldiers and had lots of ammunition. After this we made the soldiers retreat. As I charged they all fell back and they all gathered together in a little bunch over the hill there. These two boys were the bravest of all of us, for they were not bullet-proof but they did not get a scratch— they were lucky. One of my men was shot and two got wounded— one broke his leg and the other broke his arm. They retreated so fast that we just pulled up and went along after them. The battle started at about ten o'clock and we fought all day here. We went back to Pine Ridge just after dark. It was about fifteen miles by the old road. When the soldiers gathered on the hill they began to go back on that ridge over there. After the soldiers did their dirty work over there they began to march up Wounded Knee. The soldiers wanted to fight yet, but we did not care so much about charging at them. I wanted to see the place where Big Foot and his people got killed and as I followed down the draw I could see men and women lying dead all along there. Soldiers and Indians afterwards were here and there. . . . Right at the beginning of the draw there were many Indians and there were more soldiers further down.

This was a good day—the sun was shining. In the evening it began to snow. It was a very bad snow. The day was cold even though it was sunny. That night the snow covered us and we all died from the cold. As I went down toward the village, I could see children dying all over—it was just a sight. I did not get as far as Big Foot's body though. Somehow I did not feel sorry about these women and children. There was a time that I did not use my first vision, but I used the power of the vision about the Messiah. I was not sorry, I was not feeling bad about it, but I thought there will be a day. I was not sorry about the women and children because I was figuring on dying and then I would join them somewhere. I just thought I would probably die before this thing was over and I just figured that there would be a day when I could either take revenge or die. I did not recall the vision that I should have recalled at this time. . . .

75. Third-person account of Dewy Girl's remembrance of Wounded Knee, as told by Eugene Wounded Horse, 1940s

Eugene Wounded Horse told this third-person account of Dewy Girl's remembrance of Wounded Knee to Will Spindler at some point in the 1940s. Spindler was a long-time teacher at the day school at Potato Creek village on the Pine Ridge reservation. The piece appeared under the title "Dewy Girl Was There," in Real West 11 *(July 1968): 20–21, 54.*

"[After the eruption at Wounded Knee on the morning of December 29, 1890] the Indian women and children were fleeing in wild panic to reach the cover of a deep dry wash near their camp. The troopers' Gatling [Hotchkiss] guns and rifles fired at them from three directions on that tragic December morning. Those who reached the edge [of the ravine] rolled or slid down the steep bank.

Many never made the dry wash. Some were killed by the murderous rifle bullets and explosions of the shells from the Gatling [*sic*] guns fired into the fleeing mass. Others lay wounded and writhing in agony, some calling frantically for help from members of their families. Wild panic raged on the lonely prairie.

[Nine-year-old] Dewey Girl clutched her mother's dress as they dashed wildly for the dry wash. Then suddenly her mother, Clover Woman, seemed to fly into the air. A shell fired from the hill above had exploded on the frozen ground nearby, the terrific concussion lifting and throwing her, while flying fragments wounded her hip badly.

The concussion, loosening the frightened girl's grip, also threw her some distance and she rolled alone to the bottom of the draw or wash. Jumping frantically to her feet, she saw her mother lying at the rim of the bank. In a daze she limped to her, shook her back to her senses, and helped her down the bank.

Hiding with her mother in a patch of wild rose bushes, Dewy Girl heard rifle bullets and shells whistling overhead. Mingling with the wild din of gunfire were wild yells, the crying and wailing of women, and children screaming in panic and pain. Children and parents became separated. Men trying to protect their families with what weapons they had were soon slain, most of them before reaching the wash.

Dewy Girl finally succeeded in getting her mother into a washed-out hole hidden by a clump of pines. Then she covered the hole with dry sticks, all the while keeping her eyes on the soldiers as instructed by Clover Woman. The horse soldiers, as the cavalry was termed by the Sioux, were still firing on men, women and children at close range. They were all over the camp setting fires to lodges, tepees and everything that could be destroyed. Many picketed horses and dogs were shot and killed.

Then suddenly the troopers were at the bank of the winding draw, firing into both wounded and lifeless bodies, as well as at those fleeing up the draw. Dewy Girl saw two friends, a woman and a small boy known as White Owl Woman and Red Cherry, fired on by two troopers. Suddenly it was too much for the poor girl and she fled back to hide with her mother in the hidden hole.

Lying huddled closely to Clover Woman, she soon heard the voices of troopers above their hiding place but they went on. Finally she fell asleep and when she was awakened by the barking and howling of dogs she peeked out and saw that night had fallen. Both had lost their blankets and shawls in their wild flight and they were desperately cold. When daylight came at last, Dewy Girl searched the draw and found plenty of dried rosebuds for herself and her mother to eat. Placing them where Clover Woman could reach them, she then brought her some balled snow to satisfy her thirst.

As the shivering Indian girl walked up the draw in the early morning following the day of the terrible Wounded Knee tragedy, low hanging clouds hung overhead, the wind whistled through the pines, and the cold was swiftly increasing in intensity. Snow had fallen during the night and now the high wind was whipping it into deeper drifts. Otherwise the silence of death reigned over the destroyed camp. Without her blanket and shawl, she was soon chilled to the bone. Climbing to the rim of the deep draw, she saw that everything on the flat was partly covered with snow. Finally she climbed into a pine tree and from this height surveyed the battlefield for any signs of life. But only the shrieking, howling wind and the howling and barking dogs broke the grim silence. Death was everywhere. Lifeless bodies lay strewn about over a wide radius. A few smoldering lodgepoles made thin columns of smoke in the cold air.

She looked for White Owl Woman and little Red Cherry and finally found them both dead and huddled together in a clump of bushes, their bodies nearly drifted over with snow. There were many others lying along the bank. At last, numb with cold, she climbed down from her perch among the pine needles and picked more rosebuds. She ran across another woman with her small son huddled under her shawl, both dead and frozen. Not far from them lay another young woman with her small daughter in her arms. She was known as Red Willow Woman, the daughter of White Owl Woman.

More dead people lay all over the bottom of the draw. She felt like screaming in her terror but knew she must not as it would only frighten her mother more. She took the rosebuds to Clover Woman and then returned to her perch in the pine.

The cold wind and driving snow continued to increase in intensity as Dewy Girl sat in the tree. Suddenly she spotted something sticking out of the snow that seemed strangely familiar. Climbing down quickly she found it was their blankets and shawls. Happily she scooped them up and beat a hasty retreat to her mother's shelter, where she decided to stay and warm herself as best she could. "I wish your father were here," Clover Woman told her. Her mother's words made Dewy Girl anxious about her father. Could he possibly be alive somewhere? More likely, though, if she found him it would be only his lifeless, frozen body. She was reluctant to leave her mother for too long a period. If the horse soldiers should return to kill those they found alive—

Once more she returned to her seat in the pine, this time with her shawl and blanket about her. Then from somewhere in the snowstorm she heard the words of a song, a survival song of the Sioux. It was the first sign of life in the void of death all about her and she listened intently for the direction from which it came. The voice came nearer. Then suddenly she saw dimly a man on horseback leading a horse pulling a travois made of slender lodgepoles. Soon he dismounted and leading both horses began examining each frozen body that showed in the drifting snow. He wept as he viewed this terrible scene of desolation and grim death.

Dewy Girl watched intently as he neared her tree. Then, as he halted before the clump of pines hiding her mother, she suddenly recognized him. It was her father, Little Bird! Swiftly she climbed down and ran to him, tears of joy running down her cold cheeks.

Little Bird and his daughter had a joyous reunion there in the snow and the storm, and for the moment the tragedy of death and suffering was forgotten as he held her close. "Where is your mother?" he asked finally.

Dewy Girl removed the sticks and brush covering from the hole and revealed Clover Woman wrapped in her shawl and blanket. At first Little Bird was unable to speak, as tears welled up into his eyes. Then, regaining his composure, he told them the story of his long search for them, which extended into the night and the snowstorm. "When the sudden firing broke out in the camp," he told them, "everything went crazy. The fleeing people and the smoke from the black powder firing were so thick that I could not find you. First I ran to our lodge, but nobody was there. Then I thought of our horses and took time to get them to take you out of danger, as I had no weapon to defend you. But I could not find you anywhere, and soon I had to flee up the draw with the others or be killed by the horse soldiers. Those of us who got away from the soldiers set up a refuge camp on White Clay Creek. When I could not find you here I went there, asking everyone about you but no one had any information. My uncle, Ten Fingers, loaned me the lodgepoles last night and I came back here before daylight to search here again. There will be others coming soon to look for their families. The Great Spirit has been good in that I found you both alive and I am grateful."

While Little Bird got his wounded wife ready to travel, the girl gathered more dry rosebuds for food. Then she helped him lash her mother to the lodgepoles of the travois, after which she mounted the travois horse and her father mounted the other. They were ready for their long journey into the cold, snow, and storm, but where it would take them they knew not. One thing was clear: they must get out of this place of death and desolation.

Climbing out of the deep draw, they rode to their burned-out lodge. How swiftly and terribly all had happened on that fateful yesterday morning! Nothing but ashes remained of their lodge and all of their belongings. The bleak wind howled and moaned over the spot, mixing the ashes with the snow to make it a dirty gray. Dewy Girl broke down at last and wept bitterly.

The pent-up anger and bitterness erupted into words at last from Little Bird on beholding the ruin wrought by the soldiers on his people. "You horse soldiers have won your glory!" he cried from the bitterness of his heart. "You have had your revenge for Long Hair [Custer]. . . . You have destroyed human beings without mercy. You have captured us by first taking our weapons, knives, and everything. The cold, dreary winter is upon us and we are destitute. You advised us to return and we followed your advice in good faith. We suffered with lots of illness and our leader Big Foot was very ill. We faced your leader in truce because you asked us, and then you fired on us. You have slaughtered us, even our women and children. This is our land and we have every right to be here. Today is a sad day in our lives. Today we face a cold wind, a dreary winter, with very little shelter for us and no food."

As they rode on to the west, Dewy Girl could not help but look back and think of the mothers' and children's lifeless bodies in the cold snow.

76. Account of James High Hawk, 1950–1960s

James High Hawk gave this undated account of the Wounded Knee Massacre which Victor H. Runnels of Aberdeen, South Dakota, provided in Indian Country Today, *25 August–1 September 1997.*

There were some small children playing around and I was one of them. I had a little brother that was nursing then, an infant, and one brother a little bit larger and I was a little bit larger than he was. He was four years old at the time. I was wounded twice, shot twice, I have two wounds. My mother was wounded though she kept trying to take care of her little family, then they came again and shot her and also my infant brother. He lived some time but had a bad wound and suffered and then died. I have an older brother also that was in this Massacre. He is not here but he took care of me when I was wounded and after they shot our mother. He took me toward the ravine where some of the Indians were hiding from the blood thirsty soldiers. James High Hawk

I [Victor Runnels] knew James High Hawk, he was my uncle, he died in 1964. My great-grandmother, Susan Releaux, was a volunteer nurse at the emergency hospital set up in the Episcopal Church in Pine Ridge, S.D., after the massacre. She said it was a terrible scene [there] and devastating to hear the cries of the wounded, and dying children.

77. Account of Crane Pretty Voice, date unknown, as told by Ellen in the Woods

The following account by Crane Pretty Voice, as told by Ellen in the Woods, was published in South Dakota's Ziebach County: History of the Prairie *(Dupree, S.Dak.: Ziebach County Historical Society, 1982), pp. 325–26.*

Crane Pretty Voice had two daughters. The first was six weeks old when her parents took her toward Pine Ridge and Wounded Knee with Big Foot in 1890.

The father was a policeman or scout for the government, but they were on the trail with Big Foot anyway. He told his wife that it looked like they (the army [troops under Lieutenant Colonel Edwin V. Sumner]) were going to get them together and surrender them and kill them. He told her that if the army started anything [in the Cheyenne River area] the women folk should run for the creeks and get out of sight.

[Eventually] when the shooting started [at Wounded Knee], that's what she did. When she was about a mile away, she said, her baby was crying and pretty soon it looked like something hit her from the back. And then the baby wasn't crying so she wrapped it up in a blanket and she left it and she kept running. There was a lot of them running. [After the massacre] they got to Pine Ridge Station [Agency]. The army headquarters was there. The next day the army came [back to Wounded Knee] and they had found a baby. They wanted to know who it belonged to and it was theirs. The captain wanted to keep the child. They asked her and she said she was so angry because she thought they had killed her little girl, so she told them to just take her. [The "captain" was actually Brigadier General Leonard W. Colby of the Nebraska National Guard.]

In 1941, Ellen was visiting her mother, Josephine Condon, when an old time Cadillac drove up to there, where Crane Pretty Voice and another older lady were also visiting. The lady got out of the car with two grown daughters and was coming, and here it was her mother. She came looking for her mother and they told her where she was.

She went back. She just came and gave her mother $100.00 and visited her. Then she went back.[5]

5. For broader context, *see* Greene, *American Carnage*, 359–61, and, especially, Renée Sansom Flood, *Lost Bird of Wounded Knee: Spirit of the Lakota* (New York: Scribner, 1995).

78. Interview with Jim Mesteth by Phyllis Mesteth and Boyd Bosma, 1977

Phyllis Mesteth and Boyd Bosma conducted this interview with Jim Mesteth (Oglala Lakota), born circa 1880, at Pine Ridge on 1 July 1977. Then ninety-six years old, Mesteth conveys his personal recollections of the direct aftermath of Wounded Knee. Indian Historian *11 (Spring 1978): 18–21.*

I couldn't tell you what happened [in the fighting], because I was here, over here in Pine Ridge. The battle was over at Wounded Knee. . . . The only time I was there was the next day after the battle to pick up dead corpses and sick ones, wounded ones. The people went over there so I went with them. I was a young kid, but I went over there. I just seen them laying here and there all over, men, women, and kids. . . .

So they, that's quite a massacre. Even some of the little fellows, little boys, get wounded. Oh, they had that church over there, that Episcopal Church, full of sick people. They lay on the floor, you know, beds all around. . . . So a lot of them lived, and quite a few of them died.

We used to live up here in this Cheyenne Creek, way at the head of it, and that's about half way, no, quite a ways from Wounded Knee. And we used to go after wood and hay every other day from there, from Pine Ridge. And this time we went there and we saw smoke coming out of the house.

So we stopped there and they told me to go on and peep in the window and see who's there. I think I was foolish to do that, [']cause I was the only kid with them and I was foolish enough to do it. They was all grown up. They wouldn't take that chance.

So I went and peeped in there, in that window, and that man was sitting there. He motioned to come on. He said, "You-po! You-po!" Well, that means, "Come on! Come on!" So I run back and they said, "Who's there?" So I said, "There's a man sitting there and he wants us to come, motioned to come."

So they got off and they all walked in there and there sat that man all wounded. Had a cane. So we brought that fellow home with us, and he laid there, and he got all right. He was wounded three or four places, different places, and still he didn't die. On the left shoulder, up pretty high, and on this side, too, and this one's about the end of the ribs, and the arm. He was shot through his arm. And there was another place, on the leg. Yeah. Right above the knee. He didn't break no bone. Just cut the meat, I guess.

Yeah, he was shot four places. He said he had his gun with him, but he said, "I left it up here at the head of this creek where the pine tree is. Right there is a big pine tree right on the creek. I put that gun right there. How come I got to find this house, he said, "there was two oxens [*sic*] coming through there, coming down the creek. I knew that these two must be drinking water someplace. I was pretty near dead for water. I followed them and they come to this house and they went to the well. . . . This fellow said, "I went there and pulled up some water to drink. Then I went to that house."

He said he'd traveled all night from Wounded Knee to that place. It's only about ten miles, but, of course, he had to walk pretty slow, I guess. And you [know], that fellow had a little lard bucket with him. He said he packed water in that from that Fast Horse Creek. That's between the Cheyenne Creek and Wounded Knee. So he said, "There is water on that creek. I got the water there and packed it. That's all I drink [*sic*]. Yeah, White Lance, he lived a long time. He died about, oh, fifteen years ago. He was quite a warrior.

Well, after that, they brought all the corpses home, back here, those that had relatives. And the ones that didn't have no relatives around, why they buried them right there on the hill, in a trench. So they would just lay them down there. . . .

Yeah. Only time I seen that was when we went after them dead bodies and wounded people. Lots of wagons went. The army was there. They was there all the time, even scouts. Lots of Indian scouts. . . .

White Lance was [a] brave man. Those bullets, he never told about [re]moving any of them. But you could tell that he was shot, like here above the arm, that went through his back. Bigger hole in the back than it is here. You can't hardly see where it went in. Where the bullet goes in, it was small, about the end of your finger, and on the other side, it's about an inch around. One of them is terrible, but it's on the edge of his body all the time. It didn't hit him square, why [if it had], he'd bled to death. . . ."

Appendix

Readers seeking further Lakota identity and genealogical information regarding Wounded Knee are encouraged to consult Richard E. Jensen, "Big Foot's Followers at Wounded Knee," *Nebraska History* 71 (Fall 1990): 194–212. For discussion of the numbers of American Indians present and killed, *see* James Mooney, "The Ghost-Dance Religion and the Sioux Outbreak of 1890," in *Fourteenth Annual Report of the Bureau of Ethnology to the Secretary of the Smithsonian Institution, 1892–1893*, pt. 2 (Washington, D.C.: Government Printing Office, 1896), pp. 870–71; and Jerome A. Greene, *American Carnage: Wounded Knee, 1890* (Norman: University of Oklahoma Press, 2014), pp. 399–401.

1. Indian scouts present at Wounded Knee, 29 December 1890

This list of Indian scouts present at Wounded Knee, 29 December 1890, appears as given in muster roll for Indian Scouts in Company A enlisted at Pine Ridge Agency from 27 November 1890, to 30 April 1891, Folder 650, Box 657, Pine Ridge Agency, General Records, Main Decimal Files, RG 75, NA, Kansas City, Mo.

Name and Rank	Enlisted	Remarks
Charles W. Taylor, 1st Lieut.		In command to Jan. 24, 1891
Guy H. Preston, 2nd Lieut.		
******		
1st Sergent [*sic*]		
Standing Soldier	Nov. 27, 1890	To Feb. 1, 1891
Red Shirt	Do	Do
Sergents [*sic*]		
Willard Standing Bear	Nov. 27, 1890	
White Deer	Do	
Yankton Charley	Do	

Corporals
John Long Dog	Do	
Sam Last Horse	Do	
Little Bull	Do	

Trumpeter
Marshall Hand	Do	

Farrier
Short Bull

Privates
Make Trouble Ahead	Nov. 27, 1890	
High Back Bone	Do	Killed in Action Dec. 28 [29,] 189
Burning Bear	Do	
Jack Standing Bear	Do	
Poor Bear	Do	
Leon White Bird	Do	
Yellow Boy	Do	
Joe Bush Jr.	Do	
Walking Bull	Do	
Kills Brave	Do	
Peter Cazoo	Do	
Prairie Chicken	Do	
Grass Cutter	Do	
Little Cloud	Do	
Clear	Do	
Cobb (Bad Cob) [sic]	Do	
Jumping Eagle	Do	
Ghost	Do	
Bad Hair	Do	
Real Hawk	Do	
Feather on Head	Do	
His Horse	Do	
Spotted Horse	Do	
Little Spotted Horse	Do	
Whirlwind Horse	Do	
Wooden Leg	Do	
Not Afraid of Pawnee	Do	
Charles Picket Pin	Do	
Ribs	Do	
Red Sacks	Do	
Holy Skin	Do	

Black Sheep	Do
Iron Tail	Do
Charles Twiss	Do
Fool Thunder	Do
Poor Thunder	Do
White Wing	Do
Fast Whirlwind	Do
Iron Bull	Do
Elk	Do
White Elk No. 1	Do
Hawk Man	Do
Running Bear	Do
Eagle Shield (Pvt and Corpl)	Do
Eagle Chief No. 1	Do
Runs Close to the Lodge	Do
Two Tails	Do
Ike Little Hawk	Do
Takes the Enemy	December 24, 1890
White Bull	Do
Wounded Head	Do
Good Elk	Do
White Colt	Do
Looking Horse	Do
Red Dog	Do
Coming Ghost	Do
Has No Horses	Do
Albert Otto Eagle	Do
Leon Blue Horse	Do
Spotted Eagle	Do
Frank Conroy	Do
White Face Bull	Do
Eagle Elk	Do
Bird Head	Do
Big Boy	Do
Short Bear	Do
James Clinch (James Clincher)	Do
Coyotte [*sic*]	Do
Harry Shields	Do
Long Horns	Do
Pacer	Do
Eagle Chief No. 2	Do
Old Hair	Do
Allen Last Horse	Do

Deserted

Two Tails	Dec. 28, 1890
Harry Shield	Do
Wounded Head	Do
Old Hair	Do
Takes the Enemy	Do
Eagle Chief No. 2	Do
Coyotte [*sic*]	Do

This troop was in action at Wounded Knee, S.D.[,] Dec. 28 [*sic*—29], 1890, and near Pine Ridge Agency, S.D., December 29 [*sic*—30], 1890. Otherwise the Troop was at Pine Ridge [Agency] all the time.

2. Census of Sioux Indians from Cheyenne River Indian Reservation in battle of Wounded Knee and at Pine Ridge Agency, in June 1891

"Approximate Census of the Sioux Indians belonging to the Cheyenne River reservation who were in the battle of Wounded Knee and are yet at Pine Ridge Agency S.D. taken June 30, 1891," Records of the Bureau of Indian Affairs, RG 75, National Archives Microfilm Publication, M: 595, roll 33. This document accounts for 91 dead out of 227 people. All brackets in this list are from the original.

No.	Name	Sex	Age	Living or Dead
1.	Afraid of Enemy	M	37	Living
2.	Brown Eyes	F	36	"
3.	Counts	M	11	"
4.	Scares the Hawk	M	5	"
5.	Pretty Spotted Horse	F	7	"
6.	Important Woman	M	23	"
7.	Bear Woman	F	26	"
8.	Touches the Ground	F	22	"
9.	Woman	F	56	"
10.	Catches the Boat	M	9	"
11.	Brother	M	7	"
12.	I Shot the Hawk	M	41	Dead
13.	Loves her Shawl	F	64	
14.	Jumps Good	M		
15.	Red Beaver	F	24	
16.	Iron	F	61	
17.	Killed the Bear No.	1	M	70
18.	Three	M	25	
19.	Mrs. Killed the Bear No.	1	F	57
20.	Kills Against	F	12	
21.	Made to Shoot	M	69	
22.	Mrs. Made to Shoot	M	65	
23.	Black Thunder	M	42	
24.	Plenty Young Birds	F	39	
25.	Whiskers [Dewey Beard]	M	25	
26.	Eagle [wife of Wears Eagle]	F	19	Dead
27.	Blolan [*sic*]	M	10	
28.	Elk Woman	F	47	
29.	Brown Beaver	M	23	Dead
30.	Beaver	F	9	Dead
31.	Bring Many	F	36	

32.	Brings Yellow	F	4	
33.	Black Fox	M	33	Dead
34.	Brown Hair	F	29	
35.	Brings White	F	2	Dead
36.	Important Man	M	45	Dead
37.	Mrs. Important Man	F	34	Dead
38.	White Cow	F	8	
39.	Industrious Bear	M	61	Dead
40.	Small Leg Woman	F	51	Dead
41.	Frost on Her	M	12	Dead
42.	Poor	M	10	Dead
43.	Face	F	18	
44.	Big Woman	F	15	
45.	Gone [illeg.]	F	31	
46.	Yellow Horse	M	4	
47.	In Front	F	8	
48.	Brown Bull	M	68	Dead
49.	Mrs. [illeg.]	F	67	Dead
50.	Bird Shake Herself	M	23	Dead
51.	Black Shield	M	45	
52.	Deaf	F	19	Dead
53.	Pretty White Cow	F	6	Dead
54.	Bear with Small Body	M	30	Dead
55.	Mrs. Bear with Small Body	F	29	Dead
56.	Takes Away Enemy	M	11	Dead
57.	Smokes Walking	M	9	
58.	Enemy	M	5	
59.	No Name	F	61	
60.	Thunder	M	27	Dead
61.	Bear Don't Run	M	45	Dead
62.	Mrs. Bear Don't Run	F	45	
63.	Head Woman	F	21	Dead
64.	Pawnee Killer	M	17	Dead
65.	[Farms?] at the River	F	15	
66.	Bear Sheds His Hair	M	61	Dead
67.	Mrs. Bear Sheds His Hair	F	49	
68.	Red Buffalo	F	25	Dead
69.	Trouble in Front	M	22	Dead
70.	Runs Behind	M	14	Dead
71.	Elk that Looks	M	39	
72.	Mrs. Elk that Looks	F	27	
73.	Good Pipe	F	6	Dead
74.	Kills the Enemy	F	2	

75.	Frog	M	47	
76.	Mrs. Frog	F	42	
77.	Ones Call	F	15	Dead
78.	Hunts to Death	M	12	
79.	Horned Cloud	M	53	Dead
80.	Mrs. Horned Cloud	F	52	Dead
81.	Warrior	M	22	
82.	Joseph	M	20	
83.	Her Horse	F	18	
84.	The Enemy	M	14	Dead
85.	His Fight	M	41	Dead
86.	Fog [?]	M	61	Dead
87.	Twin Woman	F	61	Dead
88.	High Hawk	M	51	
89.	Bear Woman	F	46	
90.	Long Woman	M	21	
91.	Kills Twice	M	13	
92.	Kills in a Hurry	F	5	
93.	Only Man	—	4	
94.	The Scout	M	2	
95.	Red Cow	F	13	
96.	Lives [?] in Iron	F	31	
97.	Brings the Dirt	F	71	
98.	Runs Fast	F	47	
99.	Red Belly	F	53	
100.	Stands Up for Him	M	14	
101.	Brings Yellow	F	9	
102.	I Shot the Bear	M	81	Dead
103.	Her Wind [?]	F	63	
104.	George	M	21	Dead
105.	Kills Horse	F	11	
106.	Enemy	M	5	
107.	Killed Him First	M	49	Dead
108.	Mrs. Killed Him First	F	42	
109.	Wounded in Winter	M		Dead
110.	Shoots the White	F	15	
111.	White Mule	F	3	
112.	Blind Woman	F	59	
113.	Kills the Fair	M	7	
114.	Yellow in Ear	F	19	
115.	Brown Woman	F	47	
116.	Little Water	M	36	Dead
117.	White Face	F	40	Dead

118.	The Voice	F	17	Dead
119.	Light Hair Girl	F	11	
120.	Whip [?]	F	9	
121.	Sacred Blanket	M	7	Dead
122.	Animal	M	6	Dead
123.	Not Stingy	F	4	Dead
124.	Made to Stand	M	24	Dead
125.	Produce	F	57	Dead
126.	Gray Thunder	M	17	Dead
127.	Mangy Elk	M	42	Dead
128.	Trotter	M	31	Dead
129.	To Laugh	F	65	Dead
130.	Male Eagle	M	44	Dead
131.	Short Woman	F	42	Dead
132.	Warrior	M	22	Dead
133.	Two Arrows	M	20	Dead
134.	Comes Home with Red	M	8	
135.	Many Brothers	F	9	
136.	Runs After Her	F	2	Dead
137.	Mrs. On the Ground	F	34	
138.	Runs Woman	F	18	
139.	Red	M	6	
140.	Guide	M	4	
141.	Sour [?] Man	M	26	
142.	Up to His Waist	M	44	Dead
143.	Mrs. Up to His Waist	F	50	Dead
144.	Important Man	M	13	Dead
145.	Walks in the Circle	M	2	
146.	Pretty Bear	M	36	Dead
147.	Cub Bear	M	6	
148.	Pretty Shield	M	41	
149.	Mrs. Pretty Shield	F	32	
150.	The House	F	21	
151.	Her Shawl	F	18	
152.	Yellow Eyes	F	7	
153.	Goggle Eyes	M	62	Dead
154.	Fore Woman	F	51	Dead
155.	Thunder Boy	M	19	Dead
156.	Pretty Woman	F	15	
157.	Blue Spotted	M	8	Dead
158.	[illeg.] of the [illeg.]	M	34	
159.	The Ring	F	2	Dead
160.	The [illeg.]	F	4	

161.	In a Cow[']s Horn	M	61	Dead
162.	Mrs. In a Cow[']s Horn	F	51	
163.	Stands for Himself	M	21	
164.	White Bull	M	61	Dead
165.	Clown Woman	F	61	Dead
166.	Pretty Hair	F	11	Dead
168.	Blue Horse	M	17	
168.	Knocked in the Head	F	25	
169.	Long Holy	M	15	
170.	Wear Calf Skin Robe	M	51	Dead
171.	Mrs. [Wear Calf Skin Robe]	F	48	
172.	Bad Boy	M	23	
173.	Chases and Kills	M	5	
174.	Wolf Ears	M	51	Dead
175.	Mrs. [Wolf Ears]	F	50	
176.	White	M	26	Dead
177.	Feather Earring	M	17	Dead
178.	Medicine Lake Girl	F	6	Dead
179.	Walking Bull	M	61	Dead
180.	Mrs. Walking Bull	F	51	Dead
181.	Warrior	M	22	
182.	Caught in the [illeg.]	F	58	
183.	Comes and Stands	F	70	
184.	Brown Turtle	M	57	Dead
185.	First Born [?]	F	67	Dead
186.	Shot the Eagle	F	29 [?]	
187.	Close to Home	M	20	
188.	[Illeg.] Clock Hand	F	10	
189.	Little Bull	M	46	
190.	Deserts Him	M	9	
191.	Brown Girl	F	2	
192.	Missed	M	21	
193.	Stinking Foot [?]	F	90	
194.	Kills in Bunch	M	31	Dead
195.	Shawl Over Head	F	21	
196.	The M[illeg.]	M	15	Dead
197.	The Hand	F	3	
198.	Hollow Teeth	M	21	
199.	Buckskin Britch [Breech?] Clout	M	51	Dead
200.	Use His Feet	M	5	
201.	Left Hand	M	4	
202.	Runs Away with Horse	M	4	
203.	Young Prairie Chicken	F	51	

204.	White Hair	M	26	
205.	Unties Shoestring	F	71	
206.	Killed His Choice	M	13	
207.	Takes the Buffalo	F	42	
208.	Quits on Him	F	6	
209.	Send Voice Thunder	M	21	Dead
210.	Bo Blue [?]	F	61	Dead
211.	Strong Fox	M	40	Dead
212.	Mrs. Strong Fox	F	31	Dead
213.	The Quick	M	9	Dead
214.	Brown Horn	F	9	Dead
215.	White Woman Hand	F	61	
216.	Good Hand	F	81	
217.	Bear	F	36	
218.	Blind Man	M	21	
219.	Day	F	21	
220.	Red Eagle	F	2	
221.	Blue Wing	M	22	
222.	Back Bone	M	53	
223.	Mrs. [Back Bone]	F	49	
224.	White Hawk	M	11	
225.	Big Boy	M	8	
226.	King Boy	M	4	
227.	Wild Man	F	71	

3. Joseph Horn Cloud's list of Indians killed at Wounded Knee, 1903–1904

In 1903 or 1904, Joseph Horn Cloud compiled this list of the Indians killed at Wounded Knee. Excerpted from Tablet 3, pp. 12–24, Eli S. Ricker Papers, RG 1227, Nebraska State Historical Society, Lincoln. See also *Richard E. Jensen, ed.,* Voices of the American West, *vol. 1,* The Indian Interviews of Eli S. Ricker, 1903–1919 *(Lincoln: University of Nebraska Press, 2005), pp. 204–6, and Donald F. Danker, ed., "The Wounded Knee Interviews of Eli S. Ricker,"* Nebraska History *62 (Summer 1981): 176–79. Parenthetical comments in the list are from the source documents. Bracketed comments are from the volume editor.*

Chief Big Foot
Mrs. Big Foot
Horned Cloud
Mrs. Horned Cloud
William Horned Cloud, son
Sherman Horned Cloud, son
Pretty Enemy, niece
Mrs. Beard, daughter-in-law
Thomas Beard, grandson
Shedding Bear
Trouble-in-Front, son
Last Running
Red White Cow, daughter
Mother-in-law of Shedding Bear
High Hawk
Mrs. High Hawk
Little boy, son
Little girl, daughter
Whirl Wind Hawk
Mrs. Whirl Wind Hawk
Young lady, daughter
Young girl "
Little girl "
Little boy, son
Little boy, son
He Crow
Pretty Woman, daughter
Buckskin Breech Clout
Running in Lodge, son
White Feather, son

Little boy, son
Bear Woman (the oldest woman
   in the band)
Crazy Bear
Elk Creek
Mrs. Elk Creek
Spotted Chief, son
Red Fish
Mrs. Red Fish
Old Good Bear
Young Good Bear
Mrs. Good Bear
Little boy, son
Pretty Hawk
Mrs. Pretty Hawk
Baby Pretty Hawk
Mrs. Lap
Shoots the Right
Bad Wound, son
Bear Parts Body
Little boy, son
Brown Beaver
White Beaver Woman
Black Coyote [Black Fox] (The one
   who made the trouble)
Red Water Woman
Sun in Pupil
Mrs. Sun in Pupil
Henry Three, or Pretty Bald Eagle
Iron Eyes (Big Foot's brother)

Mrs. Iron Eyes
Has a Dog
Red Shirt Girl
Pretty Woman
Albert Iron Eyes
White Day
Little Boy, son
Charge at Them
Old Woman, mother
Mrs. Iron American
Mrs. Yellow Buffalo Calf
Louis Close to Home
Cast Away and Run
Bad Braves
Red Horn
Winter
Strong Fox
Mrs. Strong Fox
Little boy, son
One Feather
Little boy, son
Without Robe
Old Man Yellow Bull
Mrs. Old Man Yellow Bull
Brown Woman
Shakes the Bird
Red Eyes Horse
Shoots With Hawk's Feather
    (shot with Hotchkiss; see Beard's
    statement regarding six-inch hole
    in stomach)
His Mother
Ghost Horse
Little Boy, son
Chief Woman
Mrs. Trouble in Love
Hat
Baby boy
Mrs. Stone Hammer
Little baby
Wolf Ears [Wolf Eagle]
Good Boy, son
Edward Wolf Ears

Little girl
Shoots the Bear
Kills Seneca Assiniboine
George Shoots the Bear
Mrs. Shoots the Bear
Kills Crow Indian
Little Body Bear
Mrs. Little Body Bear
Little boy, son
Baby girl
Red Eagle (This man was in the tent
    & was killed by the cannon)
Eagle Body, daughter
Little girl
Little Elk
Mrs. Little Elk
Black Shield's little girl
White Wolf
Red Ears Horse, sister
Old Woman, her mother
Wood Shade
Mrs. Wood Shade
Running Standing Hairs
Mrs. Running Standing Hairs
Young lady, daughter
Scabbard Knife
Mrs. Scabbard Knife
He Eagle
Mrs. He Eagle
Edward He Eagle, son
Young girl, daughter
Young boy, son
Log
Mrs. Log
Really Woman, son
Brown Hoops
Little boy, son
Young girl, daughter
Mule's daughter, young lady
Red Otter Woman
Black Flutes, young boy
Takes Away the Bow
Gray in Eye

Mrs. Drops Blood
Young boy, son
Little boy, son
Old Woman
Mrs. Long Bull
Young girl, daughter
Spotted Thunder
Swift Bird
Mrs. Swift Bird
Boy, son
Boy, son
Strike Scatter
Boy, son
Wolf Skin Necklace
Last Talking, old woman. She is
    alone. Her property, two horses,
    bedding & lodge
Not Go In Among, son of Hailing
    Bear and Her Good Medicine.
    Buckskin horse and saddle, rope
Wounded Hand
Comes Out Rattling, wife
Big Voice Thunder
Mercy to Others
Long Medicine
Broken Arrow
Mrs. Broken Arrow
Young man
Young woman
Brown Turtle
Old woman, mother
Bird Wings
Not Afraid of Lodge
Bear Comes and Lies
Wears Calf's Robe
Yellow Robe
Wounded in Winter, son
Mrs. Black Hair
Bad Spotted Eagle (a Cree Indian)
Mrs. Bad Spotted Eagle
(The above were visiting Big Foot[']s
    tribe)
White American

Long Bull
Courage Bear
Mrs. Courage Bear
Fat Courage Bear
George Courage Bear
Black Hawk
She Bear, wife
Weasel Bear, daughter
(Joe Horn Cloud added Weasel Bear
    when we were running the list
    over)
180 [*sic*]
185 [*sic*]

4. Members of Big Foot's band not killed at Wounded Knee, ca. 1907

This list of those Lakotas not killed at Wounded Knee, but who were of Big Foot's Miniconjou band and, therefore, in the action, is excerpted from the Eli S. Ricker Papers. See Tablet 3, pp. 12–24. This circa 1907 list included at least some of those people who died of wounds while in treatment at the Holy Cross Episcopal Church at Pine Ridge. See also Jensen, ed., Indian Interviews of Eli S. Ricker, *pp. 206–8, and Danker, ed., "Wounded Knee Interviews of Eli S. Ricker," pp. 178–79.*

Shell Necklace
Birds Afraid of Him
Sees the Elk
Made Him Long
Made a Stand
Black Zebra
Black Shield
Fast Wolf
Gray
Dewey Beard
White Lance
Joe Horn Cloud
Frank Horn Cloud
Little Cloud
Bear Runs in the Woods
Good Bear
Gets on a Fight
Sinew Belly
Bull Man
One Skunk
Tattooed
Holy Comes (Holy and Medicine have the same word in Dakota. Medicine is holy. The word medicine is now rather more common.)
Running Hawk
You Can Eat Dog
Little Bull
Black Bugle
His War
Long Bull

Shows His Cloud
His Two Lance
Wears Fur Coat
Fat Hips
Wounded Both
Good Horse
Fast Boat
Kills in the Middle
Runs After It
Goes to War
Kills Two
Man Himself
Kills in Hurry
Shot Him Off
Scout
White Horse
Picks and Kills
He Eagle
Wind in Guts (Stomach)
Mustang Elk
White Eagle
Kills One Hundred
Hits Her On a Run
White Face Woman (the oldest in the band except, perhaps, Bear Woman)
Black Cow
Her Good Horse
Red Fingernail Woman
White Cow Comes Out
Iron Horn Woman
Comes Out Alive Woman

Little Girl
Hollow Horn Woman
Comes Crawling Woman
Elk Woman
Different Woman
Stops Her Horse
Hawk Woman
Smoke Woman
Good Natured Woman
Her Horse
Her First
Horse Nation
Brings it to Her
Her Elk Tooth
Liver Gall
Eagle Shape
Her Eagle
Her Yellow
Her White Horse
Her Roan
Little Eyed Woman
Ground Horn Woman (wounded and
   afterwards died)
Gray Owl Woman

Good Land Woman
Missed Not Woman
Brings Her Home
Her Cedar
Good White Cow
Kill Her White Horse
Kills Them First
Standing Elk
Her Neck
Her Brown Faced Dog
Her Shell Walks
She Wears Eagle
Sees the Bear
Two Lance
Young Big Foot
His Crow
Black American
Black Hair
Chief Dog
Son of Red Horn
Son of Little Body Bear
Enemy Afraid of Him
104 Little Wound [*sic*]

5. List of Wounded Knee Lakota survivors as of May 1941

James Pipe on Head compiled this list of Wounded Knee Survivors as of May 1941. Pipe on Head to Representative Francis H. Case, 5 May 1941, Francis H. Case Papers, George and Eleanor McGovern Library, Dakota Wesleyan University, Mitchell, S.Dak.

1. James Pipe on Head	(age) 62	Oglala, S.D.
2. Dewey Beard	76	Kyle, S.D.
3. Frank Sits Poor	62	Manderson, S.D.
4. Alice White Wolf	67	Pine Ridge, S.D.
5. Jesse Running Horse	52	Pine Ridge, S.D.
6. George Running Hawk	63	Wanblee, S.D.
7. Thomas Blue Leg	54	Wanblee, S.D.
8. George Blue Leg	56	Kyle, S.D.
9. Ella Ladeaux	66	Manderson, S.D.
10. Sylvia Looking Elk	86	Oglala, S.D.
11. Peter Stands	68	Oglala, S.D.
12. Julia Spider Backbone	62	Oglala, S.D.
13. Thomas Blindman	55	Oglala, S.D.
14. Charles Blindman, Sr.	57	Oglala, S.D.
15. Rough Feather	77	Kyle, S.D.
16. Jackson He Crow	61	Oglala, S.D.
17. Dora High Whiteman	60	Oglala, S.D.
18. Silas Afraid of Enemy	50	Oglala, S.D.
19. John Little Finger	66	Oglala, S.D.
20. Mrs. Young Bear	75	Porcupine, S.D.
21. Mrs. Haki Kta Win or LaVatta	61	Little Eagle, S.D.
22. Philip Black Moon	62	Red Scaffold, S.D.
23. Paul High Back	74	Poplar, Mont.
24. John Spotted Bear	68	Little Eagle, S.D.
25. Jennie Knocks Him Down	70	Bull Head, S.D.
26. James Red Fish	61	Bull Head, S.D.
27. Blue Arm	67	Cherry Creek, S.D.
28. Carl or Jackson Kills White Man	66	Cherry Creek, S.D.
29. Edward Owekin (Owl King)	61	Cherry Creek, S.D.
30. Mrs. [Nellie] Knife	69	Dupree, S.D.
31. Julia Crane Pretty Voice	70	Howes, S.D.
32. Mrs. Widow or Good Shawl	75	Cherry Creek, S.D.
33. Mrs. Circle	63	White Horse, S.D.
34. Alex High Hawk	62	Howes, S.D.
35. James High Hawk [HiHawk]	55	Howes, S.D.

36. Jonas High Hawk   53   Howes, S.D.
37. Leon Holy   50   Cherry Creek, S.D.
38. One Skunk   74   Cherry Creek, S.D.
39. Francis Eagle—Little Crow   57   Howes, S.D.
40. Jackson Roan Horse   61   Howes, S.D.
41. Henry Roan Horse   56   Howes, S.D.

Index